Nurturing Children's Talents

Nurturing Children's Talents

A Guide for Parents

Kenneth A. Kiewra

An Imprint of ABC-CLIO, LLC

Santa Barbara, California • Denver, Colorado

Library of Congress Cataloging-in-Publication Data

Names: Kiewra, Kenneth A., author.
Title: Nurturing children's talents : a guide for parents / Kenneth A. Kiewra.
Description: Santa Barbara, California : Praeger An Imprint of ABC-CLIO,
    LLC, [2019] | Includes bibliographical references and index.
Identifiers: LCCN 2018037254 (print) | LCCN 2018054851 (ebook) |
    ISBN 9781440867934 (ebook) | ISBN 9781440867927 (cloth)
Subjects: LCSH: Gifted children. | Achievement motivation in children. |
    Gifted children—Family relationships. | Gifted children—Education. | Parenting.
Classification: LCC BF723.G5 (ebook) | LCC BF723.G5 K54 2019 (print) |
    DDC 649/.6—dc23
LC record available at https://lccn.loc.gov/2018037254

ISBN: 978-1-4408-6792-7 (print)
       978-1-4408-6793-4 (ebook)

23 22 21 20 19   1 2 3 4 5

This book is also available as an eBook.

Praeger
An Imprint of ABC-CLIO, LLC

ABC-CLIO, LLC
147 Castilian Drive
Santa Barbara, California 93117
www.abc-clio.com

This book is printed on acid-free paper ♾

Manufactured in the United States of America

To my parents, Frank and Winifred; my wife, Christine; and my children, Keaton, Anna, and Samuel: Thank you for sharing your talent journeys with me and for supporting me on mine. I dedicate this book to you.

Contents

Preface: A Book for All Parents

Nurturing Children's Talents: A Guide for Parents is a book for all parents. That's because talent is made, not born, and parents are in prime position to help children find and cultivate talents. This is true for parents at varying economic and experiential levels. Talent is not restricted to those living in the glow of Manhattan's Upper West Side. You'll see in these pages that chess talent can erupt and flourish in poverty-stricken Franklin County, Mississippi, or that basketball talent can take shape on a ramshackle court in an Omaha housing project. You'll also see that musical talent can flourish in homes with already assembled musical nests but also in homes where parents and siblings have no musical background. And you'll see that writing talent can blossom at age four, while photography talent might not come into focus until adolescence. That's why talent-nurturing advice applies to new and experienced parents alike. In essence, talent can blossom anywhere when parents or other caregivers recognize that children can accomplish amazing things and lend a hand.

In addition, you'll see that talent development is not restricted to popular domains such as music and football but transcends many niche domains such as chess, baton twirling, and spelling. *Nurturing Children's Talents* covers a wide array of talent domains including academic talent, and all families seek academic success. Finally, you'll see that talent development need not culminate in gold medals or Academy Awards to be fruitful. Talent is not an end product but a process, a continuum along which all children can move. Thus, all parents are positioned to help children grow talents whether the outcome is Carnegie Hall or community band. In the end, it is the pursuit of talent that parents and children find most gratifying. Children emerge from the talent path with greater confidence, resiliency, and self-regulation skills. And children and parents enjoy the talent ride and develop a close relationship.

Parents meanwhile probably don't realize when their child is on a talent path or, when they do, are uncertain about how to best help their child.

Regarding talent realization, the parent of an Olympic figure skater said to me "If someone had told me ten years ago that we'd be where we are today, I'd have not believed it." Another said of her son that "When [he] started skating, we didn't know he was going to be this good. And we weren't even hoping he'd be this good. It just wasn't on our radar." Regarding parents' uncertainty about what to do, the parent of a world-champion baton twirler told me "It's all trial and error. You don't really know how it's going to turn out. Are you doing the right thing? You don't ever really know." The parent of a renowned musician said, "It's been a big fat accident. We wish we had known more. Did we get in the way? Did we hold him back? We didn't know enough." An Olympic figure skater's parent added "I wish there had been a manual about what was going to happen to us and what to do." Hopefully, this book can relieve uncertainty, reduce misguided trials and errors, and be that missing guide or manual parents seek for nurturing children's talents.

Nurturing Children's Talents is certainly not a book aimed at overbearing tiger moms and helicopter parents hell-bent on raising a talented child—parents who push, pressure, squeeze, and suffocate their children. They were never among the parents I interviewed. That's because the child invariably drives the talent train, and the fuel is the child's intrinsic motivation and passion, not the parent's hopes or prodding. Parents can help navigate the train, but they can't supply the steam. And the parents I interviewed knew and lived that.

Speaking of tiger moms and helicopter parents, they have given involved parents pause and have also given parents who go the extra mile a bad rap. I am among the psychologists who believe that parents need to push back against the negative overinvolvement image. I agree with psychologist Madeline Levine, who contends that the optimal parent is one who is involved, responsive, and sets high expectations and that such sweet-spot parenting produces children who are academically, psychologically, and socially more adept than children whose parents sit on the sidelines. "Many of us find ourselves drawn to the idea that with just a bit more parental elbow grease, we might turn out children with great talents and assured futures. Is there really anything wrong with a kind of 'over-parenting lite'?"[1]

Nothing at all. Every day parents are indeed pushing back against the overinvolvement stigma because they love their children, want what's best for them, and believe that great things are possible. This leaves parents seeking expert advice on parenting like never before. But most parenting books I've seen tell parents how to fix problems rather than how to help children flourish. This also leaves parents seeking life-enhancing opportunities: preschools, music lessons, soccer academies, cooking classes, chess clubs, nature organizations, private tutoring, and much more. But my research for this book indicates that simply turning children over to expert teachers and coaches is not the path toward talent development.

Talent parents do more. They don't just arrange life-enhancing opportunities; they set the talent table and nourish their children's interests, wherever those interests lead. Talent parents do things their children cannot do on their own, such as providing a talent-rich environment, securing coaches, guiding practices, sparking motivation, and guiding, managing, and committing to the talent journey. One parent I interviewed spoke for many when he said, "I've made a commitment to my son that as long as he continues to work and grow . . . , we'll use whatever resources we have to get him where he needs to go."[2]

Many parents are already aboard—or soon to ride—a talent train and can benefit from this book, the first of its kind, which proclaims that talent is within the reach of most everyone, showcases parents' instrumental roles, and chronicles talent parenting. Today's engaged and caring parents seem eager to receive this message and discover how to nurture talent.

Acknowledgments

What I have discovered about talent development would have never been revealed without coinvestigators helping light the way. They inspired and guided me and made conducting research really fun. Thank you John Creswell, Abe Flanigan, Sarah Kasson, Xiongyi Liu, Linlin Luo, Matt McCrudden, Tom O'Connor, Carol Ott Schacht, Melissa Patterson Hazley, Kyle Perry, Brittany Rom, and especially Amanda Witte, who has joined me on several talent projects. Also, a special thank-you to videographers Alexis Borchardt, Elijah Watson, and Kate Westberg, whose creative talents brought to life the talent documentary *Prodigies of the Prairie,* which so influenced this book.

Few ideas are ever original, and mine are heavily influenced by talent authorities who have written before me. I embrace their work and often reference them in this book. I hope I have done their important contributions to talent development justice. Thank you Benjamin Bloom, Geoff Colvin, Daniel Coyle, Mihaly Csikszentmihalyi, Anders Ericsson, Howard Gardner, Malcolm Gladwell, Paula Olszewski-Kubilius, Sir Ken Robinson, Matthew Syed, Josh Waitzkin, and Robert Weisberg. You are all talent expert legends.

My talent knowledge grew exponentially, given the opportunity and privilege of teaching a creativity and talent development class at the University of Nebraska. There, students challenged and refined my ideas and introduced me to fresh ideas through their talent investigations and reports. For their collaborations, I am thankful.

I am, of course, especially grateful to the many supremely talented children, their nurturing parents, and their target-zone coaches who revealed to me talent's inner workings for all to see and model. You make the world better and exhilarating.

University of Nebraska colleagues helped me produce the initial manuscript. Special thanks to graphic designer Emily Slattery and to graduate support person Cindy DeRyke, who has generously exceeded her job description and helped me fine-tune my work for many years.

This project would have never left the ground without literary agent Suzy Evans of the Sandra Dijkstra Literary Agency. She believed that an academic could write a trade book and envisioned parents eager to unlock talent nurturing secrets when others did not. She also worked tirelessly to find my book its perfect landing place: ABC-CLIO. From there, ABC-CLIO acquisitions editor Debbie Carvalko and production editor Nicole Azze were instrumental in professionally and expediently transforming my coarse manuscript into a polished book.

A special thanks to family friend Meghan Houser, a successful book editor who took time to patiently shepherd me through the trade book publishing process. Finally, a nod to my own talent heroes who have long inspired me: talent pioneer Benjamin Bloom, New York Yankee center fielder Bernie Williams, and astronomer and writer Carl Sagan, who taught us much about the cosmos, how to reason scientifically, and how to be good planetary stewards.

CHAPTER ONE

Why I Study Talent Development

When my first child, Keaton, was born, I had no intention of introducing him to chess and developing his chess talent. I was not a chess player myself, and like most parents, I just wanted him to be healthy and happy. I never anticipated that he would become a six-time National Scholastic Champion, earn a full-ride college chess scholarship, achieve the International Chess Master title, and become a leading player and coach. And I never imagined the essential roles I would play in his development.

My Story as Talent Parent

My job as a college professor was flexible and allowed me to spend a lot of time with Keaton. Whatever interested him, we did. We reenacted and embellished stories by personifying Keaton's stuffed animals. "Three Billy Goats Gruff" became a caravan of bunnies battling a venomous snake guarding the garden bridge. We drew his favorite story characters and posted his top 100 drawings on walls, counters, and cabinets in our kitchen gallery. Mostly, we talked. As we cooked, a conversation could boil up about corn and branch to farming, pesticides, and natural foods. Through our interactions, Keaton developed deep interests in revolving topics such as dinosaurs and the Pony Express. When an interest arose, I fed it. His dinosaur interest was met with new books, dinosaur-themed makeup games, museum outings, and backyard excavations for allosaurus bones. His Pony Express interest was met with trips to the Marysville, Kansas, Pony Express Barn; stick horse mail-toting gallops around our house; and a sit-down with our local postmaster general.

When Keaton was four years old, his interests turned to skill games such as tic-tac-toe, checkers, and Connect Four. As we played, I taught him strategies for where to play in certain situations. He quickly applied these strategies, discovered several more, and played these games in a deliberate, passionate, and calculating way. He became unbeatable, defeating everyone—children and adults alike—who visited our home. Recognizing Keaton's penchant for games, I soon introduced him to chess because chess is the ultimate skill game and is widely played. I retrieved my old wooden set from the basement and showed Keaton the little I knew about chess, but he did not find it interesting. After a few sessions the pieces went back in the box, and Keaton moved through other interests.

When Keaton was in second grade I reintroduced him to chess, still believing that this would be something he would enjoy and be good at. This time he took to chess like rooks to open files. He wanted to play chess with me every free minute before and after school. A few weeks later, I entered him in a local scholastic tournament. My fascination that he was the next Bobby Fischer was quickly dashed when his first-round opponent defeated him in just four moves using a standard check-mating trick we knew nothing about. Keaton limped through the rest of the tournament, winning just a few games against children his age.

The sobering result did not dampen Keaton's chess enthusiasm or mine for helping him. Quite the contrary. He wanted to learn more. Meanwhile, I realized that my scant chess knowledge was insufficient to help Keaton learn chess, so I purchased several books and began instructing him from these. Rather than play chess, we studied it—openings, tactics, strategies, and endgames—for hours a day at his request. I translated the books' themes and set up problems for Keaton to solve. He relished these sessions. A few months later, Keaton participated in his second tournament—the Nebraska Scholastic State Championship. His name appeared at the bottom of the entry list among the 80 or so names ordered by chess rating. But Keaton lost just once in the six-round tournament and finished third. His chess talent was emerging.

Buoyed by Keaton's performance, we upped the training. We purchased more books and studied them cover to cover. But as the books increased in complexity, it became harder for me to teach Keaton. He was a stronger player than I was, and I lacked the knowledge to answer his questions and help him advance. I asked our state champion, Kevin, if he would coach Keaton, and Kevin agreed. He was a serious teacher who was perfect for Keaton. Keaton did not want fun and games; he wanted chess knowledge. Keaton's coach made him earn that knowledge while molding him to think like a champion. Kevin set up difficult problems, maybe just one or two a session, for Keaton to ponder and solve. When Keaton pressed his coach for information, such as why a certain move is better than another or why a bishop is stronger than a knight, Kevin would patently reply, "You tell me."

Months later we traveled to Arizona, where Keaton competed against 1,000 students for the K–3 National Scholastic Championship. This was our first chess trip and his first serious tournament. Seven games were played over three days, and each could last four hours. Several times Keaton's game was among the last one finished. I marveled that he played with such patience and care. He won six of seven games and finished in a tie for third place— third place in the country. I was stunned by his performance; I knew then that Keaton had found his element.

When Keaton's first coach relocated I hired a second coach, another local chess expert and university professor named Tom, to coach Keaton. Tom was especially instrumental in teaching Keaton about chess theory and helping him discover and cultivate his attacking style. In time Keaton's skill level surpassed Tom's, and at Tom's urging I found Keaton another coach—one of the world's best. He was a grandmaster named Miron whom we had met at a summer chess camp. He had recently moved to New York from Russia, where he had coached the Russian National Team. Lessons with the grandmaster coach were conducted via telephone. Each set up a chess board and called out moves to one another using the chess board's algebraic notation, such as "Move White's knight to the f7 square." Keaton took these lessons in the quiet of his chess room—a converted basement bedroom adorned with chess-themed photos, awards, and wallpaper border. A wooden board and pieces sat center stage.

Over the years, Keaton took lessons from his coaches once or twice a week and studied chess another 10–15 hours per week. Oftentimes I would work with him and reinforce what was taught in lessons. In addition, he frequented school and community chess clubs, where he played practice games and socialized with other players. We occasionally traveled to places such as New York, Atlanta, and Chicago to camps for serious players. The large amount of time Keaton spent on chess prompted him to drop other activities such as music, baseball, and soccer. Chess and school dominated his life, but he had no regrets. He loved to play and study chess. It was his passion.

I linked Keaton's chess talent development to school. Keaton was identified as gifted in the first grade and received mentoring in math or language arts for an hour each day. When he was in fifth grade, I approached the school district's gifted committee and proposed that Keaton be mentored in chess. My rationale was that chess was Keaton's true gift or talent. The committee surprisingly granted my request—the only time mentoring had occurred outside traditional subjects—and Keaton received daily chess instruction for course credit from his own coaches and partially at the school's expense through high school.

For the most part, Keaton was self-motivated. He wanted to win National Scholastic Championships, win the Nebraska state title, and attain a master rating. He was also motivated to emulate his instructors, who were wonderful role models. Keaton was motivated most by his deep passion for the game. When he played, he was immersed in the game. He stared at the board so intently that it was surprising it did not ignite in flames. He was supremely confident and completely comfortable. He looked ageless. Still, I tried to boost his motivation when I could.

For instance, I reminded Keaton at tournaments how prepared and strong he was. Before each game, I reminded him to draw on that chess knowledge and to hear his coach's voice while analyzing game positions. Before leaving Keaton at the board I would say, "Everything you need to play great chess is in your heart and in your head." Only rarely did Keaton's chess motivation wane. When it did, I reminded him that my time and resource commitment can only match his commitment. But I also let him know that if he wanted to take a break from chess or even quit chess, that was his call and was okay with me. This was his show.

Managing Keaton's chess activities was time-consuming and like a second job. I attended many of his lessons and all of his tournaments and camps. Most years he played in a couple dozen tournaments throughout the state and around the country. Some tournaments, such as the U.S. Open, lasted nine days; most camps lasted a week. I made all the registration, hotel, and travel arrangements. In addition, I attended weekly chess clubs with him in our community and ordered materials and resources. Of course, I also paid the bills. The yearly price tag for chess activities in the 1990s usually exceeded $10,000. Grandmaster lessons alone cost $50 an hour, and some weeks Keaton had four hours of instruction. A typical chess trip for a national tournament cost us $1,500 for transportation, hotel, registration, and food. In the early years Keaton would win one or two giant trophies at a national tournament, and I would pay $100 to have them shipped home. Eventually I got smarter and started bringing a wrench to tournaments to dismantle the trophies and an extra suitcase to carry them home—when bags flew free.

Probably the biggest thing I did to support Keaton's chess was establishing a chess culture in our community that allowed Keaton more chess opportunities and legitimized his chess involvement. Let's face it, society values things such as football as a sport and music as an art. Although chess is part sport and part art, it is viewed by many as a game for nerds. I wanted to alter that perception for Keaton and others. To do so, I organized and taught a chess club at Keaton's elementary school. One hundred kids participated. Although Keaton was one of the youngest, he was also the best player and quickly earned the acceptance and admiration of schoolmates.

A second chore was writing a weekly chess column for the city newspaper. This was a way to inform the larger community about chess and its educational values. I also kept the press informed about Keaton's chess accomplishments as he won national and state titles. This publicity led to feature stories about Keaton that appeared on television and radio and in newspapers. I became president of a local chess organization that supports chess education. From this perch, I organized dozens of chess activities, tournaments, and camps in which Keaton could participate, instruct, or showcase his talents by playing several opponents at once or playing blindfolded. Finally, I cotaught after-school chess clubs with Keaton and helped him gain independent employment as a chess instructor in schools and at camps. These experiences helped pay for chess lessons and travel. They also legitimized chess as a profession and set the stage for his eventual chess coaching career.

As I did these things to support Keaton's talent journey, I never did so with complete certainty or conviction. I wondered if I was doing the right things, if I was doing enough things, and at times if I should be doing these things at all. But I did these things for what seemed like good reasons. First, Keaton had a need that begged to be fulfilled. As a parent, I could no more ignore this chess need than I could a medical need. Second, I treasured my involvement in Keaton's chess. I savored the time we spent together playing, practicing, traveling, and teaching. Third, chess was his passion, and I loved his chess too—not just the championships but the dazzling moves he made. Finally, I loved that Keaton was engaged in deep study and could generalize that to other life aspects. I knew that if he could master chess, he could master anything.

My Story as Talent Researcher

Hearing my personal story, you might wonder if talent is a bastion of the few—reserved for the intellectually gifted or for the offspring of a learning-crazed educational psychologist with some time and capital. I wondered too. And that is when my personal journey as chess parent merged with my professional role as educational psychologist. I wondered why some children such as Keaton develop talent, whether talent is within the reach of most children, and what roles parents play. I then set out to find answers.

My search led me to study the lives of extraordinary individuals such as Wolfgang Mozart in music, Pablo Picasso in art, and Bobby Fischer in chess and led to my colleagues and I conducting interviews with dozens of talented individuals, their parents, and their coaches to uncover how talent is nurtured. Interviews extended across various talent domains such as chess, baton twirling, figure skating, speed skating, swimming, diving, golf, gymnastics, baseball, softball, basketball, football, volleyball, fencing, bowling, rodeo, music, dance, theater, costume design, photography, art, law, spelling, fiction writing, poetry, psychology, robotics, rock climbing, business, coaching, teaching, and gifted education.

The people investigated were truly elite and often well known. They included Olympians such as Bonnie Blair and Dan Jansen (speed skating), Charlie White and Meryl Davis (figure skating), and Paul and Morgan Hamm (gymnastics). They included professional athletes such as Bo and Barrett Rudd (football) and collegiate athletes such as Andrew White III (basketball) and Mikaela Foecke (volleyball). They included renowned artists such as Joel Sartore (photography) and Jim Brickman (songwriter and pianist). They included national champions such as Anamika Veeramani (spelling) and world champions such as Steffany Lien (baton twirling). They included elite coaches and teachers such as John Cook (volleyball), Gary Copeland (fencing), and Mimi Zweig (violin). Also included are dozens of award winners and up-and-coming stars.

What Talent Research Taught Me

Talent research taught me a number of things.

1. *I was not alone in trying to navigate talent waters.* Parents everywhere were rowing the same boat without compass or sextant. Most said that they didn't plan for talent, see it coming, or know what to do when it appeared. Many also said that they wished there had been a manual available for raising a talented child and that they just muddled through the process and did the best they could.

2. *Talent is neither a starting point nor an endpoint.* People are not born with talent, and talent development is not finite. Talent is a continuum, a process of increasing growth. This process viewpoint means that all people are somewhere on that talent continuum and that talent growth can proceed indefinitely. There are no winners and losers, only developers. Talent, then, is a pursuit and growth available to all.

3. *Talent is not born but made.* Whatever biological hand we are dealt can be greatly enhanced as we draw new environmental cards that support or even override biology. Through practice and training, we can alter our bodies and our brains. We make talent. None of the famously talented people you know or whom I studied could have been who they became without a constellation of environmental talent factors firing in sync.

4. *There is a constellation of environmental talent factors.* Environmental factors include an enriched early environment to set one on the talent path, strong mentors to model and teach talent skills, a long and arduous practice routine, a center-of-excellence training ground, a singleness-of-purpose motivation to master, and a talent manager. This talent constellation is within reach of most every child.

5. *Children cannot take the talent journey alone.* Children alone cannot possibly make all of these talent factors fire. But they can if others help. Parents are in the optimal position to foster talent. They can provide an enriched early environment, secure mentors, regulate practice, locate or build a center of talent excellence, spur motivation, and manage all aspects of talent development. This is no easy task. In fact, it can be life altering and require

extraordinary actions and sacrifices. But for the parents I interviewed, the desire to fulfill these myriad roles was powerful and came from two places. One, parents saw their children displaying talent development needs that begged to be met the same way medical needs must be met. Two, parents loved their children and wanted them to be fulfilled and happy.

6. *Maximum talent development hinges on the child's commitment.* Parents play crucial roles in developing their children's talent, but elite-level talent development rests first and foremost with the child. If the child is not passionate about the talent domain and is not committed to pursuing talent, it's game over. Elite levels of talent development are only possible when the child has a single-minded passion to pursue the talent area and is willing to practice hard over an extended period. Parents cannot drive the talent train; children must do that. Parents can, however, ignite a talent passion and help keep the train on track.

7. *Talent development is not an isolated journey.* Some families might avoid the talent path in favor of a developing well-rounded children. This is a value judgment left to each family. In making this judgment, consider that most talented children I studied were happy and well adapted. Most were strong students and had friends. Some participated in activities outside their talent domain. A chess champion was a football star, and a rodeo champion was a basketball point guard. Even though most pursued their talent domain with singleness of purpose, their lives were not one-dimensional. Also consider that it might be more fruitful to spend time leveraging strengths than shoring up weaknesses. The world is fast becoming a technical place where specific strengths trump general competence.

8. *There are talent benefits.* Talent pursuit and fulfillment have myriad benefits. First, talented people enjoy their talent domain and enjoy pursuing talent—and parents love being on the talent journey too. Second, many talented people turn talent enjoyment into talent employment. Talented children emerge as professional musicians, coaches, photographers, writers, chess players, and volleyball, football, baseball, basketball, and skating athletes. A third benefit is self-growth—not just in the talent domain but as a person. Motivational speaker Zig Ziglar said, "What you get by achieving your goals is not as important as what you become by achieving your goals."[1] What talented people become are winners, confident that they can accomplish anything they set their mind to in the same way they tamed their talent domain. They know how to achieve great things. They have learned how to master any domain.

Talent development yields more than personal benefits; it also yields universal benefits. What if Mozart had not pursued music or Picasso had not pursued art? What a cultural loss that would have been. What if Charles Darwin had not pursued biological science or Sigmund Freud had not pursued psychology? What an intellectual loss that would have been. What if

Marie Curie had not discovered cancer radiation treatment or Alexander Fleming not discovered penicillin bacteria treatment? What a medical loss that would have been. And what if Bonnie Blair had not pursued speed skating or Roger Federer had not pursued tennis? What an athletic loss that would have been. The world is a better and more enjoyable and inspiring place because of talented people. Talent is for the world to appreciate and share.

The Purpose of This Book

I write this book for several audiences: talent seekers and those seeking to understand talent and its roots, talent enablers such as school administrators and teachers, and talent coaches and mentors working in the talent development trenches. But most of all I write this book for parents, because they are the prime movers in a child's talent development. They can influence the constellation of environmental factors that produce talent. This book is for parents who notice budding talent and wonder how to make it blossom and also for parents yet to unearth their children's potential. This book is for all parents, because as you will soon discover, talent can blossom almost anywhere when growing conditions are right, and it is parents who largely determine those conditions. So, you certainly don't need to be an educational psychologist to nurture talent. You simply need to know what this educational psychologist has learned. I give you *Nurturing Children's Talents: A Guide for Parents*.

CHAPTER TWO

Introduction to Talent Development

Before considering how to nurture talent, three fundamental questions are raised and answered: Is talent born or made? What factors spur talent? What role do schools play in talent development?

Is Talent Born or Made?

At first glance, it looks like talent is born. Consider prodigies such as Wolfgang Mozart, Pablo Picasso, and Bobby Fischer. Mozart learned to play the piano at age 3 and the violin at age 4. At age 5, he began composing. Soon he composed regularly and performed in Europe's leading concert halls. Picasso the child painted like an adult. American author Gertrude Stein said that young Picasso "wrote paintings as other children wrote their A, B, Cs."[1] Picasso said, "I never drew like a child. When I was twelve, I drew like Raphael."[2] When Fischer was 14, he became the youngest U.S. chess champion. When he was 16, he became the youngest player ever to earn the grandmaster title. Such talent so young suggests that some must be born with talent, perhaps a gift from the gods.

Look more closely, though, and talent appears made even among these prodigies. Both Mozart and Picasso were raised and tutored by fathers already accomplished in the respective talent areas. Mozart's father, Leopold, was a successful composer, violinist, and assistant concert master at the Salzburg court. He had also written a book on violin instruction the year Mozart was born. Leopold was devoted to teaching Mozart and insisted that his son practice hard and achieve perfection. Picasso was instructed in art by his father, Jose Ruiz Blasco, who taught drawing at various art schools. Fischer's parents were not chess players, but Fischer was raised in New York City, a chess Mecca, where he learned from elite players who frequented the same local chess clubs he did. Moreover, Fischer worked hard at chess. He sat for hours at the board and thoughtfully played both sides of games. He solved chess puzzles using a pocket chess set as he rode the bus to and from school. He taught himself Russian so he could voraciously read Russian chess literature. He often hid chess books inside his schoolbooks so he could study chess while in school and left school during lunch periods to play chess with a chess master who lived nearby. After school, Fischer would head to one of the local chess clubs and often stay there late into the night until his mother found him and dragged him home. At age 16, Fischer dropped out of school to study chess full-time. He was a child consumed by chess.

Look closer still, and it appears that Mozart, Picasso, and Fischer, although prodigious, were far from their talent peaks as children. All of them worked at their crafts for many years before making talent breakthroughs. And they were hardly alone on the long road to talent development. Psychologist John Hayes investigated many talented composers and artists to determine the time interval from one's introduction to a talent domain to one's first truly great accomplishment. Hayes discovered that there was a 10-year rule.[3] That is, no outstanding composer or artist—even the prodigious Mozart or Picasso—created a work judged significant in fewer than 10 years, with some taking closer to 20 years. The same held true for Fischer and other chess grandmasters. Even with all his passion, dedication, and resources, Fischer did not earn the world title until he was 29 years old. Researchers studying chess grandmasters confirm that most only attain the grandmaster title after about 32,000 hours of intensive study.[4] Do the math: That's intensive study eight hours a day, seven days a week, for over 11 years.

Talent Is the Result of Incremental Progress

Psychologists today believe that talent is within reach of most everyone. Robert Weisberg, who studies creativity, argues that creative breakthroughs, such as Picasso's famed painting *Guernica* and Orville and Wilbur Wright's flying machine, do not come to fruition in some inspirational gift from the gods but instead come from long, arduous, and incremental work in a domain.[5] *Guernica* is a mural that captured the horrors of war following the bombing of the Spanish town of Guernica by Nazi air forces. Although some might find the painting original and spontaneous, Weisberg debunks this genius myth and illustrates Picasso's incremental process. First, several of the painting's central figures, such as the bull and the horse, appear in the artist's previous works. Second, Picasso's working sketches leading up to *Guernica* show many variations from sketch to sketch and from sketches to final painting. This is evidence that Picasso did not create *Guernica* from a single breath of inspiration and instead created it in a deliberate and incremental way.

The same was true for the Wright brothers. Their flying machine invention came about not in one grand and inspired attempt but rather in the brothers' long and turbulent journey. First, the brothers developed the mechanical background needed to devise and assemble an aircraft by being raised in a home where they completed several home construction projects and by later owning a bicycle shop. Second, when they made their original design, they drew upon the scientific and applied work of other inventors also working to develop a flying machine. Finally, the Wright brothers' actual construction and testing of the machine took many years and was fraught with many setbacks and adjustments. Talent came slowly, with many failures and with much work.

Talent Can Be Engineered

Psychologist Howard Gardner, who has studied the creative lives of Mozart, Picasso, and others, asked talent-is-made skeptics to conduct a thought experiment called Five Experiences a Day.[6] Gardner told the skeptics to imagine taking biologically identical twins separated at conception and giving one five positive experiences a day and the other five negative experiences a day. By the time of birth, one will have had over 1,300 positive experiences, and the other would have had over 1,300 negative experiences—for a 2,600-experience disparity. Now, advance the calendar five more years, and an additional 9,000 positive or negative experiences have occurred, yielding a disparity of 20,600 experiences. Does anyone believe that these two five-year-olds would be alike?

John B. Watson, a psychologist from the 1920s, was an early advocate that environment, not heredity, determined a child's fate. Watson famously proclaimed "Give me a dozen healthy infants, well-formed, and my own specified world to bring them up in and I'll guarantee to take any one at random and train him to become any type of specialist I might select—doctor, lawyer, artist, merchant-chief, and, yes, even beggar man and thief."[7]

Watson's proclamation was remarkably tested by educational psychologist Laszlo Polgar and foreign-language teacher Klara Alberger, who made marriage plans as part of a personal experiment to see if they could raise chess champions.[8] Laszlo believed that a child's achievement stems from educational training rather than heredity. Laszlo was a recreational chess player, but he largely chose chess because chess skill is objectively measured using a precise rating system based on match results against other rated players. In addition, established titles are attained such as master, international master, and grandmaster. The Polgar experiment was carried out under challenging conditions because the couple raised three daughters—Susan, Sofia, and

Judit—and women to that point had not fared well in what was considered a thinking man's game. At the time, no woman had ever earned the grandmaster title or was ranked among the world's top 100 players.

The Polgar experiment began in earnest when Susan was four years old and Laszlo began specialized chess training. He taught Susan to play, hired an expert coach to work with her, and took her to a chess club to practice. To teach her, Laszlo relied on his modest experience, a library of 5,000 chess books, and a collection of 200,000 games and puzzles clipped from newspapers and categorized for effective study. Susan was homeschooled by her parents through high school and even in college, where she majored in chess, because Laszlo believed that schools were unhealthy and dangerous places for talented children. He said, "School has a leveling out, uniforming effect . . . [that] happens at a low standard."[9] While homeschooled, Susan spent about 10 percent of her time studying school subjects and 90 percent (8 to 10 hours a day) studying chess. Despite this heavy chess focus, Susan excelled on school exams, acquired multiple languages, cared for more than 20 pets, and participated in recreational sports. Susan's younger sisters, in turn, became curious about chess as they watched Susan study and play. In time, sisters Sofia and Judit also began specialized chess training by age four and progressed through the same chess-studying regime as Susan.

The Polgar experiment was an unequivocal chess success. Intensive and long-term chess specialization produced remarkable results. For example, all three sisters earned international master titles, and Susan and Judit also earned grandmaster titles. Susan was the first woman to ever earn the grandmaster title through tournament play, and Judit surpassed Bobby Fischer's world record for the youngest ever to attain the grandmaster title. Although none of the sisters became world champion, Judit broke into the exclusively male top 100 list and rose to number eight in the world, the highest ranking by any woman ever. The Polgar sisters' path to chess supremacy was well calculated, and the parents, especially Laszlo, led the daughters' every move.

The Conditions Surrounding Talent Development

Psychologist Benjamin Bloom was the first to study talent development comprehensively.[10] He studied the 120 most talented American adults in six domains: piano, sculpture, swimming, tennis, mathematics, and neurology. His purpose was to determine how childhood factors, including parenting, shaped talent development. Bloom's overriding conclusion was this: "What any person in the world can learn, almost all persons can learn if provided with the appropriate conditions of learning."[11]

We began by asking whether talent is born or made. This section makes evident that talent is largely made. Talent is not a beginning but an end. And talent is within the grasp of almost anyone. Philosopher Ralph Waldo Emerson perhaps said it best: "Every artist is first an amateur."[12]

What readers must understand next is how talent is developed. Bloom believed that almost anyone could become talented given the right conditions of learning, and Gardner said that five positive experiences a day can change a life. Next, we explore those factors that made Keaton, the Polgar sisters, Bloom's most talented Americans, and so many others talented.

What Factors Spur Talent?

It has been established that talent is made, not born. Cutting through these talent stories—any talent stories—are six common factors: (1) early experience, (2) practice, (3) mentors (4) centers of excellence, (5) singleness of purpose, and (6) managerial support. This section examines each factor. Remaining chapters add substance to these factors and specify what parents can do to foster talent relative to each.

Early Experience

The road to expertise usually begins early in a child's life. My own research reveals musicians beginning musical training as toddlers, figure skaters starting at age two or three, baton twirlers starting between ages two and four, and a writer learning to read at age three.[13] In some cases, this early start comes about because children are born into the talent area; parents or siblings are already immersed in the talent domain. Such was the case for Mozart and Picasso. Some of the talented musicians, artists, and athletes whom Bloom studied were also born into households where the talent area was already in force. One tennis parent said, "We always kidded that our daughter woke up in a car bed, next to the tennis courts, hearing the ping-pong of tennis balls—that was one of the first sounds she recollects probably. . . . We belonged to a tennis club and played tennis all weekend."[14]

Colleagues and I interviewed the parents of 24 nationally recognized children spanning several talent domains and found that 22 of them personally introduced their child to the talent domain.[15] Among those 22 parents, some were paid instructors or high-level competitors; others pursued the talent area as a hobby. One parent was University of Nebraska volleyball coach John Cook. Coach Cook has been named National Coach of the Year and has guided his Nebraska team to four national championships. His daughter, Lauren, was a first-team All-American player at Nebraska. Coach Cook said, "I think my daughter had an advantage because of my job. She's been in the gym a lot. She grew up around volleyball. When she was a little kid, she was playing with balloons in the basement. We set up a mini court and would play on our knees."[16] The parent of a cello player described her musical household: "We always played music in the house, all kinds of music, classical, Beatles, all kinds. We always provided an avenue for the children to enjoy music and play instruments."[17]

Sometimes it is not parents who set the talent-initiation stage but siblings. In interviews with gold medal Olympic speed skaters Bonnie Blair and Dan Jansen, I learned that both were raised in homes where their older siblings were already enthusiastic and accomplished speed skaters. Blair, who was the youngest of six children, said, "When I was born, it wasn't a matter of when I was going to be a skater, it was how quickly could they get me on skates."[18] She began skating at age two and was racing by age four. Jansen was the youngest of nine speed skating children. He believes that having so many older siblings who skated was crucial to his early start in skating and how far he progressed in the sport. Jansen said that he and his siblings were simply "given a pair of skates and off we went."[19] Weekends were spent traveling with family to speed skating meets, and for Jansen "It was a fun thing to do with my entire family."

Even when talent-destined children were not born into the talent area, most enjoyed and benefited from an early introduction, a head start, in the eventual talent area. Interviews I conducted with parents of six young chess masters revealed that chess play began as early as age three and that the average starting age was six.[20] This early start occurred even though none of the parents were anything more than recreational players, while most had no chess background at all. Early starts often came about because parents noticed that their children had a special interest or a natural connection to a talent domain. The parent of a National Spelling Bee champion noticed that her young daughter had a flair for language and a special interest in word origins and foreign languages. The daughter even carried a notebook to write down interesting words. This parent said, "I sensed early on that my daughter had this flair for language and spelling that had to be tapped."[21] The parent of an eventual Olympic figure skater remarked, "Our daughter had a special awareness of the body and was gifted in terms of movement. She walked at an early age, etc., so we gave her opportunities to try out her gifts." Finally, the father of an exceptional chess player noticed the natural connection that his son had with chess: "The way he touched the pieces was with the tenderness you would touch a woman you loved. There was actual enjoyment in just touching the pieces and moving them with such care and maturity. There was something unusual about this picture. So, I started to study with him."

Practice

Early experience can jump-start a child on the road to Carnegie Hall, but only practice, practice, and more practice can deliver her. As indicated earlier, talented people practice a lot for 10 or more years to achieve expertise in a domain.[22] Just as important as the extent of practice is the nature of practice. Talented people practice the right way. Their practice is deliberate. Let's look more closely at the extent and deliberate nature of practice.

You have already heard about the many practice hours that talented people log. Regarding chess, Bobby Fischer seemingly practiced all day. Susan Polgar studied 8 to 10 hours a day. Keaton practiced far less time but still logged about 20 hours a week, or 1,000 hours a year. This amount fits with practice times among young chess masters I studied—those who earned a master rating by age 16.[23] On average, it took those young masters 8 years and 8,000 practice hours to attain the master title. That's not quite 10 years, but there are still chess ranks to ascend beyond the master title.

I have yet to meet a truly talented performer who has not spent many years and thousands of hours practicing, even at the high school level. National High School Rodeo champion Jayde Atkins has been riding horses since she was two years old and practices every day after school until dark. State champion swimmer Olivia Calegan swims twice a day and about four hours a day in total. Six-time world-champion baton twirler Steffany Lien started practicing at age four and has practiced tens of thousands of hours since. Her mother Susan said, "We sometimes spend five or six hours a day in the gym. We usually split that time into two practices, so we're in the gym twice a day. It's just part of our rhythm of the day to go to the gym and practice. Even on Christmas Eve, we figure out how we're going to get into some gym in the morning before it closes."[24]

Psychologist Benjamin Bloom also found that heavy practice loads distinguish top American performers from others—even those with similar genetic stuff.[25] In many families Bloom studied, the talented child's siblings enjoyed the same early experiences and enriched opportunities to excel. But rarely did a sibling even come close to the accomplishment level of the more talented sibling Bloom studied. This was true even when the talented child's brother or sister seemed to possess more natural ability early on. In the end, parents reported, the one who excelled was the one who practiced most.

Simply logging a lot of playing time is not the way to practice, however. I know this firsthand. For years I played golf. My wife might say "a lot of golf," but I never improved much. Apparently, just knocking balls around the course or even spraying a bucketful around the range does not improve one's game. Psychologist Anders Ericsson, an expert on expertise, confirmed that the number of chess games played or hours spent playing the piano are weak predictors of eventual skill level.[26] More important than a lot of playing is what Ericsson calls deliberate practice, which is intentional and effortful practice aimed at improvement. Deliberate practice is focused, arduous, and intense. It requires full concentration, is often carried out alone, and is not necessarily enjoyable. In one classic study, Ericsson investigated the practice routines of expert musicians over a 15-year period.[27] The musicians spanned four groups ranging in expertise from "professionals" to "best experts" to "good experts" to "least accomplished experts," in descending order. Results showed that the four groups spent the same amount of time on music activities but varied in deliberate practice. The professionals, for example, spent 25 hours a week in deliberate practice. This amount was three times greater than that for the least accomplished experts, who simply did a lot of playing. Weekly deliberate practice differences added up over time. At age 20, the two best groups had spent over 10,000 hours on deliberate practice compared with the lower two groups, which had spent 8,000 (good experts) and 5,000 (least accomplished experts) hours. Ericsson believes that it is deliberate practice, not biology, that determines a person's talent fate. Ericsson said that "The traditional view of talent, which concludes that successful individuals have special innate abilities . . . , is not consistent with . . . evidence"[28] and that "There is no cell type that geniuses have that the rest of don't."[29]

When Tiger Woods was at his golfing best, he was a poster boy for deliberate practice. He practiced nine hours a day, and only two of those daily hours were spent walking the course and playing golf. The rest of the time was spent lifting weights, practicing putting, and shaping golf shots on the range. Even on the course, Woods did not just knock it around like a weekend golfer but practiced shots from varying lies.

Caroline Thiel, a Nebraska State High School swim champion, is a deliberate practice proponent. Theil told me that "Some days in practice you're just so exhausted. You're sore and your entire body aches, and it's hard to find motivation. But you remember your goals and you find motivation. You push through each 100-, 50-, or 25-yard sprint. Your brain shuts down but your body keeps going through the muscle aches and heavy breathing and throwing up. People don't realize how hard swimming is and how hard we practice. People think that you just get in the pool and swim a few laps."[30]

When people practice for a long time in the right way, certain outcomes are evident. Most important, performance improves, be it in swimming or clarinet playing, and certain muscles associated with the growing talent become stronger and well toned. But something else happens deep inside our bodies. We improve our neural circuitry through a process called myelination, the process at the root of talent development.

When we move or think, an electric signal travels through a chain of neurons. Myelin is the insulation that wraps these neuron chains and increases signal strength, speed, and accuracy. The more we practice and fire a neuron chain, the more myelin wraps that neuron chain and the stronger, faster, and more fluid our movements and thoughts become. Brain scans of concert pianists, for example, confirm that those who practice the most have the greatest myelin quantities.[31] Writer Daniel Coyle, in his book *The Talent Code,* writes that "The story of skill and talent is the story of myelin. . . . The truth is, practice makes myelin, and myelin makes perfect."[32] Dr. George Bartzokis, professor of neurology at UCLA, said this to Coyle: "What do all good athletes do when they train? They send precise impulses along wires that give the signal to myelinate that wire. They end up, after all that training, with a super-duper wire—lots of bandwidth, a high-speed T-3 line. That's what makes them different from the rest of us."[33] Of course, myelination is not just for the elite but for all. Anyone can amp up myelination through deliberate practice.

Mentors

My hack golfing days finally passed when I started practicing golf shots more deliberately. But I couldn't practice that way until I better understood the game of golf, and that didn't happen until I began golf lessons. Under the tutelage of a golf coach, I learned how to practice. The coach identified and repaired subtle flaws in my game. He would say things like "Try holding the club on the other end and with two hands" and "It's best to remove those head covers before striking the ball." Little adjustments like that helped me practice better and improve. I joke, of course, but the importance of coaches and mentors is instrumental in talent development.

Psychologist Benjamin Bloom found that talented children often worked with three mentors over a 10- to 15-year period, with each mentor fulfilling a successively more complex role that matched children's emerging talent level.[34] First mentors were perfect for young children. They introduced children to the domain in playful ways and made learning enjoyable and like a game. First mentors were encouraging and enthusiastic and offered a lot of praise. They unfolded the budding talent. Quite often, first mentors were the child's parents.

Eventually children outgrew their first mentor. The children's growing commitment and expanding knowledge led to a second mentor—usually at the urging of the first. Second mentors were technical experts who emphasized precision and accuracy. They worked only with talented performers committed to the talent area. They demanded a lot of deliberate practice—up to five hours a day.

Finally, some students sought a third mentor, a master teacher nationally recognized as one of the few elite teachers in the field. These were mentors who commonly worked at universities or conservatories or as national coaches. They mentored just a handful of students fully committed to the talent domain and capable of excellence. Third mentors helped students correct minor flaws, analyze their own performance, and develop a personal style

My own research generally confirms a mentoring hierarchy whereby children begin with a talent-introduction mentor and progress to one or more talent-mastery mentors. One chess parent commented on her son's first coach: "He was a wonderful coach. . . . [H]e really got the kids to laugh and enjoy."[35] The parent reported that coach and student often ate jelly beans and watched cartoons before playing chess. That chess student and every other chess player I studied was eventually mentored by an elite coach who was a top-ranked player.[36]

In music, violinist Will Hagen, the highest American ranked violinist since 1985, progressed through several mentors since his violin introduction at age 3. William was first mentored at age 4. William's mother reported that "His first teacher almost immediately said, 'Wow, there is really something here,' and she encouraged us to take him to a different, more advanced teacher."[37] The family heeded the advice and moved on to a more qualified teacher. At age 10, William changed mentors again and began working with Robert Lipsett at the Colburn Community School of Performing Arts in Los Angeles. William and his mother would fly there weekly from their home in Utah. After being mentored by Lipsett for several years, William studied for 2 years with the world's top violinist, Itzhak Perlman, at the famed Juilliard School of Music in New York. After that, William returned to Los Angeles to resume his studies with Lipsett.

Violinist Mimi Zweig, who started the String Academy at Indiana University, revealed when interviewed that she progressed through a series of mentors as she originally traveled her own talent path. Her first teacher was an amateur violinist who engendered a love for music that hooked her to music for life. Mimi's second teacher, who worked with Mimi from age 10, was a professional violinist who played in the Sacramento Symphony Orchestra and gave her a solid technical foundation. Mimi's third teacher was a famous professional violinist in Syracuse, New York, whom Mimi worked with from age 14 and on into college.

Pianist Jim Brickman credits his parents for his creative leanings and for finding him the right mentors. Brickman, when interviewed, said, "I don't come from a musical family, but my parents are creative in their own way. My mom's a poet and writer. My dad is an amazing chef and historian. So, their expressing themselves that way meant that I was nurtured by that creative expression, but for music."[38] At age four, Brickman begged his parents for a piano and for lessons. They finally relented and bought a beat-up piano and hired a first teacher, who soon told his parents that Brickman had no talent. At his mother's begging, the teacher continued teaching Brickman until the family eventually sought more insightful teachers at the Cleveland Institute of Music, where Brickman flourished. Brickman reflected on the importance of mentors, especially in developing one's personal style:

> The most important thing in a young person's life is to have a mentor, somebody who understands what is happening inside you—like a great coach for an athlete. And, I was fortunate to have somebody when I was in my early teens: A graduate student at the Cleveland Institute of Music. Although this is a classical conservatory, my mentor was more of a pop-jazz guy and he related to what was going on in my mind—that I had a

pop sensibility about my song writing. He advocated for my pop song writing and nurtured and influenced that part of me.[39]

Centers of Excellence.

Budding stars often gravitate to centers of excellence, talent hotbeds, to work with the best mentors and other rising stars who flock there.[40] Musician Mozart and psychoanalyst Sigmund Freud gravitated to Vienna, Europe's intellectual hub. Painter Picasso went to Paris, the center for the arts. Dancer Martha Graham sashayed from California to New York, the center for dance. Today, budding musicians gravitate to New York's Juilliard School of Music, while budding technology geeks head to California's Silicon Valley and tomorrow's engineers head to the Massachusetts Insitute of Technology. Tennis prodigies head to tennis academies such as the former Bollettieri Tennis Academy in Bradenton, Florida, where Bollettieri and other top coaches honed the skills of eventual tennis champions including Andre Agassi, Jim Courier, Maria Sharapova, and Martina Hingis. And chess players still gravitate to New York City hoping to become the next Bobby Fischer or study at colleges with elite chess programs such as the University of Texas at Dallas, where my chess-playing son Keaton attended college.

In my own investigations, the family of one Olympic figure skater moved 200 miles to Colorado Springs so their son could train with an elite coach and other elite skaters.[41] And elite speed skaters and skating coaches in the 1970s and 1980s flocked to Milwaukee, home of the only full-size Olympic skating oval.[42] Sometimes parents create centers of excellence at home for their talented children. Rodeo rider Jayde Atkins's family ranch in central Nebraska was a rodeo hotbed.[43] She had the perfect training ground, coaches, and nearby rodeo competitions at her disposal. And the parents of talented chess players and baton twirlers invited elite coaches to visit their homes for extended periods to provide concentrated training for their children.[44]

Singleness of Purpose

Long and daily practice sessions leave the talented individual with little time for outside activities. Among the young chess masters I studied, only two had secondary interests—both in music. The others spent the bulk of their time on chess. One chess parent said, "The extraordinary time we put toward this one activity takes him out of a lot of fun games. The kid gives up an enormous amount to dedicate himself to the sport the way he does."[45] One child had limited social relationships, and a couple of others had low academic achievement because of their single-minded focus on chess. One parent commented that "Chess is a little bit reclusive if you're using a computer and not interacting with other people." Another parent commented on his son:

He is sort of one dimensional. It's chess and the stuff outside chess is not strong. He doesn't do much outside of chess. He's just dedicated his life to chess. That's all he's done since he was a youngster. He does not perform up to his potential in school because, quite frankly, he's not interested in school, he's interested in chess. If he didn't have to go to school and you would deliver meals to his room, he would stay there all day. He just lives and breathes chess.[46]

That same parent once removed chess as a brief punishment because the child was struggling in school. "We once took chess away and he was miserable. It was like yanking the soul out."[47]

When I asked the chess parents why their sons devote so much time to chess, they were unanimous in their response: He just loves it; it's his passion. One parent remarked, "He is passionate about it . . . just thrilled by it. . . . It gives him a lot of joy and satisfaction . . . and he's not really happy when he's not [playing or studying chess]."[48] Sticking with the chess theme, I once met American grandmaster Patrick Wolff at a tournament in Sioux Falls, South Dakota. While he paced the room between moves, I seized the opportunity to ask him how he got to where he is today. Not realizing that my question was framed by my talent development interests, Wolff looked at me quizzically and answered that he flew from Boston to Sioux City, Iowa, and took a puddle jumper from there to Sioux Falls. After I apologized and rephrased, he told me that it was his singleness of purpose that made him strong. From his elementary school days forward, he awoke early every day and studied chess for two hours before school. Chess was his one passion.

Moving outside chess, musician Jim Brickman when interviewed said this about the single-mindedness that musical performance deserves:

So often artists who tour with me say something like, "Well, my wife doesn't really want me to leave for the weekend because her friends are visiting." Those aren't options. Music is a 24-hours a day, constant, constant, constant. It never ends—but in a wonderful way. It's not, I'm going to do a little bit of this, or I want to have five kids, or I want balance in my life. That's fantastic maybe twenty years down the road, but right now is not the time for doing a little bit of this or a little bit of that. Right now, there's no "or" involved.[49]

Switching to photography, wildlife advocate and nature photographer Joel Sartore believes that his Type A personality helped make him an award-winning photographer. When interviewed, Sartore said, "My success comes from being Type A. Type A means I am very driven, never put something off, do it right now, very energetic, very persistent, even aggressive about what I want and what I am going to achieve. I never put off until tomorrow what I can achieve today. All the *National Geographic* photographers have that in common. We are all Type A."[50] Sartore's fierce dedication to photography was best captured in these poignant remarks:

> As a *National Geographic* photographer, my life is measured one story to the next. I bought my first house in Nebraska while I was on assignment shooting the Gulf Coast. My son was born in the middle of a long story about the Endangered Species Act. My daughter came along with a pack of gray wolves. Twenty stories later though, it's the North Slope I'll remember best: Alaska's loss of wilderness and innocence—and the story during which my wife got cancer.[51]

To some of us, single-mindedness seems unnatural, unhealthy, or even dangerous. Still, a pinpoint focus is one hallmark of the creative and talented. Consider Mozart's sad fate after age 30. He had married but not the woman he loved. His mother died, and then his father died shortly thereafter. Mozart was unable to secure lasting employment, and his most creative works were not well received. He was poor and begged for money, and his health was deteriorating. You would think that his productivity plummeted during this trying and stressful period, but not at all. Mozart's dogged determinism and singleness of purpose sustained him.

Psychologist Ellen Winner calls this singleness of purpose the rage to master.[52] She believes that this rage propels talented children through years of grueling training with laser focus and that mastering a certain activity is more important to them than socializing or anything else. Talented individuals simply practice a lot, want to practice a lot, and like to practice a lot. Their hard work and singleness of purpose is the product not of pushy parents but of the child's rage to learn. My research confirms that parents rarely push talented children; talented children push parents. These children push for instruments, lessons, tournament fees, transportation, and parents' time. So, should parents push back and deny or limit a child's passion in hopes for a more balanced life? Maybe, but to do so might be tantamount to yanking out the soul.

Managerial Support

Psychologist Benjamin Bloom said that it is not enough for the child to commit to the talent area; other supporters must commit as well. No child can attain mastery without support, and that support usually comes from parents.

Parents of talented youngsters assume a managerial role. These parents arrange and monitor lessons, plan practice and competition schedules, make travel arrangements, access materials, and accompany the child to events, many of which are across the country or overseas. They also play the role of accountant, fund-raiser, secretary, hairdresser, costume maker, press agent, medical assistant, dietician, chauffeur, school liaison, videographer, and gopher. One chess parent nicely summed up the managerial role that parents play: "My son calls me his agent. That's kind of what I feel like. I do all the planning and everything else and he just gets on the plane or in the car and we go."[53] The parent of an Olympic figure skater said, "I'm the one who signed him up for ballet and off-ice conditioning. I was involved in the costume design and finding the costume maker . . . and helping narrow down music choices for the program. I contact specialists. . . . I do all drug testing paper-work, flight arrangements, hotel arrangements, rental cars. . . . I am like his personal secretary. I'm his assistant. For half the day, all I do is skating work."[54]

Parents don't just manage their child's talent; they foot the bill and make many sacrifices to do so. Most families I studied probably spend $10,000 or more on annual costs. The parent of one elite chess player offered this mon-etary cost estimate:

> Tournament fees in the United States can easily be $200 to $400. Add hotels and tickets for two because he doesn't travel alone. So, when he goes to Philadelphia for the World Open, do the calculation: two airline tickets, six days in the hotel, six days for food, plus the $400 entrance fee. You're talking about $2,500, give or take. If this is an international tournament, double that. Each ticket for him and his mom is about $1,500, ten days for a hotel is another $1,000, plus entrance fees. So, let's say $5,000. Now do the multiplication. Three to four international tournaments a year, three to four national tournaments a year, and let's say four local tournaments, which also require entrance fees and maybe a hotel. Add to this his study materials, coach costs, and memberships, and I would guesstimate that total cost is north of $50,000. Easily.[55]

To foot these heavy costs, families make great sacrifices such as borrowing money, forgoing retirement savings, living in smaller homes, and taking sec-ond jobs. A skating mom bluntly said, "This is an ungodly expensive sport. I can't tell you how many times we mortgaged our house."[56] A cello player's mom remarked, "We decided that money wasn't going to keep him from a certain teacher. So, we lived off borrowed money for a time."

Why do parents work so hard as managers and sacrifice so much to finance talent development? The parents Bloom interviewed said that the pursuit of talent brought their families together for a common good. One parent said that the talent area provided "a common interest and common goal. . . . It helped our family become a family because we were spending all our time together."[57] The chess parents I interviewed were unanimous in their response: They do all they do because they love their sons, and they love their chess. One parent said, "Well, I knew he had talent and I didn't want to see it wither. If you're really good in one thing, you're very, very fortunate so

I just wanted to encourage that in him. I was proud of his skill. I just knew it gave him joy."[58] Another parent remarked, "Because he's my son and I love him and I want him to be whatever he can be. And, if that happens to be chess . . . then that's what I want for him. I want him to be happy."[59] Finally, as the parent of a burgeoning young writer and public speaker remarked,

> It is a full-time job and sometimes even more than a full-time job and it can be hard. But the reason I keep doing it is that I don't just manage somebody. The person I manage is my daughter. At one point, I said to my daughter, "This is so much work for me, would you rather I hire some kind of professional? Someone who can do a better job?" And she said, "But who will rub my tummy when I have a tummy ache?" We just don't see how anyone else could take my role.[60]

What Role Do Schools Play in Talent Development?

The previous section implicated parents as the prime movers in talent development. This section largely explains why schools ordinarily take a pass when it comes to talent development.

Schools Don't Have Time

It is unreasonable to think that schools should take the lead in talent development. Schools have plenty on their plate trying to give a wide range of students a general education. Moreover, there is not as much instructional time available as people might believe. Consider these figures. During a given year, a child attends school 20 percent of the time, is asleep 30 percent of the time, and is potentially awake in the home 50 percent of the time. Moreover, a school provides just 600 hours of academic instruction per year—about 3.25 hours daily over 180 days. Given these figures, it is parents who hold the learning and talent development keys. They potentially regulate half the child's day. A parent can provide 62 percent more instruction beyond that of school by working with the child or securing a mentor just 1 hour per day throughout the year. Two hours of daily home instruction more than doubles a school's instructional contribution. Of course, if the child is not yet school age, parents potentially regulate 70 percent of the child's day. Parents—far more than schools—have the opportunity to foster talent.

Schools Focus on Academics

School reformist and talent author Sir Ken Robinson contends that schools do not focus on the entire child but instead focus on the child from the shoulders up and slightly to the brain's left side. That is, they focus on relaying core subjects such as math, science, and language and ignore other talent pockets such as the visual and performing arts. It is as if schools are trying to rear a bunch of college professors who, Robinson jokes, "look upon their bodies solely as a form of transport for their heads. It's a way of getting their heads to meetings."[61] To make his point about school's one-size-fits-all short-sightedness, Robinson tells the story of Gillian, which I retell here.[62]

Eight-year-old Gillian was already at risk. Her school performance was poor. She turned assignments in late, had terrible handwriting, tested poorly, and either fidgeted in class or stared absentmindedly out the window. The school wanted to place Gillian in a school for children with special needs. Gillian's mother brought her to a psychologist for assessment, fearing the worst. The psychologist asked Gillian's mother to describe Gillian's difficulties but asked Gillian no questions. He simply watched her as the adults spoke. After a while, he thanked Gillian for her patience and asked her to be patient just a bit longer while he and Gillian's mother left the room to speak privately. Before leaving the room, the psychologist turned on the radio.

Once in the corridor outside the room but out of Gillian's sight, the psychologist said to Gillian's mother, "Just stand here for a moment and watch what she does."[63] Nearly immediately, Gillian was on her feet moving around the room to the music. It was easy to see the girl's graceful movements and the expression of joy on her face. At last, the psychologist turned to Gillian's mother and said, "You know, Mrs. Lynne, Gillian is not sick. She's a dancer. Take her to a dance school." And Mrs. Lynne did just that. Eventually, little Gillian, the girl with the high-risk future, became known to the world as Gillian Lynne, one of the most accomplished dancers and choreographers of our time. Gillian needed music and dance in her life, and her school could not provide that. Robinson provided this analysis: "Very few schools . . . in the world teach dance every day . . . as they do with math. Yet we know that many students only become engaged when they're using their bodies. For instance, Gillian Lynne told me that she did better at *all* her subjects once she discovered dance. She was one of those people who had to move to think."[64]

Schools also could not help a Nebraska youth with a genius intelligence quotient (IQ).[65] The boy could read at age two, recite stories from memory, smash a pitched baseball, and hit a golf ball without a hint of hook or slice. When he was school age, the school admitted that it wasn't equipped to meet his needs but suggested that the parents enroll him in the school's regular kindergarten program to slow him down. The parents passed on that debilitating recourse and homeschooled him instead.

Schools Focus on General Intelligence

Schools are also misguided because they often embrace a general view of intelligence. They administer general aptitude tests and then place students in remedial classes or in gifted classes based on their IQ, which is largely a measure of verbal aptitude and logical reasoning. The consensus among school personnel is that those with high IQs are destined to accomplish great things, while those with low IQs are destined to struggle. It is not that simple. First, the relationship between IQ and eventual success is weak.[66] High intelligence does not ensure real talent. In fact, many highly creative individuals have average or somewhat above average IQs but not IQs in the gifted range.[67]

Psychologist Lewis Terman studied the lives and careers of a group of gifted students over a 35-year period.[68] He found that while most carved out successful careers, few ever made extraordinary contributions. That is because children with high IQs are well equipped to master school subjects steeped in language or logical reasoning but are not necessarily equipped to master other areas such as music, art, or chess. That is why I thought it fallacious when a private foundation offered funding to families of children with near-genius IQs. The fallacy was supporting children who excelled on a single IQ test but showed no real accomplishments versus rewarding those who were working hard and making big accomplishments in talent areas such as music and art.

Psychologist Howard Gardner spurns schools' overemphasis on general intelligence and intellectual skills in math and reading over other skill or talent areas. Gardner contends that there is not a unitary general intelligence; there are multiple intelligences—nine in all.[69] In addition to linguistic and logical intelligences—the kinds measured on IQ tests and emphasized in school—Gardner posits seven other brands: musical, spatial, kinesthetic, natural, interpersonal, intrapersonal, and existential. Gardner believes that all people possess the various intelligences in varying degrees, often with one or two of the intelligences being particularly strong. Based on Gardner's theory of intelligence, writer T. S. Eliot was high in linguistic intelligence, chess champion Bobby Fischer in logical and spatial intelligence, composer Mozart in musical intelligence, painter Picasso in spatial intelligence, dancer Gillian Lynne and golfer Tiger Woods in kinesthetic intelligence, scientist Darwin in natural intelligence, social leaders Mahatma Gandhi and Martin Luther King Jr. in interpersonal intelligence, and introspective writer Virginia Woolf in intrapersonal intelligence.

Gardner believes that a school's curriculum should expose students to all the intelligences, not just linguistic and logical intelligences.[70] Students should have ample opportunities to sing and dance, experience nature, and play chess. Moreover, Gardner contends that once a student finds her or his element, as Gillian Lynne did with dance or my son Keaton did with chess, the student is probably best served by focusing on strengths rather than shoring up weaknesses. But schools ordinarily do not leverage a student's strengths. Instead, they provide all with a general education steeped in letters and logic that targets the child from the shoulders up and slightly to the brain's left side.

Schools Can Contribute to Talent Development

Despite myriad obstacles to schools supporting talent development, some schools do contribute to talent development. Consider the true story of one such school depicted in the film *Knights of the South Bronx,* starring Ted Danson. New York City is a center for chess excellence, and many of its schools are linked to the Chess in Schools program, which provides free or subsidized chess instruction during and after school. David McEnulty, a strong player with a decorated chess instruction background, was hired to teach chess at an elementary school in the South Bronx, a New York City area with one of the highest poverty and crime rates in the United States. At first, the children who joined the chess club knew little or nothing about the game and were soundly beaten when they played in local tournaments. McEnulty's group could have easily tipped their kings and resigned from chess. After all, many were from precarious home environments. There were single-parent homes, welfare cases, or relatives in jail. McEnulty, though, convinced them that their weak play stemmed not from bad situations but from a lack of chess experience and practice. Chess pieces don't care about your color, income, or neighborhood, McEnulty told them. The children kept pushing pawns and continued to learn. Most even developed a rage to learn, and McEnulty fed that rage. In just a few years, McEnulty's chess children won city, state, and national chess titles. Here, it was largely the school that fostered talent.

In my own investigations, it is largely parents who foster talent development. Such was not the case, though, with high school basketball star Aguek Arop, as I learned from interviewing him, his athletic director, and his coach. Aguek was recruited by a Division 1 college when he was just a high school sophomore. When he was a junior, his high school team won the Nebraska State Championship, and Aguek was named the state's best player. Aguek and his large family were Sudanese refugees. Although Aguek's early home experiences and his parents' ethic for hard work shaped Aguek's strong character, it was largely Aguek's own actions that kick-started his basketball indoctrination, and it was the school that shaped his basketball talent. Aguek's first Nebraska home was in the projects, and it was there that he watched his older brothers play and soon joined in against older and bigger kids. Every day after school, Aguek would hit the courts to play or practice. When he was in seventh grade his parents dropped him and his brothers off at the YMCA, where he would repeatedly practice certain aspects of his game such as making left-handed shots. As an eighth grader, he joined the school team. His coaches made him a seasoned player. Aguek's high school athletic director, Dennis Mitchell, said, "I think our coaching staff built him into what he is now. We took a kid that was skinny and light and built a 6′6″ monster. Our coaching staff transformed him into a bonafide Division

1 college player."[71] Assistant basketball coach Bruce Chubick deflects Aguek's meteoric rise back onto Aguek's rage to learn and deliberate practice. Chubick said, "Aguek is a guy who is really self-driven. We show him what to do and he'll practice it on his own hundreds and thousands of times. We never need to show him something more than once. Show him what to do once, and he's in the gym practicing it to perfection."

Like several talented individuals I studied, school played a supporting role in the talent development of high school swimmer Olivia Calegan, who set five state swim records in the Nebraska State Championship meet when she was a junior. Olivia had all the ingredients for stardom. She was born into a swimming family; was mentored by her father, who quit his day job to coach Olivia for many years; was single-minded in her extensive and deliberate practice; and was part of a swim club talent hotbed with outstanding coaches and teammates. But Olivia also flourished because she was part of a strong swim program in school. In the previous five years, Olivia's high school team was undefeated in meets and won three state titles. In the latest state championship, the team captured gold in 9 of 11 events. Olivia's team has an elite coach, Leigh Ann Witt, who was a 15-time All American swimmer at the University of Texas and is a former Olympian in the same sprint event that Olivia swims. Coach Witt fully understands the importance of deliberate practice in terms of both technique and pushing beyond one's comfort zone:

> I focus on the little stroke technique things like the pitch of the hand and the height of the elbow. Little things make a big difference. I try to use my swimming background to paint a picture for my swimmers of what a good stroke feels like. I ask them every day to go all out full speed off the blocks. The higher the intensity, the more their muscles start building up lactic acid and making them tie up and get sore until they feel like they can't lift their arms above their head. They're constantly building up that lactic acid in practice and trying to recover from that and overcome that so when they race they'll be able to swim through that fatigue and pain even when they feel like they just can't go another stroke. Our practice routine moves them outside their comfort zone. They learn to keep pushing on when they feel like they can't go any more. Doing that makes good athletes great athletes.[72]

Schools can certainly play a supportive role when they provide enrichment opportunities that spark or nourish talent. Many schools, for example, offer before- or after-school programs in nonacademic domains such as music, chess, art, dance, and athletics. Several of the chess players I studied discovered chess not at home but in school clubs. Grandmaster Robert Hess started this way. His father called Robert's entrance into chess a happy accident. "One day when my son was in the first grade and I was picking him up from school, a kind of funny guy with a Russian accent gives me a business card and says, 'Your son, he's sort of good at chess, you should call me.'"[73] He made the call, and soon Robert was training twice a week with grandmaster Miron Sher, who became Robert's primary coach.

Some schools also identify highly gifted students and provide them with mentors in conventional school subjects such as math or science. Such programs are exemplary for linking students with mentors but fall short because a general intelligence test score is often the gatekeeper, while nonacademic talents are usually ignored. Fortunately, as reported in Chapter 1, my son's school permitted chess mentoring. This support was a major departure from school regulations but a monumental overture to join with families to support talent development.

CHAPTER THREE

Early Experience and Parents' Roles

There are three reasons why an early introduction to one's eventual talent domain is beneficial. First, talent takes 10 or more years to develop, and the earlier one sets out along the talent path, the earlier one might arrive at a chess master designation, a martial arts black belt, an Olympic trials cut time in swimming, or an early spot on a National Basketball Association (NBA) roster, as was the case for LeBron James and other highly talented players just graduating high school. Among chess players I studied, most began early and attained international master or grandmaster titles as teenagers.[1] Among baton twirlers, all began early and were soon winning national or world titles.[2]

A second reason pertains to accumulated advantages. This is the idea that certain early advantages produce greater opportunities that in turn produce more advantages, and on and on. Advantages beget advantages; the rich get richer. Consider the accumulated advantage story of a fictitious boy named Kyle. Kyle was born to athletic parents, so he was blessed with an athletic body (Advantage 1). He grew up in a household where his parents participated in and valued recreational sports, especially soccer, and involved Kyle in their training and games (Advantage 2). When they signed Kyle up for Youth Soccer at age five, he was already the best soccer player on the team (Advantage 3). Because of Kyle's early physical stature and soccer skill, his coach played him more than others on the team. Moreover, he positioned Kyle in the center of the field, where he touched the ball more than his teammates, and assigned him to take all the team's free kicks. That's a lot of extra practice (Advantage 4). Because Kyle got more experience than his teammates, he progressed faster than they did. The difference in skill level between his teammates and him widened (Advantage 5). Because Kyle was the strongest player on the field that year, he was noticed by a regional coach, who coached a select team of seven-year-olds. He suggested that Kyle try out for that team the next season, which Kyle did, and he made the team (Advantage 6). Playing on that team afforded Kyle strong coaches, yearlong soccer training, and intense competition in practices and games against strong players (Advantage 7). This experience led to Kyle attending several national camps, where he progressed even more and met premiere national coaches (Advantage 8). It was at one of these camps that Kyle's play caught the eye of a national team coach, who invited Kyle to join the national team for his age group (Advantage 9). From there, Kyle was immersed with the best coaches, teammates, competitors, and facilities in the United States. He gained untold experience playing nationally and internationally (Advantage 10). Within a few years, Kyle made the U.S. Olympic team.

Sociologists have found evidence for the accumulated advantages idea in the sciences. Here is how it might work. A scientist publishes a landmark paper. That paper leads to greater notoriety and greater opportunity, such as procuring research grants and attracting strong graduate students to assist on subsequent projects. These advantages lead in turn to other significant works, greater notoriety, and increased opportunities. Sociologist Robert Merton indeed found that eminent scientists are given disproportionate credit in cases where they collaborate or compete against lesser known scientists.[3] The rich get richer.

Psychologist Benjamin Bloom found evidence for a special form of accumulated advantages among musicians.[4] Bloom found that musicians' long-term and single-minded commitment to music might stem from an early feeling of specialness and competence that ignited further advantages. He concluded that the more special and accomplished young musicians perceived themselves to be, the more willing and eager they were to invest more time in musical training. Similarly, the more special and accomplished parents thought their child to be, the greater their investment in the child's talent development. The advantage of early competence brought about the advantage of even greater child and parent commitment.

A third reason that early experience is beneficial pertains to myelination, the advantageous wrapping of neuron chains due to deliberate practice. As described in Chapter 2, practice increases myelination, which in turn makes our thoughts and actions stronger, faster, and more fluid. Writer Daniel Coyle reports that there is a critical period for myelination, which begins before birth and extends into our 30s, when it slows down but continues to build until our 50s. The earlier the myelin-wrapping process begins, though, the better. Developmental psychologists have long reported critical learning periods during youth associated with language, vision, music, and memory. As Coyle said, "Anyone who has tried to learn a language or a musical instrument later in life can testify that it takes a lot more time and sweat to build the requisite circuitry. This is why the vast majority of world-class experts start young. Their genes do not change as they grow older, but their ability to build myelin does."[5]

From this introduction, it is evident that an early start on the road to talent development is a good thing. The remainder of this chapter provides parent recommendations for getting your child off on the right foot.

Display Your Passions and Talents

Before they were even teenagers, Lexi, Kelcie, Trina,[6] and Steffany[7] had combined to win a boatload of national and world twirling championships. What all have in common are mothers who were twirlers. All of these twirlers were raised in homes where twirling was on display. Lexi's mom, Julie, was a twirling coach and competition judge. Julie said, "Lexi's been involved in twirling since she was born." When Julie would try to leave Lexi at home with a sitter to go to the gym to coach twirlers, Lexi wouldn't allow it. Julie said, "Lexi refused to stay with the sitter. She would throw a fit. She desperately wanted to come with me to the gym and be with the twirlers. She had baton in her heart."[8] Kelcie's mom, Maura, was also a twirling coach and national-level judge when Kelcie was born. Moreover, Kelcie's older brother was a twirler and helped pave the way for Kelcie. Maura was not surprised that Kelcie followed her mother's and brother's twirling lead: "Twirling seems to me like a family thing. It's very rare that I (as a coach) ever get a student who doesn't have twirling in their family."[9]

Kayden Troff's father was a recreational chess player and taught Kayden's older brothers how to play so that he had playing partners.[10] Young Kayden sat silently on his father's lap and watched the family play. When Kayden was barely three years old, he announced that he was ready to play. Kayden's father tried to be a good sport and humor the baby, so he set up the board and allowed Kayden to try to play. The family was amazed when they saw that Kayden knew how all the pieces moved and how to attack without being taught directly. From that moment on, Kayden was a regular player in the Troff household. Thirteen years later, Kayden became one of the youngest players ever to earn the grandmaster title.

Nebraska softball and singing star McKenzie Steiner was raised in a household where softball and music were family interests and passions. McKenzie was raised on softball, because her older sister was an elite player and her father, Scott, was her coach. Scott said, "McKenzie's older sister was really athletic and really good at softball. Our family would travel the country and watch her play. So, McKenzie was practically raised on a softball field, and I think her love of the game came from that."[11] McKenzie's love for singing simply emerged because Scott enjoyed singing. Scott, who admitted that he had no singing talent, said, "I honestly think that she learned to love singing as a child from listening to me singing in the car. She saw me being happy with it. And occasionally I'd hear her singing in the back and think, 'Wow, she's really good.'"[12]

National rodeo champion Jayde Atkins was raised by parents, who trained and rode horses on their Nebraska ranch. Jayde's mother said, "Our kids have just kind of grown up around that and been on horseback from the start. Jayde has always had a pony or something to ride since she could walk and it's just always been part of her lifestyle."[13]

Olympic speed skaters Bonnie Blair and Dan Jansen were raised by parents who were recreational skaters and had already set a long line of Blair and Jansen children on speed skating paths. Jansen said, "Skating was just something the Jansen family did all winter. Winter would come and we would skate. . . . [As children], we were simply given a pair of skates and off we went. . . . It was a fun thing to do with the entire family."[14]

What all these stories have in common, of course, is that children were influenced early by their parents' activities and interests. This is not surprising. Parents who enjoy tacos and enchiladas tend to have children who enjoy tacos and enchiladas. As psychologist John Watson intimated when he essentially said "Give me a baby and I'll shape its future in any way I choose," one's environment is a powerful force.[15] Parents who have talents, interests, and passions should put them on display for children and not be surprised when children grab a taco or enchilada and join them in those pursuits.

Offer a Talent Menu

Psychologist Howard Gardner, who has written extensively about multiple intelligences and creativity, believes that parents can help children find their niche by exposing them early to a wide array of experiences—a sort of talent menu.[16] This exposure comes through natural interaction as parents and children do things such as read, play games, prepare meals, care for pets, visit new places, and enjoy nature. Gardner especially praises children's museums as places where children are exposed to a wide sampling of eventual talent areas.

Sandy Hamm, father of Olympic gymnast twin brothers Paul and Morgan, was himself a competitive diver, but he was intent on exposing his boys to a wide range of experiences and allowing them to chart their own courses. When interviewed, Sandy said, "We did normal stuff when the boys were young. We took them to swimming, t-ball, soccer, and piano to see what they liked. We didn't try to direct them into a sport but just expose them to different activities and see what they liked, eventually it was gymnastics that stuck."[17]

Thomas Rudd, a former National Football League (NFL) player and the father of NFL-playing brothers Bo and Barrett, was careful not to push his boys into football but instead exposed them to other options. When interviewed, Thomas said, "I actually tried to downplay football because trying to force somebody to do something like football is just not possible. You can't force football down someone's throat. So, I tried to make them well-rounded and experience other things. In the end, they picked what they wanted to do."[18]

It is impossible to know what early experiences might influence children and eventually set them along a talent path. Nature photographers Peter Essick, Joel Sartore, and James Balog were all in high school when they discovered their passion for photography, but when interviewed in their productive primes, all three credited childhood experiences for their eventual course as nature photographers. Essick believes that his interest roots were planted as a child when his father exposed him to the beauty of the outdoors and especially to that of Yosemite Park, a place that Essick later photographed for *National Geographic*.

As a youngster, Sartore found inspiration to become a nature photographer in a single book his mother showed him titled *The Birds*:

> My mother had a set of Time-Life picture books. One was called *The Birds*. In that book was a look at several birds that have gone extinct. . . . The very last passenger pigeon, a bird named Martha, was shown alive in a photo taken just before her death in the Cincinnati Zoo back in 1914. I was astounded. This was once the most numerous bird on Earth, with an estimated population of five billion, and here it was reduced to this single female, with no hope of saving it. I couldn't understand how anyone could tolerate this. I still feel the same way, and I work hard to prevent this from ever happening again.[19]

Balog said, "Everything I've done in photography as an adult has in some way seen or unseen, known or unknown, conscious or unconscious been a reworking of all my childhood experiences. Every single one, whether it was trees, the technology, or the ice, the seed of all those projects go back to my youth."[20]

The implication is that parents should expose children to a wide array of experiences in a natural and enjoyable way. It is possible that one of these experiences will someday open a talent door.

Recognize and Foster Natural Abilities

I made the point in Chapter 2 that talent is largely made and that considerable evidence confirms this. Still, one's biology cannot be completely ignored. When psychologist Anders Ericsson said that "Nothing shows that innate factors are a prerequisite for expert-level mastery in most fields,"[21] the operative word was "most." In some athletic fields such as basketball and volleyball, where height is an advantage, having the tall gene can increase people's success potential if they practice like crazy. In short, being tall won't get you to the NBA, but being skilled and tall is a good combination.

When psychologist Howard Gardner put forth his multiple intelligence theory,[22] he wasn't just saying that there were varied intelligences, such as musical and kinesthetic, and that people are likely to find their talents in one or two areas. He was also saying that the various intelligences likely have a biological root that equips one to flourish more in some areas than in others. In other words, Pablo Picasso had some biological gifts that favored art, whereas Bobby Fischer had different biological gifts that favored chess. It is unlikely that Fischer could have been Picasso or that Picasso could have been Fischer.

The biological underpinnings of talent do not change the talent-is-made pronouncement. Think of talent as a rubber band. If you buy Gardner's multiple intelligence theory, think of talent as nine unique bands. The band sizes and shapes you receive at birth might be biologically determined. But rubber bands stretch, and they stretch a lot. Humans can stretch those bands many times their original size through critical environmental factors such as early experience, practice, and mentoring. The rubber band view posits that genetics disperses the bands but that human hands stretch those bands—some more so than others.

Based on these ideas, Gardner believes that we are best served if we pursue activities and eventually talent areas where we have a biological advantage or leverage—a bigger and stronger rubber band.[23] Educator Ken Robinson agrees and calls the intersection of biological advantage and personal passion one's element.[24] Robinson argues that talent is best realized when one first finds or discovers his element. What might have happened to Gillian Lynne (introduced in Chapter 2) had she not been seen by a psychologist who discovered her dancing element? Imagine if Bobby Fischer's older sister had not stopped by a store and purchased a little plastic chess set for Bobby and her to play with while their mother was at work. Without that encounter, without Fischer discovering his chess element, American chess might have never had a world champion. Had I not noticed my son Keaton's penchant for games, I might not have retrieved an old wooden box of chess pieces from the basement. What would Keaton's life have been like then?

The point is that parents need to be talent scouts. They need to recognize their children's biological advantages and help them find their element, where biological advantage meets passion. There is no shortage of examples of element finding among the talented individuals I studied. Nebraska Basketball Player of the Year Aguek Arop is 6′5″ and has hands the size of trash can covers. Volleyball star Mikaela Foecke was the National Collegiate Athletic Association (NCAA) Championship Most Outstanding Player as a freshman the year her college team won the national title. Foecke is 6′3″ and is built powerfully—part genetics, part tossing hay bales around her parents' Iowa farm. Swimming star Olivia Calegan, who set five Nebraska swimming records in one meet, admits that she has the perfect sprinter's build: "Tall, lean, huge shoulders, and a muscular body type."[25] Her coach, a former Olympian, said, "Olivia has crazy flexibility in her hips and knees, and I think that's what helps make her such a strong breaststroker is that flexibility and power that comes from her legs and knees."

The mother of a daughter with precocious verbal gifts helped her find her element as a nationally acclaimed writer and public speaker. The mother said, "I knew she had some sort of writing talent when she was five because she would write pages after pages, even though it was a childish type of writing, but I knew kids that age don't just keep writing."[26] Upon discovering her daughter's budding talent, the mother purchased a computer for her and soon helped her pursue her dream of publishing a book.

The mother of a figure skater foresaw that skating might be a good fit for her son's boundless energy, so she signed him up for skating lessons:

> When my son was little, he was a really difficult kid, he was so energetic. He just didn't sit still. So, when every other kid was playing in the sandbox, he'd be climbing on top of playground structures and other parents would be like, "Whose kid is that?" He never watched TV and was not a computer kid, so I never got a breath. He was just go, go, go. So, when I watched him skate, I just felt like, oh, this could work out great.[27]

Accrue Advantages

As described earlier, accumulated advantages represent the chain of events that occur when certain advantages lead to greater opportunities that lead to more advantages. Parents should be proactive in securing advantages for their children. Psychologist Benjamin Bloom shared the following account chronicling how concert pianists benefited from the chain of accumulated advantages.[28]

Most showed some early musical inclination such as singing in their crib. Such inclinations could have been easily missed or ignored, but instead parents responded by providing social and material resources not normally available to toddlers. Parents sang to children, played musical games with them, bought them musical toys, listened to music with them, and pointed out musical styles. Because of these early advantages, children became increasingly interested in music, which brought on the next wave of advantages. Parents bought their children musical instruments and started them in music lessons.

The pianists' early home experience with music gave them the head start that parents hoped for. When the children began lessons, they were among their teachers' best pupils. Because these children stood out, their teachers gave them extra time and attention, special encouragement, carefully selected material, and choice spots in recital programs. Advantages continued to accumulate.

Due to their favored treatment by teachers and their increasing skills, the pianists developed enormous self-confidence. During early recitals, they strode confidently to the piano and commanded the stage. Their confidence further raised their stock of advantages. There was additional social validation that they were good musicians and increased visibility in the local music community.

The young pianists' progress led to another advantage: increased parental support. The more the children's musical passion and talent grew, the more support parents provided. For example, parents would attend their child's lessons and then reinforce those teachings at home during daily practice sessions. In this regard, children had the advantage of being doubly instructed by teacher and parent. Parents also sought a stronger teacher for their children—one with more music knowledge, higher standards, and better connections to the music community. Of course, this jump in commitment and instruction led to more opportunities and advantages. The new teachers arranged many new experiences—such as competitions, adjudications, and music ensembles—that made music a real and vital part of students' lives and afforded them greater notoriety. That notoriety, in turn, led to more and better opportunities to perform in public and build their name even more.

By the time the pianists were in their teens, there had been countless opportunities presented and seized for successful talent growth—a long and unbroken chain of accumulated advantages. Just for a minute, imagine someone who tries to begin musical development not as a toddler but as a teenager. The chain of accumulated advantages afforded to the early beginner just would not be available to the late beginner. The late beginner could not reasonably expect the same parental interest and support, the same preferential teacher treatment, or the same community support and adoration. The time to strike and flash has long passed.

The lesson for parents: Respond to children's inclinations and interests with corresponding interest and resources. Feed the passion; kick-start the chain of advantages.

Live the Life

Many parents of talented children, as with committed poker players, are all-in. They go to great lengths to support their child's emerging talent and often make sacrifices to do so. Family life revolves around their child and the talent area. The family becomes a chess family, a swimming family, or a music family. A music family, for example, fills the house with music, attends musical performances, studies musical styles and composers, converses about music, and plans meals and other family activities around the talented child's all-important practice and lesson schedule. Family vacations are even music-oriented—perhaps a trip to Nashville's Grand Ole Opry.

A chess family, like ours was, participates in after-school and community chess clubs; attends weekly tournaments; prepares for and takes lessons; studies chess books, magazines, and software; plays chess over the board or against a computer or online opponents; peruses chess websites; and invites chess players to their home.

Fred Waitzkin, the author of *Searching for Bobby Fischer* and father of chess prodigy Josh Waitzkin, said this about chess transforming family life:

> All the top players have at least one parent behind them, encouraging, assisting, worrying. In a sense, the child is only part of the team. Regardless of his gift for the game, he can't compete at the highest level without a good teacher and supportive parent. . . . [As the parent], I decide which tournament we'll play and how much practice he should have the week before. I log his weaknesses and strengths and point them out to [his teacher]. I remind [his teacher] to give him homework, and I pester Josh to do it. I make sure he is asleep early on Tuesday night so he won't be tired for his Wednesday lesson.[29]

Fred Waitzkin also said,

> When it is time for Joshua's lesson, I pray that the neighbor won't sing the blues or that the super's kid won't jump on the trampoline. It is a special time. We take the baby to the sitter so she won't pull the pieces off the board. [Josh's mother] can't run the dishwasher or washing machine. She tries to prepare dinner quietly because a dropped pot might cause Josh to lose his train of thought.[30]

Waitzkin also said this about his son: "His precocious ability for this board game has seized control of my imagination. I used to worry about my career, my health, my marriage, my friends, my mother. Now, I mostly worry about Josh's chess. . . . His sedentary activity has displaced many priorities in my life."[31]

Another example of living the life also comes from the chess world and involves Gary and Yee-chen Robson, parents of chess prodigy Ray Robson, America's youngest ever grandmaster. In Gary Robson's book *Chess Child,* we learn that the Robson house was completely child and chess centered.[32] Yee-chen quit her teaching job and became Ray's primary homeschool teacher. Gary spent his free time—and even work time—serving as Ray's chess coach and manager. Gary, a college professor, altered or changed jobs several times, always with the goal of spending more time with Ray and furthering Ray's chess development. For example, Gary once decided to attend Ray's international chess event even if it meant losing his job. He reasoned, "As much as I loved my students, the job was less important to me than Ray's development."[33] Another time, Gary gave up his professorship and worked part-time as an instructor to spend more time managing Ray's chess career. Gary said, "Chess was on my brain, and I found myself wishing I could be Ray's manager full time."[34] Gary silently repeats this live-the-life mantra each day: "Enjoy your time with Ray while you are here and now and while he is here and now, for this is the only time you have."[35]

Robert Calegan, father of six-time Nebraska state champion swimmer Olivia Calegan, did all he could to lead the swimming life and foster Olivia's talent development—including quitting his day job. Robert said, "I was always there during Olivia's practices so I figured I would become more involved. I became vice president of her swim club and eventually president. But the more I was around the practices, the more I felt like I could contribute more, so I started coaching Olivia's team."[36] Robert was not a swimmer, so he took classes to learn about swimming. At first Robert coached around his workday—in the evenings, on weekends, and in the mornings before work. He was putting as much time into coaching Olivia's team as he was devoting to his job. Eventually, Robert became a full-time swim coach: "I tried to maintain my day job but little by little my life transitioned more into coaching than my day job could handle. So, when an opportunity arose to coach a couple clubs, including Olivia's, I quit my job and became a full-time swim coach."[37]

The mother of a National Spelling Bee champion said that spelling was a family affair. Every day after dinner, the speller's parents quizzed her on words, her brother identified new words for her to learn, and the speller would present new information about word origins to the family. Spelling practice dominated their family time.

Why do parents alter lifestyles, make sacrifices, and spend time, money, and energy cultivating talent? One reason is that the pursuit of talent development brings families together for a common interest, a common goal, a common good. A parent in the Bloom study said, "It helped our family become a family because we were spending all our time together."[38] Parents I interviewed conveyed the same talent-brought-us-closer theme. The spelling bee mother said, "Spelling brought my daughter closer to the family. We took up spelling as a family."[39] The mother of a violinist said, "My husband was not an affectionate father when the kids were born. He did not grow up in an affectionate household and did not know how to be close. But through music, my son has formed a great connection with his father." Finally, the mother of a figure skater said, "Skating has brought our family the greatest joy. It has made the family united. Skating competitions have allowed us to see the world, learn so much, and join together. Skating has helped make us what we are as a family."

Impart Values

Parents set the talent development stage by modeling and imparting values that guide their youngsters' talent pursuits. The parents in Bloom's study modeled and advocated hard work and the pursuit of perfection.[40] Parents were tireless workers. Even at home, their leisure time was filled with constructive activities such as reading, carpentry, sports, music, or photography. Parents spurned idle activities such as watching television. While pursuing constructive activities, parents also modeled the values and means for studying a domain, establishing priorities, and managing time. Parents pursued perfection in their work and held their children to the same standards. If something is worth doing, they would say, it's worth doing right. When parents monitored children's homework, household chores, or practice in the talent domain, the expectation was always a job best done.

Parents I interviewed shared this same hard-work ethic and expectation with their children. Here is a sampling of what they said:

- "We have a failure is not an option mentality. Good work begets good work."
- "Everybody in our house is a hard worker. We strive for excellence, making sure what we do, we do well."
- "We expect our children to put in maximum effort."
- "In the environment we provide for her, there's no limit to how much she can learn—there's no impossible goal."
- "We have taught our kids from the time they were teeny that they can do anything they want to do. There's no limit to what they can accomplish if they are willing to work hard for it."
- "It was just an expectation in our family that when you get to play an instrument, it's a privilege, and with that privilege comes the expectation that you must practice."
- "When you watch TV, you're losing out on your dream."[41]

Parents' values get passed along to their talent-pursuing children. Olympic speed skater Dave Cruikshank described his father, an independent businessman and insurance salesman, as being highly driven, organized, strategic, and detail-oriented and credits his father for passing these characteristics on to him, where they guided both his athletic and business careers. Cruikshank said, "Because I saw my father do it, I learned how to dedicate myself toward a rigorous work ethic."[42]

Richard Mayer, the world's most productive educational psychologist, credits his upbringing, particularly the core values his parents instilled, for his success. Mayer said,

As a kid, I was brought up in the Midwest in a Jewish home. There was a lot of emphasis on social justice, ethical behavior, the value of hard work, and the love of learning. All those core values influenced me. An interest in social justice is reflected in me trying to address practical problems in education, and an interest in the value of hard work and love of learning are reflected in my enjoyment of academic life.[43]

Other top educational psychologists I interviewed credited their parents for imparting values that helped them succeed. Barry Zimmerman said, "My father was a wonderful model who stressed that personal dedication and practice pay dividends."[44] And Dale Schunk credited his parents for establishing his general drive for success and his specific interest in self-efficacy—belief in one's competence. Schunk said, "They were wonderful role models who demonstrated how effort, persistence, and self-efficacy promote success."

In addition to instilling a hard-work ethic, parents should instill in children a sense of entitlement through a parenting style called concerted cultivation. This last sentence clearly needs some unpacking. Let's take a closer look at what entitlement and concerted cultivation mean relative to raising a talented child. The word "entitlement" carries a negative connotation. It commonly conveys people who believe that they should get some special privilege or consideration simply because of their family name or skin color or because they simply showed up. Some college students I see these days carry that sense of entitlement. They feel like they should receive A grades simply because they paid tuition. When I speak of entitlement here, I follow the writings of sociologist Annette Lareau, who described childhood entitlement as an ability to comfortably and effectively manage one's interactions in the adult world.[45] Entitled children are not intimidated by authority. Rather, they politely assert themselves to obtain the needs, desires, or advantages they seek. They know how to negotiate their way and feel entitled to do so.

Certainly, we want children to have this positive sense of entitlement. When your child goes to a doctor, you want her to speak comfortably with the physician and describe her illness. When she visits a friend and the friend's family goes out for ice cream but there are not enough seat belts for all who are traveling, you want her to speak up and say "Sorry, but I don't ride in cars where people aren't seat-belted; it's not safe." And when her teacher assigns a grade that seems unjustified, you want her to seek justification and to politely argue her position if need be.

This positive sense of entitlement seems crucial for children trying to develop talent in domains largely inhabited and controlled by adults. My son Keaton certainly displayed this sense of entitlement as he negotiated an adult-filled chess world. Keaton played regularly in adult tournaments and had to negotiate many things with opponents, spectators, and directors.

With opponents, there were issues such as which chess set and clock to use and even instances of cheating. Once an opponent moved a bishop to a new square, released his hand from the piece (thus completing the move), immediately noticed that he had blundered, returned the bishop to its original square, and denied having removed his hand from the piece. Keaton called him on the illegal move and needed to appeal to the tournament director. Sometimes spectators get too close or too loud and need to be addressed. One time a spectator placed his drink next to Keaton's board several times, and Keaton had to resolve that. Keaton sometimes had to summon tournament directors during games to handle time issues or to get rule clarifications or had to speak with directors between rounds about player pairings. Keaton also had to interact with adult mentors and colleagues. In Chapter 1, I described how Keaton's chess coach would often respond to a question by saying "You tell me." In that same vein, it was important for Keaton to seek information from his teachers to draw out and grasp their thoughts. He needed to get them to fully explain why a certain move was preferred and how such a decision was reached. Keaton often had people over to the house to play and study chess, but they weren't age-mates. They were engineers, college professors, corporate managers, and the unemployed. Keaton was completely comfortable arguing against their game analysis and advocating his own.

Concerted cultivation is the process parents use to help children attain this positive sense of entitlement. "Concerted" means "planned or arranged"; cultivation is the process of trying to develop a quality or skill. Parents can apply concerted cultivation in two ways. First, parents can model positive entitlement. They can model for children how adults negotiate for themselves in an adult world as they come to terms with a house painter, arrange a lesson for their child, request sour cream for their baked potato at a restaurant, or dicker with a furniture salesperson. Second, parents can teach their children the importance of and means for negotiating in an adult world. Concerted cultivation parents tell children they have a voice every bit as important and worthy of reception as the adults around them. Parents also prepare children to speak with doctors, teachers, friends' parents, and chess opponents. Parent and child together anticipate forthcoming situations such as a doctor visit or a teacher conference and practice what might be said.

Former chess prodigy Josh Waitzkin, the subject of *Searching for Bobby Fischer* and the author of his own book, *The Art of Learning*, said this about his concerted cultivation upbringing: "I'm sure I was a tough kid for my teachers to teach. My parents raised a willful child. Even as a young boy, I was encouraged to take part in the spirited dinner party debates about art and politics in my family living room. I was taught to express my opinion and to think about the ideas of others—not to follow authority blindly."[46]

Consider Redshirting

Let's play a thought game. Two children are somehow born in the same year with the same genetic material and raised in identical home environments. The only difference is that Child A is born on January 1 and Child B is born on December 31. Both children begin to play tennis on their fourth birthday. Both become impassioned by the game and practice a lot—about 20 hours a week, which is about 1,000 hours per year. Fast-forward two years, and the two children join a tennis league for anyone who turns six in that calendar year. Upon entering the league, Child A is naturally bigger and stronger that Child B; after all, Child A has lived and developed nearly a full year longer. Child A has also logged more practice time than Child B—twice as much, 1,000 hours more. Given these circumstances, Child A is a somewhat better tennis player than Child B upon joining the league. Of course, Child B might someday catch up, but don't count on it. As you learned in the "Accrue Advantages" section, the rich get richer. Child A's early and coincidental birth-date advantages of being older, bigger, and more practiced are likely to accumulate into other advantages. Child A is the one likely to have early success, get noticed, and be moved to a higher league with better coaches, players, facilities, and opportunities as well as year-round practice. Child A's earlier birthday was a fluke advantage that set off a chain reaction of other real advantages.

This thought game represents the real-world relative-age phenomenon discovered by Canadian psychologist Roger Barnsley and reported by Malcolm Gladwell.[47] Barnsley was attending a premiere division junior hockey game in Canada and noticed in the player program an incredible proportion of January, February, and March birthdays among the elite players. This observation spurred Barnsley to examine the birth months of every player in the Ontario Junior Hockey League. He found the same trend. More players were born in January than any other month. February was the second most frequent birth month, and March was third. There were nearly five and a half times as many players born in January than in November. When Barnsley investigated junior all-star team rosters and National Hockey League rosters, the same trend emerged: Among elite players, 40 percent were born between January and March, 30 percent between April and June, 20 percent between July and September, and 10 percent between October and December.

All of this occurred because the cutoff for age-class hockey in Canada is January 1. This means that two boys born on January 1 and on December 31 in the same year become junior hockey teammates and compete for playing time and other perks. And in most cases, it is the older boy who claims the advantages: selection to the traveling squad where there is better coaching, better teammates, better competition, and many more games and practices. The advantage of being older and a bit more practiced multiplies to the point where the child born earlier in a calendar year eventually becomes a lot better than the child born later in the calendar year. What began as a small and coincidental birth-date advantage accumulates until the older one is skating for the Montreal Canadians.

Perhaps the biggest example of the relative-age phenomenon takes place with kindergarten entry. Schools have an entrance cutoff date that have some children beginning school on the younger side (let's say barely five years old), while some enter on the older side (let's say about six years), creating nearly a full-year age difference. Author Malcolm Gladwell claims that the younger students are at a disadvantage and that the disadvantage persists. Gladwell said, "It's just like hockey. The small initial advantage that the child born in the early part of the year has over the child born at the end of the year persists. It locks children into patterns of achievement and underachievement, encouragement and discouragement, that stretch on and on for years."[48] Gladwell points to studies showing that (a) older fourth graders outscore younger fourth graders by 12 percent on standardized math and science tests (perhaps the difference needed to place higher achievers in gifted programs where more advantages lie), (b) older calendar-year students have a 12 percent more likelihood of college enrollment than younger calendar-year students, and (c) relatively younger students are disproportionately diagnosed with learning disabilities.

Age-related grade-level disparities increase further when we consider what is commonly called kindergarten redshirting. Redshirting is a term first introduced by college athletic programs that sat players out of competition their first year of college so redshirt players could use that first year to learn the team's system and to get bigger, stronger, and more practiced. Because college players get five years to complete four years of eligibility, the redshirt year did not count against their eligibility, and it made them older and stronger competitors when they did play. Kindergarten redshirting is like athletic redshirting. Some parents delay kindergarten entry one year so their children do not lag behind older classmates and perhaps rise to the top of their class. Kindergarten redshirting creates a nearly two-year age gap among classmates.

Kindergarten redshirting has grown more common and controversial. Its fairness and potential advantages and disadvantages have been contested by researchers, parents, and the popular press. A recent view regarding academic outcomes comes from education professor Diane Whitmore Schanzenbach: "Redshirting at the kindergarten level bestows few benefits and exacts some substantial costs. Both research and experience suggest that the gains that accrue from being an older student are likely to be short-lived."[49]

Even more controversial perhaps is redshirting used to gain advantages in sports or other talent domains. In many communities and organizations, children participate by grade level, not age. In my community, children join soccer and baseball teams based on grade level, not age. Students get to participate in high school football, gymnastics, and swimming through 12th grade despite their age. National scholastic chess tournaments are based on grade level, not age. One can become a Grade 6 champion so long as one is in that grade.

Some parents looking for a talent edge redshirt their children in kindergarten or redshirt them later by having them repeat a grade. Such was the case for Bryon Fields, who repeated eighth grade to give him a competitive advantage in football. He later starred in high school and earned a scholarship to play for the Division 1 Duke Blue Devils.[50]

Prospective parents who are considering timing their pregnancy so the birth occurs in January or parents who are considering redshirting a child in kindergarten or later because of potential advantages that might accrue should also consider these sobering statistics from the NCAA.[51] Among 8 million high school athletes, only 6 percent will play in college, only 2 percent will earn any sort of athletic college scholarship, and only 1 percent will earn a full-ride college scholarship. Continuing into professional sports is even less likely. Among college athletes, fewer than 1 percent are drafted by professional teams.

Where does this leave parents? Parents interested in redshirting their children should read the redshirting literature thoroughly and carefully and should consider their child's personal profile and best interests. In the end, and as this book hopefully demonstrates, parents committed to supporting their child's talent development have many ways to build and accrue advantages that do not necessitate redshirting.

Begin Later Rather Than Never

According to an old Chinese proverb, the best time to plant a tree was 20-years ago; the next best time is today. When my chess-playing son Keaton trailed other young players on national top 10 rating lists or fell to a hotshot chess prodigy in a national championship title game, his coach calmly repeated this mantra: The race does not always go to the swiftest. What he meant was that talent takes time, and each budding talent has its own timetable. Moreover, that timetable might not begin at the same time for all.

This chapter has sung the praises of an early start, and for good reasons. There are places to go, advantages to be accumulated, and myelin to be wrapped. But an early start is not always essential, as my study of six young chess masters suggested.[52] Table 3.1 shows the players' starting age, age when attaining master status, and number of years needed to attain master status. Note that all the young masters were introduced to chess at a relatively young age—between ages 3 and 9. Beginning at an earlier age, however, did not open the chess master door sooner. For example, Player 1, who began the earliest at age 3, required

Table 3.1   An Early Start Is Not Required for Chess Success

Player	Starting Age	Age When Attaining Master Status	Years Needed to Attain Master Status
1	3	15	12
2	5	11	6
3	5	12	7
4	7	18	11
5	8	15	7
6	9	14	5

12 years to attain master status, whereas Player 6, who began the latest at age 9, required just 5 years to attain master status. Although Player 1 began 6 years earlier than Player 6, both attained master status in their early teens. Overall, results suggest no clear advantage for beginning chess in the preschool years.

Keaton's own path to master status fits with these results. He began at age 7 and attained master status at age 16. Moreover, his coach was right about the race not always going to the swiftest. Over the years, Keaton passed and defeated many of those once ranked ahead of him. Several of them tumbled out of chess completely. In Bloom's talent study,[53] rarely did a talented child's siblings ever ascend the talent ladder, even though talented child and siblings had similar genetic stuff and a comparable home environment. What mattered most was that the talented individual had more passion for the talent domain, practiced more, and stuck with it the longest.

Even when talent strikes early, there is always room for growth. Garry Kasparov is considered the greatest chess champion of all time. He became the youngest undisputed world champion in 1985 at 22 years of age, but it was 1999 when he achieved his highest chess rating. Even from his world-champion perch, Kasparov continued to improve. The same goes for LeBron James, considered one of the greatest basketball players ever. James was an immediate NBA star in 2003, averaging 21 points his rookie season. But James improved. His best scoring average occurred in his 5th season. His best three-point shooting and rebounding was in his 10th season. The race does not always go to the swiftest or the one with the earliest start.

There are plenty of compelling stories about people with late starts on the talent road. Several are chronicled in Ken Robinson's book *The Element.*[54] There was best-selling author Susan Jeffers who did not begin her writing career until she was in her 40s. Jeffers had a doctorate in psychology and was a hospital executive in New York City when she had the opportunity to confront her many personal fears by teaching a course on fear. That experience moved her to write the eventual best seller *Feel the Fear and Do It Anyway* and many subsequent books despite her late introduction to the writing field. Harriet Doerr meanwhile dabbled in writing while she raised a family. When she was 65 years old, she returned to college and obtained a history degree. The prose courses she took while obtaining that degree spurred her to later enroll in Stanford University's creative writing program. That experience prompted Doerr to write her first novel at age 73, the National Book Award–winning *Stones for Ibarra*. Julia Child, the chef credited with revolutionizing home cooking and originating television cooking shows, worked as an advertising copywriter and then in the U.S. government before discovering French cuisine and beginning professional culinary training in her mid-30s. Child was nearly 50 when she published *Mastering the Art of French Cooking* and her storied career was launched.

There are certain domains where an early start might matter and certain domains where it does not. Psychologist Howard Gardner contends that there are three areas where prodigies—youngsters performing as adults—are most likely to strike: math, music, and chess.[55] The reason for these three areas is that they are restricted in their symbols and governing rules. Although it might take a lifetime to master any of these domains, each can be reasonably scaled in just a few years. Moreover, all three domains are ones that children traditionally find interesting and inviting and are introduced to early in school or at home. Such is not the case for less structured domains such as literature, political science, and business, which are brimming with domain information and are not the types of subjects taught early in school. These are the types of domains that students only begin to study in high school on up through college and graduate school.

The takeaway here is that it is never too late for children and even adults to discover their element and pursue their passion. Plant that tree today or even tomorrow.

CHAPTER FOUR

Parents' Roles in Practice

"Practice makes the master."

Patrick Rothfuss, Science fiction writer[1]

We saw in Chapter 2 that talent depends on practice—a lot of it, for a long time, done in a deliberate way. Author Matthew Syed, in his book *Bounce,* tells three compelling practice-makes-the-master stories involving famous athletes. One involves soccer superstar David Beckham, best known for his bending kick and a movie whose title reflects that famous kick, *Bend It Like Beckham.* As a child, Beckham would kick a soccer ball from the same practice field spot hour upon hour trying to get the ball to move and bend at his will. His father said, "His dedication was breathtaking. It sometimes seemed that he lived on that field."[2] Beckham said, "My secret is practice. I have always believed that if you want to achieve anything special in life, you have to work, work, and then work some more."[3] Commenting on Beckham's trademark bending kick, Matt Carre, a sports engineering researcher, said, "It may look completely natural, but it is, in fact, a very deliberate technique. He kicks to one side of the ball to create the bend and is also able to effectively wrap his foot around the ball to give it topspin to make it dip. He practiced this over and over when he was a young footballer."

Another story involves tennis champion Andre Agassi's practice routine. Agassi said, "My father says that if I hit 2,500 balls each day, I'll hit 17,500 balls each week, and at the end of one year, I'll have hit nearly one million balls. He believes in math. Numbers, he says, don't lie. A child who hits one million balls each year will be unbelievable."[4]

The last story is also from tennis and involves the Williams sisters, who have dominated tennis for more than two decades. Their father, Richard, set out to make his daughters tennis champions. He began their daily practice routine when Venus was four and Serena was three. Richard stood on one side of the net and fed the girls 550 balls he wheeled onto the court in a shopping cart. When the balls ran out, they picked them up and began again. To build their swing precision, the girls were sometimes made to hit with baseball bats, which are narrower than rackets. When they served, landing serves in the service box was not sufficient. They aimed at traffic cones placed throughout the box.

We also saw in Chapter 2 that practice can cause fundamental body changes that aid future performance. Talent writer Geoff Colvin reports that through practice, endurance runners develop larger hearts and more slow-twitch muscle fiber important for distance running, sprinters develop more fast-twitch muscle fiber important for sprinting, ballet dancers gain the advantage of turning their feet out more than average people, and baseball pitchers gain the advantage of extending their throwing arms farther back.[5] And of course, there is myelination. All types of practice increase the wrapping of myelin around the neurological circuitry that governs practiced skills. The more one practices, the greater the myelination and the better the skill.

Practice does something else: It transforms snippets of information into meaningful chunks that influence perception (the way we view things) and ability (how we perform).

Practice Builds Chunks

Look at the following sentence: *I Love Paris in the Springtime.* How did you perceive this sentence? If you were already familiar with the sentence, then you perceived it, or took it in, as 1 chunk of information—I Love Paris in the Springtime. If you were not familiar with it, then perhaps you perceived it as 2 chunks of information: (1) I love Paris (2) in the springtime. If you were unfamiliar with the sentence, then it is also possible that you perceived it as 6 chunks of information—1 chunk per word. Now, suppose that you don't know how to read but can recognize letters; then you might perceive the sentence as 30 chunks of information—1 chunk per letter. Finally, let's suppose that you cannot identify letters; then you might perceive the sentence as around 100 bits of information. The "L" in "Love" might be perceived as a vertical line and a horizontal line extending rightward from the base of that vertical line. The letter "m" might be perceived as two equally sized upward humps joined at the base. You get the idea—how you perceive something depends on what you know. The more you know about letters, words, and phrases, the more and faster you can perceive printed material. And the more and faster you can perceive printed material, the better your ability to read, learn, and remember. Good perception is a doorway to talent. And that talent door swings through practice.

Look at the chess position in Figure 4.1. What do you see? Just like the previous sentence task, what you perceive depends on what you know. In a

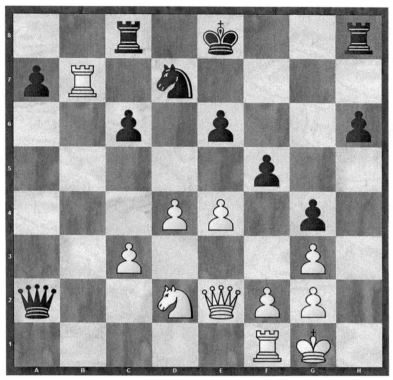

Figure 4.1

classic experiment by Chase and Simon, chess positions, such as the one in Figure 4.1, were shown to chess novices and chess experts who were asked to memorize the placement of as many pieces as possible.[6] After they viewed a position for just five seconds, the pieces were removed, and participants had to replace them on the board in their original positions as best they could. Chess novices usually replaced about four or five pieces correctly. Chess experts usually replaced all or nearly all of them correctly. Why the big difference?

Perhaps the performance ability difference between novices and experts is due to experts having superior hardware: Expert brains are bigger and faster than those of novices. This might explain why chess experts got involved in chess in the first place—they have biologically better brains than the rest of us. Nope, that's not it. The talent-is-born theory is wrong. Chess experts and novices—and almost everyone else for that matter—have comparable brain equipment, and that equipment is not all that impressive as far as perception goes. The human brain has a limited capacity to perceive and hold information—perhaps just four or five newly presented items at a time.

How, then, do chess experts remember the presented positions so well? The answer is that they don't see what novices see. Through years of practice, chess experts see much more.

Look again at the chess position. If you are a chess novice who knows a bit about chess such as the piece names and how they move, then your five-second perception might go like this: "I see the White king on the g1 square. It has two pawns in front of it. The Black king is on the e8 square." That might be it. Here is what the expert might quickly perceive: "White has castled his king to the king side and is safely tucked behind his castle of pawns, although the h-pawn is doubled on the g-file and that can become a weakness. Black has failed to castle his king and lies vulnerable in the center. The Black king is flanked by his rooks, but neither is powerful because both rest on closed files. There is tension in the center. White is threatening to capture Black's f-pawn, which is unprotected because Black's e-pawn cannot recapture, as it is pinned to the king by White's queen. Meanwhile, White's knight is pinned by Black's queen." The expert does not see individual bits of information, such as each word in a familiar phrase; the expert sees meaningful chunks of information. The expert sees in one swipe of perception what most others see in several swipes or never see at all.

By the way, the prospect that chess experts might have better brains was proven wrong in a clever follow-up to the experiment just described. Chase and Simon conducted the same study but instead placed chess pieces on the board in random positions rather than gamelike positions as was done in the original experiment.[7] This time, experts and novices performed equally bad, correctly recalling just a few piece placements. When pieces were randomly placed on the board, experts could no longer use their vast chess knowledge to perceive the position in a meaningful way. They could not meaningfully chunk the chess position information.

Let's consider what occurs in an actual chess match. Most chess matches finish in four to six hours if players use their allotted time. That time limit usually affords players about three to four minutes, on average, to consider each move. That time is helpful because there are many move options to consider. After just two moves, about 800,000 unique positions are possible. A few moves later, the number of possible positions is in the trillions. But there is another brand of chess called bullet whereby players, as the name suggests, must play quickly. Players get just one minute each to complete all their moves. The average move time is about one second. I have watched my son Keaton play bullet games, and *watching* is not easy. Time clocks are banging, and pieces are flying everywhere. How can players play a thinking game with so many possible moves so fast? First, know that these bullet games are played at a fairly high level by expert players, with move quality nearly equal to that in longer games. Second, expert players quickly recognize familiar patterns, just as the chess experts did in the chess piece repositioning experiment just described. They see meaningful chunks, not individual pieces. Third, chess experts know where to look. They can't possibly consider all move options, and they don't. They understand where the action is and what to consider. They see the tension in the center or the vulnerable king on the back rank. Chess computers, by the way, can evaluate 200 million moves per second, while the strongest chess-playing humans can evaluate just a handful. Computers, though, operate by brute force and consider many move sequences that make no sense. Well-practiced humans know what to consider as they draw from a wealth of chess knowledge. They look at a little and see a lot. Practice creates this knowledge, and such knowledge bears automatic and accurate moves that stand up in one-minute games or in standard games against the strongest chess computers.

Automatic and accurate chunk recognition is the hallmark of expertise in other talent domains too. Professional tennis players can return a 130 mph serve. This lightning-quick skill is not the product of mere reaction time. Professional players do not have inherently quicker reaction times than you and me. Instead, they have superior perception. They see meaningful chunks. Professionals read the subtle visual cues of their serving opponent, visual cues that we are blind to, such as posture, foot placement, and racket angle— all grasped in an instant. Watch the defense-minded libero in a college volleyball match. Her job is to anticipate where the opposing team is about to spike the ball and then be there to dig it before it hits the court. Digging is the easy part. Club players can dig a hard-hit ball. The difficult part is reading the cues of the opposing team—where striking players are positioned, how the ball is set—and moving to the spot where the ball is likely to land before opponents' even hit it. Wayne Gretzky, the greatest hockey player ever, credited superior perception derived through practice for his remarkable play: "I wasn't naturally gifted in terms of size and speed. Everything I did in hockey I worked for. . . . The highest compliment that you can pay me is to say that I worked hard every day. . . . That's how I came to know where the puck was going before it even got there."[8]

Author Josh Waitzkin, who excelled in both chess and martial arts, provides an excellent martial arts example displaying how practice builds perception and ability.[9] Let's say that Waitzkin is competing against a less experienced, less practiced opponent and is about to initiate a throw that, for Waitzkin, involves six well-practiced and integrated steps: (1) Push forward with my right hand on opponent's chest, causing a reactive push back. (2) Simultaneously pull his right arm forward and across his body, slip my left foot in front of his right foot, pull down with my right hand on his lapel, and sit back while spinning to my left. (3) His right foot is blocked, so he falls forward. As he does, my right foot slips between his legs. (4) As he falls on top of me, I pull his right arm in toward me and kick against his left inner thigh with my right foot, flipping him over. (5) I roll, following his fall, and end up on top of him. (6) I take his head in what is called a scarf hold and trap his right arm in a submission lock.

The throw happens in a blink, and the opponent experiences an indecipherable flurry. This was what bullet chess looked like to me, while chess experts saw and executed all the important elements in a blink. For Waitzkin, the throw was an orchestrated pattern practiced to perfection:

> First, I . . . [practiced] each step slowly, over and over, refining my timing and precision. Then, I put the whole thing together, repeating the movements hundreds, eventually thousands of times. . . . In time, each step of the technique has expanded in my mind in more and more detail. The slightest variations in the way my opponent responds to my first push will lead to numerous options in the way I will trigger into my throw. My pull on his right wrist will involve twenty or thirty subtle details with which I will vary my action based on his nuanced microresponses. As I sit back on the ground and trip his right foot, my perception at that moment might involve thirty or forty variations.[10]

Waitzkin's experience allows him to see and do more in the moment than his less experienced opponent. Waitzkin said, "The key, of course, is practice."[11] Practice allows the talented to see full sentences instead of words or letters or symbols. Practice allows the talented to see the story of the chess board with just a glance. Practice allows the talented to see when a throw might work and to execute it in the blink of an eye.

In summary, experts see and do chunks. They operate on a higher plane than novices, who see unconnected pieces and muddle through tasks in slow and uncoordinated ways. Experts come to see and do chunks through practice. Here are some practice-related parent guidelines.

Help Children Make Practice a Productive Routine

Talented children make practice a daily habit like brushing teeth. Former American miler Jim Ryun said, "Motivation is what gets you started. Habit is what keeps you going."[12] We know that bad habits such as smoking and leaving clothes strewn on the floor are hard to break, but good habits are hard to break too. Talented performers in Bloom's study echoed the daily good habit sentiment. Here's what some said:

- "I would get up and practice just like you would get up and wash your face in the morning. It was a very natural thing to do, and you just accepted it as something very normal."
- "When you're studying four or five years, habit has taken over quite strongly."
- "Christmas was the only day off."[13]

There are plenty of stories about practice routines of talented children. Wolfgang Mozart practiced 3 hours a day beginning at age three. By age six, his routine netted more than 3,500 practice hours. Eric lo Shih-kai was 13 when he became the youngest golfer to ever play in a PGA European Tour event. Eric's daily practice routine looked like this: Jog to park at 7:00 a.m. and practice approach shots until school; after school, spend 5 to 6 hours practicing golf drills—sometimes hitting 300 golf balls in a session. Juilliard School of Music teacher Dorothy DeLay has worked with violin prodigies such as Itzhak Perlman. She insists that students practice a minimum of 5 hours a day, but most practice 10–12 hours daily. Musician Jascha Heifetz famously said, "If I don't practice for one day, I know it; two days, the critics know it; three days, the public knows it."[14]

The parents I interviewed were instrumental in helping their children make practice a productive routine. They were involved in practice at least as observers, more often as facilitators. The mother of an Olympic figure skater said this about observing practice: "I lived at the rink so I could watch him practice. I drove him there every day and stayed and watched him while he was skating. . . . For years, I would just stay and watch him every day at the rink. . . . It was a lot of fun, but it was tiring too."[15]

Robert Calegan regularly attended and observed his state champion daughter Olivia's club team practices. Eventually he became Olivia's club coach. Robert said, "I was always there during Olivia's practices so I figured I would become more involved. I became vice president of her swim club and eventually president. But the more I was around the practices, the more I felt like I could contribute more, so I started coaching Olivia's team."[16]

Loree Hagen, mother of violin virtuoso William, sat in on all his lessons and practices when he was younger. She said, "I attend his lessons and take notes for him on what the teachers ask him to do. Then I sit with him while he practices and sometimes I will say, 'Hey, I thought he asked you to do this here, or have you done this?' I sit there following along with those notes and make sure he is doing what he should."[17]

Susan Lien, mother of world-champion twirler Steffany, attended Steffany's twice-daily practices and helped by handling music, timing routines, and offering pointers. Steffany said, "During practice, my mom reinforces my coach's lesson tips and makes sure I practice as the coach intends."[18] Steffany also reported that her mom has a keen eye and can see things that Steffany needs to adjust while practicing. Steffany said, "My mom will sometimes watch me from off to the side and correct my patterns or spot errors that can result in point deductions. There are just a lot of little things that most people would never catch that she sees because she has been around for everything—all the lessons and training. She knows just what to look for."

Another twirling parent, Kathy, observes and films lessons so she can view those recordings with daughter Trina throughout the week as she helps

Trina practice. When Kathy practices with Trina she looks for things to correct. Kathy said, "I probably drive Trina crazy with the 'fix this, fix that, watch your freehand, point your toes up' comments. But, all the moms in the twirling world do that."[19]

Sammie is another twirling parent involved in her daughter Savannah's daily practices. Sammie was never a twirler but attends Savannah's coaching sessions so she can assist Savannah when she practices. Sammie films coaching sessions and records notes used to guide practice throughout the week. She also makes sure that Savannah has adequate practice space. Sammie converts the family's living room, with its high cathedral ceiling, to a daily practice space by moving furniture to clear room for Savannah to practice. Sammie admits that there have been errant throws and collateral house damage, but practice takes precedent over all else. When Savannah needs more practice space, Sammie drives her to a local gym where the family has a membership. Sammie watches Savannah practice at home and in the gym. Sammie said, "Now that she has gotten older, I try to give her more space, but my eyes are always there. . . . And, Savannah keeps me involved. She'll call me in and ask me to watch. She'll say, 'Am I doing this right?'"[20]

Finding practice space for twirling is not easy. A room with high ceilings and ample floor space is a must. Here is what another twirling mother said about arranging practice space for her daughter Kelcie:

> Sometimes finding space for Kelcie to practice is a nightmare. Where we live, it's hard to get gym space. If you're not playing basketball, soccer, or lacrosse, you're not getting in a gym, especially if you're a twirler. One Saturday during winter, the day before a competition, we were driving around trying to find some place for her to practice, even offering to pay, and the schools and gyms were like, 'no, go away.' I was very frustrated, so I came home, took out the phonebook and started calling indoor tennis facilities seeing if I could rent a tennis court. I rented a court for $70 for an hour so she could practice her routines. . . . After that incident, my husband drew up plans to add a great room to the back of our house so that Kelcie would always have a place to practice. And, that's just what we did. We built a room with a 25-foot ceiling. The room is big enough and high enough so that she can do her solo without breaking anything. It's a huge relief.[21]

Sonya and J. B. Atkins practiced every day with national rodeo champion Jayde. Together, the family trained, exercised, and cared for their prized horses. The parents also observed Jayde's practices and offered pointers. Sonya described a typical practice session this way:

> Today, for example, Jayde's going to want to run her barrel horse, Slim. So, she'll warm him up, set up barrels, and do some drills. Meanwhile, I'll

exercise one of her other horses. When Jayde finishes with Slim, I'll cool him down while Jayde next rides her cow horse and practices some calf roping. After that, Slim is rested and she'll take another run on him. We trade off that way. Also, sometimes Jayde gets frustrated with something her horse is doing and can't see what to do to fix it. So, we'll switch horses and I'll ride the horse, tell her what I feel, and what she might try.[22]

Finally, the mother of a talented volleyball player said this about her husband's involvement in her son's practices: "The practices were pretty much run by the coaches but they welcomed input from my husband. He was very open to voicing his opinion on practice strategies. Definitely. If he didn't like something or saw something needed improvement, he would not hesitate to say so. There were about three dads from the team that they named 'The Volleyball Mafia.' And they were vocal about what they thought."[23]

A key theme running through these parental practice-support examples is parents reinforcing the instruction that children received from their talent mentors. Although formal lessons usually took place once a week, parents were hammering those lessons home daily. Parents attended lessons, took notes, and filmed lessons so they could review lesson points with their children and guide daily practice accordingly. Thus, children gained the huge advantage of being doubly instructed, by both mentor and parent. This meant that practice time was maximized, because mentors' teachings were practiced and applied, and that the entire talent team—child, mentor, and parent—were all pulling in the same direction.

Help Children Practice in the Learning Zone

Children need deliberate practice designed to improve performance. Any old practice won't do. Talent author Geoff Colvin makes a convincing case that a great deal of practice is not sufficient for improvement. Strange as it seems, people work at their jobs for decades but don't necessarily improve. The ability of clinical psychologists to diagnose personality disorders did not increase with experience. Experienced surgeons were no better than residents at predicting patient's postoperative hospital stays. Colvin writes, "In field after field, when it came to centrally important skills—stockbrokers recommending stocks, parole officers predicting recidivism, college admission officials judging applicants—people with lots of experience were no better at their jobs than those with very little experience."[24] Stranger still, people sometimes got worse with experience. More experienced doctors scored lower on medical knowledge tests than less experienced doctors. Heart and X-ray diagnostic skills declined with experience among general physicians. Auditors became less skilled at making certain evaluations. The reason why performance does not improve and sometimes declines as experience grows is that most experience is not beneficial. Most experience is hollow, thought-less, and not aimed at improvement. It is me mindlessly playing nine holes of golf or hitting a bucket of balls on the range without a clear purpose. I do not practice critical skills or execute them properly or get expert feedback about my performance. I do not improve, and sometimes I play worse.

An excellent example of what deliberate practice looks like was offered by talent author Daniel Coyle. It involved a 13-year-old clarinetist named Clar-issa who was studied by music psychologist Gary McPherson. I draw from Coyle and McPherson's description of one of her recorded practice sessions, what Coyle labeled "The Girl Who Did a Month's Worth of Practice in Six Minutes."[25] Clarissa is working on a new song that she has listened to but has not played. She draws a breath and plays two notes, stops, pulls the clarinet from her lips, and stares at the music. Her eyes narrow, and she plays seven more notes, the song's opening phrase. She misses the last note, stops imme-diately, and jerks the clarinet from her lips. She sings the phrase softly, accenting the missed note: "Dah dah dum *dah.*" She starts over and plays the segment a few notes farther. She misses a note, backtracks, and makes the fix. She continues in this way until the opening has some verve and feeling. It is not good music, though. It is broken up, fitful, and riddled with missed notes. It might seem like Clarissa is failing, but McPherson says, "This is amazing stuff. . . . This is how a professional musician would practice." Clar-issa leans into the sheet music and continues. She puzzles over a G-sharp note she's not played before. She hums difficult riffs between playing attempts. She replays segments again and again, each time adding an incre-mental improvement. "Look at that," McPherson says. "She's got a blueprint in her mind she's constantly comparing herself to. She's working in phrases, complete thoughts. She is not ignoring errors, she's hearing them, fixing them. She's fitting small parts into the whole, drawing the lens in and out all the time, scaffolding herself to a higher level. . . . Good God. If somebody could bottle this [sort of practice], it would be worth millions."

Clarissa's practice is the price she must pay to attain talent; the same is true for all people. Her practice is everything my golf practice is not. Claris-sa's practice is deliberate. There is clear purpose, painstaking execution of challenging skills, and much thinking. Clarissa is in the moment. Musician Leopold Auer, when asked if he was practicing enough, famously said, "Prac-tice with your fingers and you need all day. Practice with your mind and you'll do as much in one and a half hours."[26]

When you think about Clarissa's practice—or any practice event—it is helpful to think about practice's three concentric zones: comfort, learning, and panic. The comfort zone is the innermost zone and represents the mind-less and worthless practice that most people do. Practice is simple and offers no challenge and no improvement. Next comes the learning zone. This is the target zone, the sweet spot. This is where deliberate practice resides. When you engage in challenging practice just beyond your comfort zone, you learn new things; you improve. This is where Clarissa's practice played out. The panic zone lies beyond the learning zone. Here practice is too difficult and not helpful either. Practicing returns against a 130-mile American-twist serve when you are barely learning how to grip a tennis racket places you in the panic zone, trying to accomplish skills well beyond your present ability. Think about "Goldilocks and the Three Bears": You don't want practice that is too hard or too soft, but just right. Oddly, many people practice in the comfort zone, where success is ensured, or in the panic zone, where failure is ensured, because doing so avoids challenge. But practicing in those zones rarely brings improvement.

Two-sport champion and author Josh Waitzkin stresses practice in the learning zone, where challenge and growth reside: "Growth comes at the point of resistance. We learn by pushing ourselves and finding what really lies at the outer reaches of our abilities."[27] Waitzkin tells the tale of the anorexic hermit crab. As hermit crabs grow bigger, they must temporarily leave the comfort of their shell and seek a bigger one. It is during this time that they are vulnerable to prey. A crab afraid to grow might starve itself—the anorexic hermit crab—and remain forever in the comfort zone. Crabs need to grow, shed their shells, and face the challenges brought about in the learning zone.

Waitzkin provides an illuminating example of his learning zone practice in the martial arts. In practice, he sought out bigger and stronger fighters to spar with. He knew there would be no growth sparring in the comfort zone with fighters he could easily handle. When he was ready to advance his training, he sought to train with Evan, a 6'2", 200-pound second-degree karate black belt with years of fighting experience and a real mean streak. Waitzkin wrote:

> This was brutal. Evan would have me plastered up against a wall, my feet a foot or two off the ground, before I even saw the attack coming. It is the spirt of Tai Chi training for more advanced students to stop when their partner is off-balance. But Evan had a different style. He liked to put you on the ground. Week after week, I would show up in class and get hammered by Evan. No matter how I tried to neutralize his attacks, I just couldn't do it. He was too fast—how could I dodge what I couldn't see? I knew I should avoid tensing up, but when he came at me my whole body braced for impact. . . . A freight train was leveling me fifty times a night. I felt like a punching bag. . . . I spent many months getting smashed around by Evan. I was being pummeled against walls—literally, the plaster was falling off [the walls].[28]

Over time as Waitzkin got used to taking shots from Evan, Waitzkin relaxed. He stopped fearing impact, his body built up resistance to getting smashed, and he learned to absorb the blows. After that, Waitzkin could sense an attack before it began and learned to perceive Evan's intention. Things were slowing down. Next came greater skill at neutralizing Evan's attacks. Finally the tables turned, and it was Waitzkin who triumphed. Waitzkin said, "Evan came at me like a bull, and I instinctively avoided his onslaught and threw him to the floor. He got up, came back at me, and I tossed him again. I was shocked by how easy it felt. After a few minutes of this Evan said that his foot was bothering him and he called it a night. We shook hands, and he would never work with me again."[29] This made sense because Waitzkin operated in the learning zone, dangerously close to the panic zone, while Evan preferred safety in the comfort zone—where he never had to shed his restrictive shell and grow.

Parents should help their talented children understand what it means to practice in the learning zone and help them do it. When parents attend lessons, they get the sense of what teachers want students to learn and can help children practice accordingly in the learning zone. Two illustrative examples of parents directing practice into the learning zone come from chess. Gary Robson described how he used chess books to help son Ray practice in the learning zone: "I read [the book] first, practiced what I learned on the board against Ray, and, after I'd won, explained to him the concepts presented in the book that I'd applied in my win. Ray would then apply those same concepts in his games against me. [After the games], we'd analyze as best we could, and then I'd read more and start the cycle all over again."[30] Similarly, Dan Troff studied chess on his own 10 to 15 hours a week during his lunch hour and at night after the kids went to bed to prepare chess practice materials for son Kayden. Dan read books, watched videos, and studied grandmaster games that allowed him to create a chess book with specialized lessons that he and Kayden used to practice chess. Kayden's mother, Kim, helped too. When Kayden took lessons from teachers via the Internet, Kim listened in, took notes, and compiled those notes so that Dan could incorporate the teacher's ideas in the materials he prepared to help Kayden practice in the learning zone.

Help Children Regulate Practice

Try something. Draw a three-inch line on an unlined sheet of paper. You cannot use a ruler to the draw the line. Now draw a second three-inch line. Now, draw two more. How did you do? With all that practice, you must have improved. By the end, your line must have been perfect. After all, practice makes perfect, right? Chances are, your last line was no better than the first. You did not make corrections or improvements along the way because there was no feedback, no one telling you if your latest attempt was too long or too short. Without corrective feedback, people tend to stay on course, doing the same thing over and over and repeating their errors. Of course, feedback can also come from within. As you drew the lines, you might have thought "There is no way I can improve at this task without measuring the lines. Instructions said that I could not use a ruler to draw lines, but they said nothing about using a ruler to measure lines. I'll measure each time and use that feedback to make adjustments as I go."

When people practice something—be it line drawing or bowling—they need to regulate. Regulation means monitoring, even supervising, one's own thoughts and actions. It is an inner conversation. A bowler might think "How am I doing? My pin total is lower than usual. I'm not hitting the pocket. My ball does not seem to be hooking enough. Let me try rotating my fingers farther and finishing taller."

Regulation is an important everyday skill. An employee who gets a memo that the boss wants to see him might regulate: "Why does she want to see me? Could it be about the Perkin's account? Does she think that I did not sell enough product? How will I respond to that claim?" A student who gets an essay returned with a C grade but few comments might regulate: "What went wrong here? I guess I needed to spend more time on this. It was kind of short, and I can see now that my argument for socialism was not developed and convincing. I can do better than this." People who fail to regulate struggle and don't grow. They walk into meetings clueless and unprepared. They don't improve their writing because they never figure out what's been wrong in the past.

Regulation is especially important in talent development. To improve, the budding expert must regulate practice. Regulation, when done right, should occur before, during, and after practice.

Regulate before practice. Practice should have a purpose, and one way to determine that purpose is to regulate about what is to come: "Under what conditions must I ultimately perform?" A distance runner plans to run a marathon race in six months. The race begins early in the morning, traverses hilly terrain, and takes place at high altitude. Knowing this, the runner regulates her training to meet race demands. She trains early in the morning, does a lot of hill work, and wears an elevation training mask to simulate altitude running as she trains.

A chess player reads the pairing chart and sees who his opponent is in tomorrow's next round. Knowing this, the player regulates his game preparation and practice. The player consults a chess database and finds all his opponent's recorded games. He clicks through dozens of games and determines what opening system his opponent is likely to play. He then studies how his opponent plays games in this opening while looking for weaknesses he might exploit.

Josh Waitzkin regulated his martial arts practice plan for two years as he prepared for the world championships. He studied film of the anticipated top competitors and analyzed their strengths, weaknesses, and most subtle tendencies. Waitzkin saw that his toughest competitors were faster and more powerful than he was. He would plan practices aimed at becoming strategically superior. Waitzkin said, "I would have to bring water to their fire."[31] For two years Waitzkin practiced this reactive style that he called the anaconda, which involved pressuring his opponent, stifling his opponent's attacks, slowly inching him out of the ring, and cutting off his escape paths. "If my opponent breathed, I would take space when he exhaled."[32] Waitzkin had practice opponents imitate the aggressive fighting style he would encounter while he perfected his anaconda responses. He also recorded these daily practice sessions and studied them every evening frame by frame. For two years, he regulated all his training relative to the world tournament and the competitors he would likely face.

Regulate during practice. Those seeking to develop talent must also regulate as they practice. For the runner: "Is my conditioning improving as I run more hills? Is my hill-running form efficient?" For the chess player: "How will I respond if he plays g3 on move 11? I should look at other grandmaster games and see how they continue if queens get traded." For Josh Waitzkin or others preparing for a martial arts championship: "Is this feign working to create an overextension? Is my hand placement too low to initiate that throw?"

Just like Clarissa practicing the clarinet, experts are all in when they practice. They practice with body and mind. Nature photographers said they do not practice and improve by taking a lot of photographs. Instead, they build the eye and the mind by reflecting about photography. Photographers practice using their minds to see design, color balance, and composition in existing photographs they study and in landscapes yet to be photographed. Photographer Joel Sartore described regulation when interviewed:

> There was a year or two that I didn't shoot much . . . but I got better at seeing because I was looking at lots of other people's work. . . . I was thoughtful and thinking about the world around us and thinking about what great pictures are and how people get great pictures. . . . I learn from looking at other people's work. So, I think it's a matter of just being thoughtful and that's more of a factor than shooting every day.[33]

Regulate after practice. Learning does not end when the race is run, the game is played, the battle is fought, or the photograph is captured. Learning begins anew. Talented individuals regulate these experiences and shape future practice accordingly. The marathon runner assesses her performance and notes that pace fell in the middle stages: "I must practice maintaining concentration and pace on longer training runs." She realizes that she lost too much time on the uphills: "I must incorporate more hill repeats in my workouts."

The runner was also outsprinted to the finish line: "I must add more 60-meter sprints to my training and work on sprint form." The chess player regulates his performance. The regulation process usually begins immediately after the game, when opponents remain at the board for a chess postmortem. They replay the game, looking for where they went wrong and for move improvements. Later, the player feeds game moves into a computer program that analyzes each move and spits back alternate moves and plans. He practices these improved move sequences when he plays quick games, where the improved moves can be practiced again and again. Josh Waitzkin returns to his filmed tournament matches and scrutinizes that film looking for pluses and minuses. He regulates his performance and might say "I was impatient there. I need to stick with my anaconda plan no matter how much my opponent turns up the heat. I can practice that. I dropped my shoulder. I sent a calling card that a right-hand attack was next. I need to practice keeping a level shoulder." And nature photographers such as Sartore closely examine the 20,000 to 40,000 images they shoot on assignment and regulate why maybe half a dozen constitute the perfect shot worthy of publication. Perhaps it was the lighting or the filter that enhanced or diminished a shot. They learn from this regulation and improve future efforts accordingly.

Notice in all these regulation accounts that there was no self-talk about failure, losing, or giving up. That is because talented people understand that failure is inevitable and even helpful. Failure is the gateway to growth and success. General Colin Powell said, "There are no secrets to success. It is the result of preparation, hard work, and learning from failure."[34] Writer James Michener echoed that sentiment: "Character consists of what you do on the third and fourth tries."[35] Consider some of history's luminaries. Abraham Lincoln was a poster president for failure. Before his election to the presidency, Lincoln failed in business, was defeated in his run for the legislature, failed in business again, suffered a nervous breakdown, and was defeated, in succession, for elector, Congress, Congress, Senate, vice president, and Senate. Ty Cobb was one of baseball's all-time greatest hitters. He had a lifetime batting average of .367, but that meant that he failed to get a hit two of every three times at bats. Author F. Scott Fitzgerald once had more than 100 rejection slips pinned to his walls. Had he quit then, we would have never read *The Great Gatsby*. Michael Jordan was cut from his high school basketball team. Good thing he went out for the team the following year.

Back to parents, what might you do to aid regulation? First, you can be children's inner voice of regulation. This is exactly what many parents I interviewed do. They attend lessons, understand how their child should practice, and offer regulatory practice reminders along the way. Regulate before: "Your coach said that judges are really emphasizing head posture during spins. Practice spinning with head back and chin up." Regulate during: "Your teacher said you are supposed to shape that note like it's coming through a tube, perfectly formed and sustained. Try again." Regulate after: "Your coach didn't like you playing knight takes pawn in that position. Think for a while and see if you can find a better response."

Second, parents can teach children to regulate practice activities themselves. Here is why that is so important. You have heard the old adage "If you give a man a fish, he eats for a day, but if you teach him how to fish, he eats for a lifetime." When you regulate practice activities for your child, you feed her for a day. When you teach her to self-regulate, you hand her the pole and teach her how to feed herself for a lifetime. Here is how you do it. At first, you simply regulate for her as before: "Your teacher said you are supposed to shape that note like it's coming through a tube, perfectly formed and sustained. Try again." But then you add a twist. As you regulate for her, you (a) draw attention to the regulation process, (b) sell its benefits, (c) provide practice opportunities, and (d) suggest its use in other settings. Let's see what that might look like:

- "Hold on Sandy, your teacher said you are supposed to shape that note like it's coming through a tube, perfectly formed and sustained. Try again." (Regulate for the child.)

- "Do you see what I did there Sandy? I got you to think about what you did. I got you to hear what your teacher would say if she was here with you. But you need to say such things to yourself as you practice. Talking to yourself this way is called regulation." (Draw attention to the regulation process.)

- "It is important that you self-regulate because you won't always have teachers or parents sitting beside you as you practice. If you want to get the most from practice and improve, you must provide that teacher voice yourself." (Sell the benefits of self-regulation.)

- "Why don't you practice regulation now as you play through the rest of this section? Hear your teacher's voice guiding you to identify and repair mistakes. For now, say those things out loud so we both can hear them." (Provide practice opportunities.)

- "This regulation strategy is powerful and works in all sorts of ways. For instance, you have a competition in three weeks. We can regulate what that might be like and how to practice accordingly. We read in the program that French horn players must stand when they play. You never do that. You should anticipate doing that and practice standing up until the competition." (Suggest the use of self-regulation in other settings.)

Deliberate practice, the engine driving the talent train, improves the body's physical composition and mind and chunks bits of information into meaningful wholes that aid perception and yield efficient and automatic routines. Parents can help children make practice a productive routine, practice in the learning zone, and regulate practice.

CHAPTER FIVE

Parents' Roles in Mentoring

Paul was a former college basketball star turned part-time coach. I watched him working privately with a talented young player. Paul made the game fun. He smiled, laughed, and was upbeat. There were fun contests pitting coach and student. Paul modeled basketball passion and what was someday possible as he playfully dribbled like a Harlem Globetrotter with eyes closed or tossed in a string of three pointers without a miss. "You know why I can make that shot?" Paul would ask. "Because I've practiced it thousands of times. That's all it takes." Throughout the lesson, Paul focused on technique and fundamentals. He modeled the jab-step, fall-back jumper and broke down its components. As the student practiced, Paul delivered short bursts of pointed gold: "Thrust forward at the waist to maintain balance. Make him think you're going left." "It's a dance. Lead him left and glide right." "You create and take space. That's the key to success in all sports." Paul often revealed his inner thoughts. "As a pass comes to me in the corner, I gage where my defender will be. If he gives me a breath of space, I think fake, draw him in, and drive by him to the rim. If he suffocates me, I think jab, create space, and shoot the three." Paul did something particularly interesting. He invited the student's parent to observe and spoke to the parent throughout, things like "Notice how the elbow is vertical. Help him remember that when you guys practice." "It's better to shoot five shots with good form when you practice than a hundred with bad; it's *much* better." When the session neared the end, Paul asked the student to give him "one more solid high-post run, corner-fade, receive-the-pass, and shoot-the-three sequence." Time after time, the student repeated this energy-zapping pattern but missed the shot. But Paul would not let the student take that memory home. As the young player repeated the drill, Paul shouted encouragement: "You got this." "I missed this shot a hundred times in college, but I never stopped taking it." "Good shooters believe in their shot. I believe in yours." "They can turn the lights off in here, but I'm not going home. I trust *you* to take and make this shot." "Bang!"

What makes a good mentor? Certainly a mentor must be knowledgeable about the talent domain, but there is much more, just as there was much more to Paul's mentoring. This chapter describes three characteristics of a good mentor. After that, four suggestions for choosing and working with mentors are provided.

The Mentor Believes That Talent Is Made

Imagine two children introduced to running track. One believes that talent is born and that running ability is fixed. This is called the fixed talent mind-set: what you were born with is all you'll get. The other believes that talent is made and that running ability is modifiable through training and practice. This is called the growth talent mind-set: what you have can be improved through effort. All other things being equal, which child is more likely to develop running talent? To help answer, let's examine a famous research experiment conducted by psychologist Carol Dweck.[1]

Elementary school students were given a questionnaire that determined their talent beliefs and whether they had a fixed or growth mind-set. Students were next given a series of problems. The first four were simple; the next eight were difficult. As expected, all students performed well on the easy problems. Regarding the difficult problems, students with fixed mind-sets performed poorly on these. When asked why, fixed–mind-set students attributed failure to not being smart in the first place. They said things like "I'm not good at math" or "I'm not very smart." These inherent self-doubts were especially surprising, because just moments before they were solving simpler problems with ease. Meanwhile, students with growth mind-sets performed well on the difficult problems. They realized that the problems were harder, so they worked harder and manufactured new strategies to solve them. They did not give up or assign blame ("I can't do this, I'm not smart."). Their growth mind-sets led them to find ways to handle tough problems.

So, which child is likely to develop stronger running talent? The child with the growth mind-set, of course. A growth mind-set is better because it tells the learner that learning and improvement rest in the palm of your hand. Everything needed to become talented is within your grasp: simply believe you can, and apply effort. Talent is a rubber band just waiting to be stretched. Those with a fixed mind-set never stretch their band. They never leave the starting blocks. They are grounded by the flawed belief that effort won't work because talent is born, not made. As soon as the fixed–mind-set runner fails, he gives up because he's not cut out for running.

While it is vital that those entering a talent domain have a growth mind-set, it is also imperative for mentors to have that mind-set. After all, children likely derive their mind-set from parents and teachers. When a parent says "You somehow missed the music gene" or "Athletic ability does not run in our family," they are fostering a fixed mind-set. Similarly, when a teacher says "It seems like science is not your thing" or "Girls can't do math," the teacher is fostering a fixed mind-set. Even when that fixed mind-set is positive, such as "You were born to run" or "You have a math mind," danger still lurks. People who believe that talent is born tend not to try hard. Why should they if talent is born? Talent-is-born proponents are also reluctant to learn new strategies, such as a new problem-solving approach. Why should they if talent is born? A talent-is-born mind-set dismisses the two things most needed for improvement: effort and strategies.

National fencing coaches who were interviewed were unanimous in their emphasis on growth mind-set. Coach Gary Copeland said, "None of my athletes were talented because they came through the door with a fencing gene. They were talented because of the work they did. It is foolish for them or me to look for their advantage beyond practice."[2] Coach Mike Pederson stressed that a growth mind-set is important for success: "I have a student with a fixed mind-set. If something does not go as wanted, there is no effort to change or grow in a new way. Will the student have long-term success? I don't think so. I think it is rare, rare, rare for a fencer to have that fixed mind-set and become successful." Finally, Coach Ro Sobalvarro stressed that coaches, parents, and students maintain a growth mind-set. He said that defeats should not be construed as negative. They are going to occur. They can't be interpreted with a fixed mind-set that concludes that more defeats are inevitable. He said, "Some fencers excel early and some excel later." It is important that all believe that fortunes can change. "Without that mind-set, losses become a disaster because a kid is afraid to lose, afraid to try."

So, if you hear a prospective or present mentor say things like "Only gifted children can accomplish this" or "I only work with talented students," don't walk away. Run! Understand that children, all children, are a lump of clay to be molded, bands to be stretched. Find the mentor who believes in molding and stretching—who believes in growth, who believes that talent is made. Author Daniel Coyle asked a music teacher which of two students was better. Their musical performance that day certainly favored one over the other. The teacher gave a surprising reply: "It's difficult to say. When I teach, I give everyone everything. What happens after that, who can know?"[3] The teacher is right. How far students go rests in their own hands so long as student and mentor share a growth mind-set.

The Mentor Is a Target Teacher

When a student has difficulty solving a math problem or composing a concluding paragraph, what is a teacher to do? The best thing a teacher can do is look closely at what a student is doing, identify problems, and offer pointed suggestions. For the math student: "As I look over your work, I see you are calculating area using a rectangle's opposite sides, but you need to multiply adjacent sides—the top side and right side as I've done here. Now you practice one." For the student who is writing: "Your conclusion is just a summary restating points made in the paragraph. A conclusion is more than that. It reaches some sort of consensus about the points. You might say, 'World powers had markedly different reactions to the ban.' What else might you conclude?" These teachers are target teachers, able to quickly target problems and solutions.

Author Daniel Coyle offers a great example of target teaching: John Wooden, former UCLA basketball coach known as the "Wizard of Westwood." Wooden is considered one of the best coaches of all time. His UCLA Bruins won 10 national titles in 12 years, 7 of them in a row. What was Wooden's secret? In the 1970s, two educational psychologists aimed to find out. They were granted permission to watch practices and study Wooden's methods. The researchers were surprised by what they observed. There was no fire and brimstone, no punishing laps, no rah-rah speeches. In fact, there were no speeches of any type. When Wooden coached, he did so in short and pointed bursts of targeted information. He rarely spoke longer than 20 seconds. Here are some of Wooden's targeted teachings:

- "Take the ball softly; you're receiving a pass, not intercepting it."
- "Crisp passes, really snap them. Good, Richard, that's just what I want."
- "Hard, driving, quick steps."[4]

The educational psychologists recorded and analyzed Wooden's teachings throughout the season. Their data revealed 2,326 discrete acts of teaching. Of these, 7 percent were compliments, 7 percent were expressions of displeasure, and 75 percent were bursts of targeted information intended to identify and solve problems. What made Wooden a great coach wasn't praise, criticism, or pep talks. It was the targeted information he fired at players that helped them see and fix errors.

Speaking of educational psychologists, legendary Nebraska football coach Tom Osborne, who guided his Husker team to three national titles, received his doctorate in educational psychology. This might explain his targeted coaching methods. Osborne was much like Wooden and was a keen observer who identified and fixed problems in a quiet and controlled way. Osborne said, "I always felt that catching somebody doing something right and reinforcing it was a better way to change behavior than to punish, humiliate. So, I tried to never make criticism or correction personal. If a guy tackled with his head down, I'd say, 'Here's how you do it right.' Often people criticize, but they don't tell the person clearly what they did wrong and then how to do it right."[5] Osborne, like Wooden, eschewed the rah-rah, pep-talk aspects of coaching:

I always felt that pre-game speeches and all that stuff was really overrated. I know what it's like to line up for the kickoff, and on the kickoff, you're not thinking about what the coach said back in the locker room. . . . It's just you and the other team out there. As I told players all the time, "A pep talk isn't going to do it. I can't get you ready on Friday. It's got to start [with practice] on Monday."[6]

I saw Osborne's targeted and controlled approach firsthand. I was in the locker room as he gave players their send-off before a big game. Everyone was hushed, but I could barely hear Osborne speak as he quietly reminded players to do the jobs they were coached to do throughout practices and to play hard for 60 minutes because they would be the stronger team in the fourth quarter thanks to all their dedicated training. That was it. Osborne's words hit their target, and Big Red rolled.

Coyle offered another illuminating example of target teaching that occurred between music mentor Linda Septien and a vocal student. Let's listen in on some of Septien's target teaching:

- "Okay, it's a dance song, it's not pretty, it's not a power ballad. It moves quick, so be quick. Sing it like a trumpet."
- "Fade the ending. It should be like a balloon running out of air."
- "Use your diaphragm, not your face. Hold your tongue tighter there for a clearer sound."[7]

Another example of targeted teaching comes from Bonnie Baxter, who coaches world-champion twirler Steffany Lien. Coach Bonnie supplies Steffany with the fundamental and advanced technical knowledge needed to excel and does this not by modeling twirling skills but by keen observation, analysis, and feedback. Steffany said, "Coach Bonnie took me back to the basics of twirling. She made sure that my wrist was in the right position and that all my individual moves were unified and on pattern. She focused on and adjusted all the little things that contribute to the overall effect."[8] Coach Bonnie said, "If you're going to teach someone to spell, you first have to teach them the alphabet. So, I am strict and diligent when it comes to teaching good, strong basics, a good foundation." Regarding her teaching methods, Coach Bonnie said,

I don't have to get out there and spin for her. Instead, I give her the knowledge she needs to internalize the move and do the move herself. I watch and analyze. I might say, "That trick is not working because the baton's off-balance. The baton has to have a certain balance." Or, I'll say, "That trick is not working because you're moving too slowly. It won't work at that speed. You've got to double your speed." I pass along knowledge.[9]

Daniel Coyle calls these target-aiming teachers: talent whisperers. Talent whisperers, such as Wooden, Osborne, Septien, and Baxter, are quiet, reserved, usually older, and experienced—having taught for many years. They listen more than they talk, and they stray far from pep talks and inspiring speeches. Instead, they spend most of their time offering insights and small, highly specific adjustments targeted at a student's individual needs.

The Mentor Provides Cognitive Apprenticeship

Throughout history, one of the best teaching-learning methods has been the apprenticeship. An aspiring plumber, carpenter, or musician learns at the feet of an experienced master who models and teaches the craft. The best apprenticeships are cognitive in nature, such that the master reveals his inner conversation and thinking—his cognitions. A chess mentor should do more than model strong moves. She should speak her thoughts aloud as she contemplates various moves, thereby allowing the pupil "inside the head" of the mentor. A tennis mentor does more than model and teach tennis strokes. The tennis mentor reveals the thinking that goes on while awaiting service, deciding whether to come to the net, and when facing a second service break point.

As the mentor's inner thoughts bubble to the surface, the student's inner thoughts should too. The mentor draws out the pupil's inner conversation. In chess, the mentor might say "Tell me what moves you are considering. Say what you are thinking about bishop takes knight. What do you think about that move's positives and drawbacks?" The inner thoughts of mentor and pupil rise to the surface in reciprocal fashion. Here is a hypothetical mentor-pupil exchange pertaining to basketball free-throw shooting.

> *Mentor:* "As I stand at the foul line, I bounce the ball several times like this to loosen and prepare my muscles. My eyes never leave the target, which is just over the front of the rim. This keeps me focused on the target instead of noise and movement in the gym that might distract me. A real key for me is gripping the ball softly like this with my fingertips. This will give me better control when I spin it back and release it like this. When I shoot free throws, I just do three simple mental checks: bounce and relax, find the rim and focus, and gently grasp the ball for control. Now you try and tell me what you think."
>
> *Pupil:* "When I step to the line, I feel winded and nervous. I know all eyes are on me."
>
> *Mentor:* "That's why the ball bounce is good. It gives you time to catch your breath and relax your muscles."
>
> *Pupil:* "I think I stiffen up as I shoot sometimes because foul shooting is unnatural, because you just stand there and shoot."

Mentor: "Good point. That's why I think about and practice taking the shot in rhythm. I just bring the ball up and shoot it after my final dribble like this rather than wait. Try it."

Pupil: "Yeah, that feels good. I think I sometimes worry that my shot is going to fall short like that last one."

Mentor: "We can fix that. That's a follow-through problem. As I release the ball, I'm thinking about that follow through and extending my fingers out and then down into the basket. Practice that image and motion a few times without the ball."

This is not simple instruction and practice. This is mindful, cognitively reciprocal practice. The mentor reveals his inner thoughts and passes those along to the pupil, who in turn reveals her inner thoughts. This reflection speeds and solidifies learning. In time, the mentor's wisdom becomes the student's. The student thinks and acts like the mentor.

Parents should seek mentors who believe that talent is made and operate with a growth mind-set, who are target teachers competently spotting and correcting student errors, and who provide cognitive apprenticeships that reveal the mentor's and the student's inner conversations. In addition, parents should consider these four guidelines: (1) provide initial mentoring, (b) select a mentor who fits, (c) work closely with mentors, and (d) make sacrifices to obtain optimal mentors.

Provide Initial Mentoring

We learned from Benjamin Bloom's talent investigation that talented children usually progress through a series of mentors who make distinct and increasingly vital contributions.[10] An initial mentor makes the talent area introduction and instills passion for the domain. A subsequent mentor builds technique. A third mentor helps one cultivate a personal style and attain mastery. Parents are in an ideal position to serve as the initial talent mentor. Personal talent is not required; what is required is moderate knowledge about the talent domain and a deep interest in guiding one's child.

In some cases parents are already interested or immersed in the talent area, so introducing the domain and providing early guidance is easy. Such was the case for the baton twirlers I studied, as all but one had mothers who were former twirlers or even present-day twirling coaches or judges. Much the same occurred in chess, where three-fourths had fathers familiar with chess and served as initial mentors. Two-thirds of the volleyball players hailed from families with volleyball interest and were initially coached by a parent. Both swimming champions had parents or siblings with swimming talent or interest. The rodeo champion was raised on a ranch by parents with horse-training and riding talent. Two of five musicians were raised in musical homes and were initially mentored by a parent. The musically inclined mother of a violinist said, "My husband and I decided that when we had children they would have music lessons. I started giving them lessons . . . by the time they were able to stand."[11]

In other cases, the child discovers the talent area in some other way—perhaps through friends, a book, or a movie—and parents do not feel readily equipped to further the introduction and guide. Such was the case for one chess father whose son discovered chess during an after-school program. The father knew nothing about chess but did all he could to learn chess and serve as his son's initial mentor. Much the same happened in the Robson household after father Gary innocently introduced son Ray to chess when Ray was three years old. Gary Robson wrote:

> Ray learned on the flat tiled floor of our kitchen in Sarasota, Florida. I'd bought a combination checkers-chess set at a nearby K-mart for a few dollars, thinking that we'd start with checkers and would have chess to graduate to in a few years. However, Ray was drawn to the chess pieces [because there were] horses and castles and teepee-shaped objects. He wanted to know how to play *that* game, so I set up the board and showed him how the pieces moved. . . . He learned how the pieces moved almost immediately and, when I'd come home from work, I'd find him squatting on the floor, moving the knights and other pieces around the board and playing out games of his own creation. And he'd challenge me. Every single afternoon, I'd walk through the door and my three-year-old son would look up from the floor and say, "Baba, do you want to play chess?" Of course, I said yes.[12]

From that point on, Gary studied chess to teach Ray and become Ray's first chess mentor.

Kate Strickland, a National Junior Golf champion I interviewed, discovered golf at age three when she and a neighbor hit balls in her neighbor's yard. Soon balls were flying over the fence, and her parents took notice. Her father, Craig, was a former Oklahoma Sooner football player but not a golfer. Still, he studied and practiced golf so he could teach Kate the game. He bought her clubs and a net for indoor practice and became her first coach and caddy.

Select a Mentor Who Fits

For parents who don't yet know, most talented children have mentors. Navigating the coaching system is something parents must learn. One chess mom told this introduction-to-mentoring story:

A fellow came up to us after a tournament where my son had placed fifth and said, "Does Mark have a coach?" I said, "I've never heard of a chess coach. I've heard of a tennis coach but a chess coach?" He said, "Oh, yeah. How do you think those other kids came in fourth, third, second, and first?" And I said, "I don't know. I guess they're just really good at chess?" And he said, "No, they all have coaches."[13]

Selecting a mentor is not as simple as finding an expert. There are many prospective mentors out there, but not all are right for your child. Parents should be careful to match their child with mentors who care for the whole child while nurturing talent. One skating parent said, "I believe the most important thing in developing talent is finding the right coach, especially when you're dealing with children. You're dealing with a role model, a teacher, somebody that your kid is going to be with more than anyone else in their lives, even more than their parents."[14] Caleb Alexander, father of Nebraska state champion diver Austin Alexander, agrees that choosing the right coach is paramount, because the coach-student relationship is a major part of the child's life: "For the last ten years, Coach Hoffman has been like a second father to Austin. He has probably spent more time with my son than I have. The personal level between my son and his coach is, fortunately, very, very tight."[15]

The parent of a cellist echoed the importance of finding the right mentor:

It is important to not just find a teacher, you need a mentor, someone that can help the child grow and develop in different ways. For instance, when my son went to his very first cello teacher, one of the things that kind of raised alarms for me was that when he would play around on the cello and make sounds that were unusual, she got upset, and I didn't like that. I thought, I want my son to be able to explore. Even though he had to learn technique, I didn't want that creative part of him stifled.[16]

Author Josh Waitzkin described a similar bad-fit mentoring experience from his chess-playing days. He had a coach named Mark who was a world-class player and "the most important author for chess professionals in the world. . . . On the page, the man is a genius."[17] The problem was that Mark tried to fit all students into his comprehensive training program, and his method was to "break the student down rather brutally and then stuff him or her into the cookie-cutter mold of his training system."[18] Waitzkin owned an attacking chess style, but Mark tried to break him of this style and transform him into a defensive, positional player. Mark's shock-and-awe approach and one-size-fits-all agenda eventually dulled Waitzkin's natural shine and quieted his natural voice. Chess was no longer fun. Waitzkin felt alienated from his love for chess.

Anne Nagosky, a concert violinist and award-winning music teacher, reflected on the importance of teacher fit in her own talent journey. Anne said this about Mimi Zweig, her teacher for 11 years who founded the prestigious Indiana University String Academy:

> Mimi was the picture of patience. She tolerated everything, but had a way of letting you know if you weren't really living up to your potential. She never raised her voice. She never yelled. She never scolded. Her teaching philosophy was based on a nonjudgmental style and meeting students at their level. That was fabulous because I was shy when I was little and barely spoke to her at all. At the time, it was the perfect pairing for me, because I don't think I would have stuck with it if I felt a lot of pressure from my teacher.[19]

Parents must also find increasingly well-qualified mentors as the child's talent grows. Every talented person I ever studied eventually had an advanced if not elite, well-qualified mentor. These well-qualified mentors were usually current or former stars and well-established teachers in their fields. For example, most chess mentors were grandmaster level, twirling mentors were former national and world champions or had mentored others who were, figure skating and speed skating mentors had Olympic skating backgrounds, and music mentors were professional musicians at leading institutions or conservatories. A skating parent was surprised by how quickly her daughter progressed from taking group lessons for fun to spending six hours a day with various coaches including a primary coach, a coach for special tricks, and a ballet instructor. The skating parent said, "In the beginning it was just group lessons and over time coaches would say, 'Oh, your child's so gifted. She should take private lessons.' But nobody ever tells you where this is going to go, and you have no idea."[20]

Here is where it went for twirling champion Kelcie.[21] She was raised in a twirling household. Her mother, Maura, was a professional twirling coach and a national-level twirling judge. Maura began coaching Kelcie at age two but eventually turned the coaching reins over to more qualified and discipline-specific coaches. Kelcie worked privately with three elite out-of-town coaches, each of whom flew to Kelcie's home in New York about four times a year to work with her on specialized routines for a few days at a time. A coach from Tennessee helped choreograph and perfect Kelcie's free-style routines, while coaches from Texas and Ohio focused on her solo routines and other events.

Sandy Hamm, father of Olympic gymnasts Paul and Morgan, also brought elite coaches to his sons: "People expected us to ship the boys out for training but we were not going to do that. We brought coaches in. We were not going to give up our children when they were young kids."[22] Sandy ran for and was elected to the board of directors at the gym where his sons trained so he could take an active role in identifying and bringing in top coaches. Sandy successfully attracted top Soviet coaches who lived in his family's home for up to a year.

It can be hard for parents to change mentors, but doing so is often necessary to meet the child's burgeoning talent. Over time, children likely outgrow their initial and even secondary mentors. The parent of a figure skater said, "If my son wanted to get serious, and he did, he could not stay with the same teacher. We loved the teacher. We wanted to stay with her, but he just needed coaching beyond her level."[23] The parent of another figure skater said, "In the beginning, it was just lessons in the local mall, but as [my daughter] got better she needed better and better coaches." A third skating parent remarked, "We kind of saw the handwriting on the wall when my daughter was nine. The style of her primary coach was not allowing her to achieve the more difficult tricks. It was a more old-fashioned coaching style. It was time to move on to another coach." A volleyball parent said, "When my son felt like he'd learned everything he could from a particular coach, it was time to try someone else. But it's very difficult balancing the loyalty that you've built with coaches over many years with choosing what's best for your child. And we struggled with that a lot."

A figure skating parent described the negative ramifications that sometimes come when a prized student leaves a coach:

> I had to step in because I knew the coach was no longer the best thing for my kid. There was a long and successful relationship between that coach and [my daughter], but we had to decide to leave him. He was very angry about our decision. It was one of the hardest things I ever did in my life. But just as with a kindergarten teacher, [my daughter] had to move on. But when the Olympics came, we bought him tickets and took him with us to the Olympics. So, he knew that he had a magical part in her life.[24]

Work Closely with Mentors

I have heard mentors say that parents need to turn their children over to qualified coaches and then stay on the sidelines, stay out of the way. Some draw a bold line separating coach and parent. One coach I interviewed said this about parents, "They need to back up and let me do my job."[25]

Others draw a slender line that protects them from parents seen as being overinvolved. One swim coach said,

> There's been cases where parents can be too involved. It's that classic helicopter parent. They need to let kids go out and make mistakes, let them work through problems on their own. Parents can't fix everything in a heartbeat, and adversity can help kids grow. Doing poorly in a meet is part

of life. Kids experience that sometime. No matter how good they are, they are going to fail at a meet. Parents can't fix that. They need to let kids go through that. So, there's been times I've talked to some parents and reminded them there's no coaching from parents on deck. It's one of those things where I must say, "I'm the coach, you're the parent, go sit in the stands, and quit trying to tell your kid what to do." It's a matter of letting parents be parents, letting kids be kids, and letting coaches coach. That's the best setup when that happens.[26]

A trio of national team fencing coaches who were interviewed echoed the parents-should-back-off sentiment:

- "The growth of overly involved parents is alarming and nobody finds it helpful."
- "I often wonder how a child ever learns when there seems to be so much ownership by parents in the fencer's bouts and training."
- "It is okay for parents to push the kid when they need a little push, but they should stay pretty much in the background. It is up to the child how far they want to go in this sport."[27]

I concur that parents must trust coaches and allow them to coach. When I coached youth soccer, I asked parents not to direct their children when they are playing, and I told players not to listen. The chief reason was that parents' counseling voices were often wrong. Most did not understand soccer and would yell for their children to "get in there" when that was not what they should do at all. Soccer should not be played like a single tumbleweed rolling down the field collecting debris as it goes; it should be played with players spread out and holding their relative positions.

Although I asked parents to remain spectators during games, I fully invited their participation at practices. Not only could they assist with drills, but I also wanted them to learn soccer along with their children. Most important, I demonstrated and explained how parents could practice with their children. The team practiced just once a week, but parents could practice with their children daily and reinforce the skills acquired at team practices.

Music teacher Anne Nagosky's own musical path began with her teacher, Mimi Zweig, insisting on parent involvement in lessons and practice. When interviewed, Anne said, "Mimi's policy mandated that at least one parent attend all lessons and take notes and subsequently supervise the student's practice."[28] In her own teaching, Anne teaches the parent right along with the child so that the parent knows what to look for and correct during home practice. In fact, Anne sometimes trades places with the parent during lessons and guides the parent as to how to instruct the child at home.

I believe that such partnerships are best for coaches, parents, and children. Parents should be involved with coach and child in positive and appropriate ways. I believe that twirler Steffany Lien and her coach Bonnie Baxter had it exactly right. Steffany said, "I truly believe that it takes the right parent, the right coach, and a student who is willing to put in the work and time needed to excel. In my opinion, that's the recipe for success. That's how it happens."[29] Coach Bonnie concurred: "You have to have a good balance of all three. It begins with a student who is passionate about her sport and who is motivated to excel. Part of that comes from the coach who is encouraging and inspiring, and part of that comes from the parent. So, it is a combination of all three. If one of those is missing, it is not going to happen." Susan Lien, Steffany's mom, said, "I think one thing that I did correctly was that I did not assume to be the coach. I put Steffany in Coach Bonnie's hands, trusted in that, and let go."[30] Well, yes and no. Susan ceased being Steffany's coach and relied on and trusted Coach Bonnie to mentor, but Susan remained part of that winning student-mentor-parent triangle. Susan, like many parents I interviewed, attended all lessons, filmed instruction, took detailed notes, and then used that valuable information to guide Steffany through her daily practices. Susan reinforced what Coach Bonnie taught. Susan doubly instructed Steffany. And Coach Bonnie noticed and appreciated Susan's involvement. Coach Bonnie said, "No child does it alone. There's got to be parent support, encouragement, and nurturing. Susan does all this. She is what I consider the ideal mother."[31]

I believe that parents need to walk the fine line between overinvolvement and being a productive member of the winning triangle: student, mentor, parent. Let coaches coach. That's their job. But develop a positive and helpful relationship with the coach. Let the coach know that you are there to help and guide your child. A twirling parent said she wanted to maximize the mentoring that her daughter received: "Because we travel so far . . . her lessons are four hours away, I'm taking notes and video recording. And, then my daughter and I look at the video and look back over the notes when she practices. We want to make sure our time is well spent."[32] Another twirling parent had a twirling background that the daughter's coach welcomed. The parent said, "I sit in the stands and I'm intense. I text the coach and say things like, 'Look, this is what I think needs fixed.' And, she texts me things like, 'What do you think? Should we throw this trick in?' And, we work like a team."[33] A figure skating parent said, "I never wanted to be perceived as a stage mother so I try to stay in the background. But there are times I disagree with what is happening and I approach the coach privately when the time is right. I advocate for my daughter, but I pick my battles." Finally, here is what Fred Waitzkin said about his relationship with son Josh's chess mentor:

> The child is only one part of the team. Regardless of his gift for the game, he cannot compete at the highest level without a good teacher and a

supportive parent. . . . I am the coach and Bruce is the teacher. He drills Josh on the openings, hones his tactics, and trains him in endgame technique. I decide which tournaments we'll play and how much practice he should have the week before. I log his weaknesses and strengths and point them out to Bruce. I remind Bruce to give him homework, and I pester Josh to do it. I make sure he is asleep early on Tuesday night so that he won't be tired for his Wednesday lesson.[34]

Make Sacrifices to Obtain Optimal Mentors

Talent development is a costly endeavor. Securing, working with, and paying for mentors is usually the most taxing part. Parents devote a lot of time and money to children's mentoring, and some make large sacrifices to do so.

Working with elite mentors is not a simple thing. They usually don't live right down the street. Families sometimes relocate, travel great distances, or fly mentors in to secure the best training for their children. One figure skating family relocated 200 miles from Aspen to Colorado Springs so their son could train with an elite coach. The parents quit their jobs and slowed their career advancements to make the move. The mother said, "I was offered a new job in Colorado Springs, but my husband sacrificed everything for our son. He gave up a good job and derailed his career."[35] One middle school violinist was invited to an elite summer camp designed for college students in another state. For him to attend, his mother accompanied him to the camp and lived in a nearby cabin throughout the summer. Another talented violinist and his mother flew weekly from Utah to California for weekly lessons with an established mentor.

Savannah won more than a dozen national or world twirling titles, and mother Sammie credits the outstanding mentoring Savannah received.[36] That mentoring did not come easily. Although Savannah worked with a local coach in Kansas City for nine years, she eventually needed more advanced coaching. Sammie arranged for Savannah to work with two elite out-of-town coaches, one in Ohio and one in Georgia. About once every six weeks, Savannah and Sammie flew to one of those destinations for a full weekend of training. Sammie said, "Both coaches are phenomenal in their areas of expertise. The Ohio coach is an older woman with a wealth of experience who coaches a lot of top kids on the east coast. She has developed the mental side of twirling for Savannah. The Georgia coach is young and is the featured twirler for the University of Georgia. She is a Grand National collegiate champion who specializes in two- and three-baton."[37] But there is more. To perfect her twirling routines, Savannah also worked with a twirling cleanup coach twice a month who lived a few hours north. Because twirling competitions require tumbling and dancing skills, Savannah also took weekly tumbling classes and weekly ballet classes. Sammie said, "People don't realize but a baton twirler is really a gymnast and dancer with a 27-inch stick twirling above her head."

The flying-for-lessons thing can work both ways. As mentioned earlier, another twirling family flies three different coaches to their home in New York. Each coach works privately with Kelcie on a specialized routine over a period of days about four or five times a year.[38] A coach from Tennessee helps choreograph and perfect Kelcie's free-style routines, while coaches from Texas and Ohio focus on her solo routines and other events.

In the chess world, Vladimir arranged for his son Daniel to work with grandmaster-level coaches who had "an insatiable appetite for chess" that matched Daniel's.[39] One was from Kentucky, and the other was from Israel. Daniel took regular lessons from these coaches via the Internet. Vladimir also arranged for the Kentucky-based coach to fly to their California home and work with Daniel there for several days a few times a year. In addition, Vladimir arranged for Daniel to train with former world champion Garry Kasparov in New York. In our own chess home, Keaton took lessons from grandmaster Sher via telephone, but other more burdensome training arrangements occurred too. We flew grandmaster Sher to Nebraska for intense training a couple of times a year. Keaton and I also traveled to week-long camps for elite players throughout the United States where he was instructed by top grandmasters.

Elite coaching comes at a great financial price unless one is part of a national team. Such was the good fortune of Olympic speed skaters Bonnie Blair and Dan Jansen, whose elite-level training was supplied by national coaches funded by Team USA. For most others, mentoring costs come from a family's pockets, which are not always deep. Most hour-long training sessions with elite mentors today cost $100 or more. When you consider that talented children might be taking several lessons per week, costs can elevate quickly and burden families. To fund coaching, families have made great sacrifices such as borrowing money, forgoing retirement savings, living in smaller houses, and taking second and third jobs. A figure skating mom stated bluntly that "This is an ungodly expensive sport. It really is. I can't tell you how many times we mortgaged our house."[40] The mother of a cellist said, "We decided that money wasn't going to keep him from a certain teacher, so we lived off borrowed money for a time." And one chess parent remarked, "Lessons with a grandmaster require a price and it's a very high price. We've done some absolutely, unbelievably crazy things to be able to make that work. We have taken second jobs—worked janitorial jobs at office buildings. We've sold things on eBay. When we travel, we take a suitcase filled with food."

Finally, Gary Robson wrote of the financial strain and sacrifices associated with son Ray's $25,000 annual chess expenses. "Our home in sunny Florida had been without a working air conditioning unit for the past two years, and we endured the summers with windows and doors open, fans running in each room, and shorts and tee-shirts as our daily attire."[41] To save money when they traveled for tournaments or chess training, father and son took the cheapest flights even if they had many stops and long layovers, used public transportation or walked, and used a home-stay network that allowed them to bunk on a stranger's couch or floor. Gary said, "We slept on a hard floor in an unkempt room where cats wrestled over us and chewed our hair each night and where cat dander was so heavy that Ray had mump-like bumps on his face."[42]

In the end, parents were more than willing to go to such lengths and make such sacrifices and had no regrets about doing so. These two parent statements capture the sentiments of those I interviewed:

- "I've made a commitment to him that so long as he continues to work and grow and do his best, we'll use whatever resources we have to get him where he needs to go."
- "I knew he had talent and I did not want to see it wither. If you're talented in one thing, you're very, very fortunate, so I encouraged and supported that. I was proud of his skill. I just knew it gave him joy."[43]

CHAPTER SIX

Parents' Roles in Creating a Center of Excellence

Full disclosure: My college days began a bit like *Animal House*. Although I was never placed on Double Secret Probation, there were rough academic patches. I carried a B average into a meteorology final but got slapped with a final grade of D. I asked the professor how this could be. His sobering response: "Your grade on the final was an F minus, minus, minus." Oh. Then there was the English writing exam. Prospective English teachers had to pass it to earn their teaching certificate. I failed it, failed it, failed it. Three strikes and no certificate.

But something life-changing occurred toward the end of my college career—year seven or eight perhaps—and it wasn't a toga party. My *Animal House* script shifted to *Finding Forester*. Like the struggling main character, Jamal, I found my element. I found educational psychology. And I found my first mentor: Professor Nelson DuBois. My first day in his educational psychology class was the crystalizing experience that signaled my educational psychology calling. The material was delicious, infectious. I loved learning about the teaching-learning process and how people become experts. I stopped skipping classes and started auditing educational psychology classes not even on my schedule. Dr. DuBois meanwhile was a model of outstanding teaching and college professing. I wanted to do what he was doing. He convinced me that I could and guided me.

Educational Psychology Centers of Excellence

Dr. DuBois stressed that I attend graduate school, but not just any graduate school. It must be an educational psychology center of excellence—the best programs, faculty, and students. Eventually we chose Florida State University because it had the nation's best program in instructional psychology and the best mentors, including Professor Robert Gange, who pioneered the science of instruction. While I dawdled through college, I raced through graduate school, taking just three years to go from bachelor's degree to doctorate. During that tenure, I mixed with brilliant, compelling professors and with bright, motivated students grappling to find the cutting edge. And I also learned to write thanks to another mentor, Professor Harold Fletcher. When I wrote something, Fletcher invited me to his home for a Sunday afternoon conference, where I read my latest work to him out loud. I wondered, "Could he not read?" Fletcher sat back pensively, pipe in hand, and listened. But never for very long: "Stop. You can't have an if without a then. That's why they're called if-then statements." "Stop. That sentence is not parallel. This is how it should read." "Stop. That verb is passive. Rather than say he did it, say he accomplished it." "Stop, wrong word. You don't mean 'anxious,' you mean 'eager.' You were eager to meet her, not anxious about it." Professor Fletcher was a rapid-fire target teacher, a talent whisperer, identifying and correcting errors. Over time, he transformed my "I can't write" fixed mind-set to a "With practice and feedback, I can write" growth mind-set. I was an evolving writer hungering for another crack at that English writing exam. I had found my educational psychology center of excellence.

Staying with the educational psychology theme, I investigated the most productive educational psychologists in the United States and Germany to learn how they became so productive. In each case, a center of excellence played a critical and career-propelling role. There was Richard Anderson, who received his doctorate at Harvard University, where he was mentored by a famous psychologist linked to a long line of other famous psychologists rolling back to the dawn of psychology.[1] Upon graduation, Anderson gravitated to another center of excellence, the University of Illinois, where he joined several productive and like-minded educational psychologists studying reading. It didn't stop there. Anderson's work and reputation attracted dozens of emerging scholars clamoring to study with him, thus strengthening the Illinois center of excellence. Another productive American educational psychologist, Michael Pressley, left his own graduate school for an extended period and gravitated to another university center of excellence, where professors were studying Pressley's intended topic, memory strategies.[2] In Germany, all four productive educational psychologists I investigated were linked to a single center of excellence: Ludwig-Maximilian University Munich.[3] Three of the scholars gravitated there to work with the fourth, Heinz Mandl. In about a decade, the quartet produced over 200 collaborative works. Professor Alexander Renkl, one of the four, said this about the benefit of working in a center of excellence: "I grew up in a rich academic environment where it was clear that you had to be productive. . . . It's important for young students to go to a productive group because you adapt to what others do. If you're in the Mandl group and all others are publishing, then you want to do the same. If you're in a group with people who are only publishing once a year, then you do the same."[4]

Speed Skating Center of Excellence

Speed skaters, with their fluid movements, bent forward posture, and breakneck speed, are fascinating to watch. They are the fastest humans on Earth who use neither gravity nor mechanical devices to propel them. Elite speed skaters reach speeds of more than 30 miles per hour while countering the centrifugal force trying to throw them off the track. Speed skating competition requires cold weather to make and maintain ice and a skating oval. But an ordinary oval, such as that used for hockey, is too small. Olympic-size skating ovals are 400 meters long, much like an outdoor track for running. In the 1960s there was just one such oval in the United States, and that was in Milwaukee, Wisconsin. That was where the best skaters and coaches congregated or lived. Milwaukee was the center of speed skating excellence. I interviewed three four-time U.S. Olympic speed skaters with strong Milwaukee ties: Bonnie Blair, Dave Cruikshank, and Dan Jansen.[5]

Gravitating to the Milwaukee oval was easy for Jansen; it was located just two miles from his home. Jansen said,

> I grew up in West Allis, a suburb of Milwaukee that happened to be where the first 400-meter speed skating rink was in the country. It was the only one in the country until 1980 when they built the second one in Lake Placid. That was a huge part of why I started skating, more so a bigger part of why I continued skating because . . . it was right there; it was just two miles from my home.[6]

Jansen also reported that the oval drew elite skaters from the region and throughout the United States. "People like Bonnie Blair and others I got to know from Minnesota, Illinois, and other states would come to Milwaukee. Some would stay at our house and even enroll in school there so that they could train at the oval with other top skaters. If you weren't from there, you came and trained there. If you were a serious speed skater, you just had to be there."[7]

As a child, Bonnie Blair lived and trained in Champaign, Illinois. But she also trained and competed extensively at the Milwaukee oval, three and a half hours from her home. Blair said, "Milwaukee usually had ice by Thanksgiving time so that was where we would come and train. The track was outside then so we were skating in nature with wind, rain, snow, and sun, whatever faced us. Then in December of 1991, the Milwaukee facility was covered, and the national team and I trained there even more."[8] Blair, like other Milwaukee-based skaters, benefited from the elite coaching available there: "The best coaches were based in the Milwaukee area. . . . I would go up there and live at my sister's house for an extended time to train daily with [my coach] and the other skaters who lived in the area."[9]

Dave Cruikshank grew up in Northbrook, Illinois, a Chicago suburb with a strong speed skating tradition of its own. Cruikshank said, "The Northbrook area has produced an incredible history of speed skaters. We had a speed skating Olympian in every Olympics from 1952 until I retired in 1998."[10] Although Cruikshank and other top Northbrook skaters had their own center of skating excellence, they traveled to Milwaukee several times a week to train with the best on the premiere oval. Cruikshank said, "Milwaukee was the Mecca of speed skating. There is just an incredible history of speed skaters and coaches who came out of that area. It was also the biggest and best facility around. Every other day, skaters from Northbrook would drive about an hour to Milwaukee to practice."[11]

It was in Milwaukee that Cruikshank first crossed paths with his future Olympic speed skating teammates and mentors. That group included Dan Jansen and Bonnie Blair. Cruikshank said,

> When I won the junior world championship in 1987 that immediately put me onto the national team and allowed me to train in Milwaukee with Dan Jansen and Bonnie Blair and all the other great American athletes who were going to the 1988 Olympics. That was huge because, at the time, I did not know what it took to be a top speed skater. Suddenly, I'm watching and learning from Dan and Bonnie who are perhaps going to win Olympic medals, they're favorites, they're serious, they're seasoned, and they're just coming into their primes. And, I'm like, "Wow, these people really know what they're doing." So, I just got into their draft. I studied what they did, how they trained, and how they lived. That opportunity was incredibly influential for my career. And, it was one of the most fun times ever as a speed skater because I'm in there with two of the greatest speed skaters of all time.[12]

Some Talent Hotbeds Ignite

Where do centers of excellence, also called talent hotbeds, come from? Some seem to ignite, almost erupt, from nothing, but it is usually a certain person or event that sparks a center-of-excellence formation. Such was the case when one road in England produced more table tennis champions than all other English roads combined. Author Matthew Syed helps us take a closer look. Mr. Charters was a primary school teacher with a fanatical passion for sports. He coached almost all the after-school sports clubs, but his all-consuming passion was table tennis. He was a top table tennis coach and a senior figure in the English Table Tennis Association. Syed writes, "The other sports were just a front; an opportunity to scout sporting talent wherever it emerged so he could focus it—ruthlessly and exclusively—upon table tennis."[13] Charters gave every child who passed through the primary school a tryout, and those who showed potential were persuaded to take their ping-pong skills to the local Omega table tennis club. Omega was a ramshackle table tennis hotbed. It was a single table in a gravel-floored enclosure that was frigid in winter and sweltering in summer. Plants grew through the roof and floor. But what it lacked in charm, it compensated for with ping-pong talent-bearing essentials. Omega was open 24 hours a day, and all the patrons had keys; it had Mr. Charters, a talented and enthusiastic coach, and also had a cadre of talented and motivated players who pushed one another to ping-pong greatness. Most of those players hailed from Silverdale Road, the road where Mr. Charters taught school and recruited ping-pong disciples.

Sometimes a single victory can ignite a talent hotbed. Author Daniel Coyle tells the talent-ignition stories of golfer Se Ri Pak and tennis player Anna Kournikova.[14] On May 18, 1998, 20-year-old South Korean golfer Se Ri Pak won the McDonald's LPGA Championship and became a South Korean icon. Before her no South Korean had succeeded in golf, and Pak was the only South Korean on the LPGA tour. Pak's victory ignited a South Korean golf storm. South Korean girls were inspired to play golf. When they witnessed Pak's win, their mind-sets were all growth as they collectively said, "If Pak can do it, why not me?" Ten years later there were 33 South Korean golfers on the LPGA tour, and South Koreans were winning about one-third of tour events. In one victory stroke, South Korea had become a golf hotbed.

A similar talent-igniting moment occurred that same year in Russian women's tennis. Seventeen-year-old Anna Kournikova reached the Wimbledon semifinals. The combination of early tennis accomplishment on tennis's biggest stage and supermodel looks made Kournikova the world's most downloaded athlete. That notoriety sparked a firestorm of Russian tennis interest and eventual success. In 1998, just three Russian women were ranked among the top 100; in 2006, 16 were among the top 100. By 2007, Russian women occupied 5 of the top 10 rankings and 12 of the top 50. Russia had become a tennis hotbed.

Another example comes from chess. Americans were indifferent to chess until Bobby Fischer's world championship match in 1972 sparked chess mania. The match had all the trappings of a modern-day reality TV show. In one corner, there was the Russian chess machine running smoothly on centuries of chess superiority and chutzpah. In the other corner there was Bobby Fischer, the brash and brilliant chess upstart. The backdrop was the Cold War. Which superpower would emerge most super? There was drama. At the last moment, the temperamental Fischer was dissatisfied with tournament policies and conditions and refused to travel to Iceland to play. A Hail Mary visit by Secretary of State Henry Kissinger finally got Fischer on the plane to Iceland after he already forfeited the match's first two games. Fischer outlawed cameras in the tournament room, so commentators on live U.S. television and radio announced and analyzed every move as a nation desperately followed a foreign game that suddenly became its own. Intrigue turned to frenzy when Fischer dismantled the Russian chess machine. After his victory, he was on the cover of *Sports Illustrated, Life, Time,* and *Newsweek* and starred on popular late-night shows. The game of chess exploded in popularity. Chess sets and books flew from store shelves, and chess became the thing. Author Fred Waitzkin wrote that "Mothers pulled their sons out of Little League and ferried them to chess lessons," and "shy, introverted chess players basked in the national glory along with running backs and rock stars."[15] Fischer's championship sparked chess interest and made American chess competitive. Since Fischer, there have been other U.S. world top 10 players. Today, Americans ranked 2nd, 9th, and 14th in the world nip the heels of the world's top player. Fischer got the Russian chess king to tumble and crowned America as a chess talent hotbed.

Some Talent Hotbeds Are Established

While some talent hotbeds spring up naturally because of a charismatic figure or monumental event, others arise and are established systematically. They are businesses meant to hone talent and make money. America has exploded with talent academies in recent years, perhaps a reaction to parents' increasing commitment to help children get ahead and succeed. Scan the Internet. There are academies for mainstream talent domains such as baseball, dance, music, and gymnastics and for fringe domains such as cup stacking and circus. There are also academies for the academically gifted and for those who are inclined toward math and science. Some academies are residential, providing intensive year-round training; others offer summer camps, weekend classes, and after-school programs.

One of the best-known and most well-established talent academies is the IMG (International Management Group) Academy in Bradenton, Florida. The academy began in 1978 when legendary tennis coach Nick Bollettieri started the first full-time tennis boarding school, where aspiring players lived, trained, and attended school. Now, the academy is a residential multisport training destination that has trained and developed some of the world's top student athletes in eight sports: baseball, basketball, football, golf, lacrosse, soccer, tennis, and track and field. The academy's website reports that "Graduates have gone on to pursue academics and athletics at many of the schools on the *U.S. News & World Report's* annual Top 50 list, including Princeton, Harvard, Brown, West Point, Cornell, and John Hopkins."[16] Moreover, "Graduates have earned more than 133 professional all-star nods, 3 Heisman trophies, 108 major championship titles, 63 MVP awards, 14 national titles, 29 world championship titles, and 32 Olympic medals over the past 35+ years."

The IMG Academy is not just for high school student-athletes; the academy offers full-time schooling and athletic opportunities that begin at the prekindergarten and elementary school level. Boarding school opportunities begin in middle school. The annual residential cost for high school students is nearly $75,000, while the cost is about $55,000 for those who live at home—a hefty price tag indeed. Across all ages, the academy enrolls about 1,000 students annually who hail from more than 80 countries.

One recent IMG graduate is Florida State University quarterback Deondre Francois. While at IMG, Francois was coached by former Florida State quarterback and Heisman Trophy winner Chris Weinke and was rated the nation's number one dual-threat quarterback by Rivals. In Francois's redshirt freshman season at Florida State, he was named Atlantic Coast Conference freshman of the year.

Another recent IMG graduate is Broc Bando, who was recruited to play football at the University of Nebraska. Broc is a mountain of a man, standing 6'5" and weighing 280 pounds. Broc attended high school and played football in his hometown of Lincoln, Nebraska, for two years before transferring to the IMG Academy for his junior and senior years. When I asked him why he made the switch, Broc said, "You can't not go to a place like that. It's an opportunity to learn from the best and train with the best. I would not have been recruited by Nebraska and other Division 1 schools without that experience." Broc also said that "The coaching staff was phenomenal" and was composed of several former "NFL players who really knew their stuff." Broc emphasized that "you can't just go there and drink the water and get better, you have to work really hard, but the coaches know how to work you." Brock said that the IMG Academy was special because there was a genuine closeness among the players, and "all the guys on the team have the same goal and that's to play college football." The team was special too. They went undefeated during Broc's two seasons and were ranked number three in the nation by *USA Today*. The team plays a national schedule against top competition much like a college team. "Our team is the best of the best and we play other teams considered the best of the best," Broc said. The academic side mirrors college too. "It's high school but with the mentality of college. We have morning classes, practice, meetings, and lifting in the afternoon, and then homework."[17] Broc also praised his teachers, saying they were accommodating and helpful. Broc's mother was supportive of the move, knowing that this was Broc's dream and knowing that the academy works with families to make tuition affordable.

I recently spoke with former Syracuse University basketball star and NBA player Andrew White III, who also took the prestigious boarding school route to basketball stardom. Andrew was raised in Richmond, Virginia. He said that he was five years old when his father, a former college player, introduced him to basketball but that he was not serious about basketball or good at it for some time. Andrew's single-game scoring record as a middle school player was just five points. He began taking basketball seriously in ninth grade, and his father did too. Andrew's father told him that basketball could be his ticket to college and led him through intense daily two-hour workouts and had him watch instructional game films. Andrew's father stressed fundamentals so that years later Andrew still "heard" his dad's constant shooting reminders: "Get the ball to the right." "Toe, knee, wrist in parallel. All work as one."

At his family's urging, Andrew gravitated to a private boarding school his junior and senior years in Charlottesville, Viginia, that was academically rich and boasted a track record of basketball success, outstanding coaching, and big-time college recruitment. Every morning, Andrew was awakened at 5:45 by coaches who lived one floor above him. Andrew rolled out of bed and reported for an hour of conditioning and basketball practice. After a full day of intense classes, there was another two-hour practice. Andrew thrived there academically and athletically and became a top 50 national recruit. He credits his father's early training and the boarding school center of excellence for his still emerging basketball success.

The next section offers three center-of-excellence guidelines: (a) take advantage of what is available in your own backyard, (b) gravitate to a center of excellence, and (c) assemble your own center of excellence.

Take Advantage of What Is Available in Your Own Backyard

You have already heard stories about families taking advantage of talent hotbeds right in their own backyards. There were the ping-pong players on Silverdale Road who took advantage of the nearby Omega table tennis club, with its all-day access, enthusiastic coach, and talented young members. There was Olympic speed skater Dan Jansen taking advantage of the famed Milwaukee skating oval, just two miles from his home, where top coaches and skaters gravitated. Here are two other examples of families taking advantage of talent opportunities in their own backyard.

Olympic volleyball star Jordan Larson was raised in Hooper, Nebraska, population 800. She was the number two–rated prep volleyball player in the country and could have played anywhere collegiately, but she played for the University of Nebraska Husker team just 60 miles from her home. Larson was a four-year starter, first-team All American, and national champion at Nebraska. While Larson and teammates reigned, Nebraska Twins Amber and Kadie Rolfzen were eighth grade volleyball stars being recruited to play college volleyball for the University of Nebraska. The sisters signed on and were also eventual four-year starters, All-American players, and national champions. Like Larson, the sisters never traveled far to reach volleyball stardom. They were raised less than an hour from campus. To understand this trio's early volleyball talent and Husker recruitment when they could have starred for any school in the country, you need to understand Nebraska's volleyball culture. Let's start with that Husker volleyball team. Consider these amazing statistics:

- Since the team's inception in 1975, the Husker team has more wins than any other Division 1 school, has claimed five national titles, and has produced 43 All-Americans—the most by any school. One-fourth of the 2016 Olympic team were former Huskers.
- The team has been ranked in the top 25 volleyball poll every week since 1982. Its 34-year home record is 511–36.
- Nebraska has been called the epicenter of volleyball fandom. The team has had a 200+ game sellout streak since 2001. The average attendance for the 2017 season was 8,200 per match. The 4 largest-ever crowds to watch a volleyball match, and 7 of the top 10 were in Nebraska watching their beloved Husker team. That includes the 16,670 fans who watched the Huskers claim the 2015 national title.[18]

Husker volleyball passion has flooded the state and produced statewide volleyball involvement and success. The state boasts several high school and club volleyball powerhouses staffed with experienced coaches and loaded with eventual Division 1 college talent. When interviewed, Teresa Rolfzen, the twins' mother, said that getting the girls involved in volleyball was an easy and popular choice to make. Nebraska has a strong club system, and girls throughout the state want to play volleyball. The twins played recreational volleyball for a year before joining a local club as fifth graders. In seventh grade, they gravitated to a more competitive club in their area. That lasted two years, and then they advanced to another club in Lincoln, about an hour from home, while also playing in high school. Teresa recognized that receiving such high-caliber training so close to home was a convenient and productive thing. The twins' storied volleyball careers never extended more than an hour from their homes. They took full advantage of the volleyball center of excellence that existed right outside their door. Of course, they weren't alone. Dozens of Husker stars, Larson included, are homegrown products. That is because girls across the state clamor to play volleyball like the Husker heroes they follow passionately. And the local club and school teams are the junior volleyball talent hotbeds providing the training needed to become the next Husker star without ever leaving home.

Let's swing from volleyball to chess. You know about Bobby Fischer, the American world chess champion who popularized chess in the United States. From previous chapters you know about Josh Waitzkin, who was the subject of his father's famous book *Searching for Bobby Fischer*. Waitzkin was a chess prodigy seeking to become the next Fischer. Perhaps you never heard of Fabiano Caruana or Hikaru Nakamura, but either American player could become the next Fischer should he become chess world champion. With both ranked in the top 15 (Caruana is ranked 2nd in 2018), the notion is conceivable. What do all these talented players plus several others I studied have in common?[19] They were all raised in or around New York City—for them, a backyard chess talent hotbed.

How dominant is New York compared to the other 49 states in producing chess talent? To find out, I reviewed national scholastic rating lists from the United States Chess Federation from the 1990s and early 2000s when the players mentioned or investigated were schoolchildren honing their chess talents (other than Fischer, who grew up with chess in the 1960s). I looked at the top 10 players in six scholastic age groups ranging from ages 8 to 18 for 1991, 1996, and 2001. In 1991 and again in 1996, one-third of the top 10 players were from New York. In 2001, 42 percent of top 10 players were from New York. New York was indeed a chess Mecca.

Back in the Fischer days long before the Internet, chess was a live struggle. To compete you had to find competitors, and those were found in brick-and-mortar chess clubs. New York's chess clubs—Manhattan, Marshall, and Brooklyn—were renowned for their activity and player caliber and were largely responsible for making Fischer world champion. Biographer Frank Brady, in 1973, wrote:

> It is even possible that [Fischer] would not have become what he is today if he had grown up elsewhere. This is not mere provincialism but a fact of contemporary chess life; in America, great players just don't seem to develop outside the New York City area, and if they do, they quickly leave their hometowns. As painters and sculptors flocked to Florence during the Renaissance, and writers learned their craft in Paris during the last two centuries, most young American chess players eager to test their skills against the foremost masters, and possibly make a reputation, eventually find their way to Manhattan. About four-fifths of the leading masters in the country today are New Yorkers either by birth or adoption, and the remnant is widely scattered.[20]

Not too many people can walk through a park a few blocks from home and discover their element. Maybe baseball, but chess? Josh Waitzkin discovered chess in New York's Washington Square Park, where a corner of the park was inhabited by fast-moving, clock-slapping, money-exchanging chess players. "It was a bizarre school for a child, a rough crowd of alcoholics, homeless geniuses, wealthy gamblers hooked on the game, junkies, eccentric artists—all diamonds in the rough, brilliant, beat men, lives in shambles, aflame with a passion for chess."[21] That is how chess began for the young Waitzkin, but within months he was training with fellow New Yorker Bruce Pandolfini, regarded as one of the premiere chess coaches and writers in the country. Soon after, Waitzkin was national elementary school champion. Only in New York was Waitzkin's chess introduction and meteoric rise possible.

Samson Benen, Robert Hess, and Marc Arnold discovered chess the same way. They were students in New York City schools that included chess in the curriculum and offered after-school programs. Samson's mom said, "He was exposed at school where they have a very strong chess program. In kindergarten, they had a chess board in the room and this guy (an international master) came around and taught the kids the moves. . . . He called us up and said, 'Your son shows real talent,' and we said, 'at what?' and he said, 'at chess.' And we said, 'Oh come on.' 'No,' he said, 'I'm telling you, he's very talented . . . he sees a lot.'"[22] By first grade, Samson was taking lessons from an elite New York coach and often played in the famed Marshall Chess Club a few blocks from his home.

Robert Hess discovered chess much the same way as a New York City first grader. Robert and his classmates were taught chess as part of the school curriculum, the same way other schools teach physical education or art. The chess teacher was no ordinary teacher. He was Russian grandmaster Miron Sher, former coach of the Russian National Team and personal coach of eventual world number two–ranked Fabiano Caruana of New York. Robert's father recalled that "One day during first grade I picked Robert up from school and a kind of funny guy with a Russian accent gives me a business card and says, 'Your son, he's sort of good at chess, you should call me.' I made the call and soon Robert was training twice a week with GM [grandmaster] Sher who has been Robert's primary coach ever since."[23]

Growing up in New York City also jump-started Marc Arnold's chess career. Marc's school offered chess instruction as part of the curriculum. Marc was introduced to chess in kindergarten and within months of that introduction began attending the school's after-school chess club. Like Samson Benen and Robert Hess, Marc was soon singled out as someone with potential. The chess program director said to Marc's Mom "Marc has a very good demeanor at the board." His Mom asked how she knew that a five-year-old has good demeanor at the board, and the director replied, "I know. I've seen enough. I know who has the capability and Marc does."[24] Soon Marc was taking full advantage of the many New York City chess tournaments held most weekends and even weekdays at nearby clubs. Mixing with local players and coaches led to Marc's family hiring an elite New York City coach.

Like Dorothy said in the *Wizard of Oz*, "If I ever go looking for my heart's desire again, I won't look any further than my own backyard." Looking in one's own backyard is a good place to begin seeking talent opportunities.

Gravitate to a Center of Excellence

Several years ago I was at my annual neighborhood association meeting. A neighbor stood up and asked permission to build a lighted tennis court in his backyard. The request ran counter to our sacred covenants, but he hoped for an exception. He said that his son, Jack, enjoyed tennis and was getting pretty good at it. He might as well have asked to build a feedlot. Request denied. Stamp!

Years later, I wonder if the neighbor's argument might have been more convincing had he said "Look, we all know that American tennis has gone to hell in a handbag since McEnroe, Connors, and Sampras last reigned. Well, we have a chance to do something, right here, right now. My son Jack is fired up about tennis, and my wife and I are committed to doing all we can to help him succeed. It will take a while, but I image he'll someday be the Junior U.S. Open champion, the highest-ranked American player, a Davis Cup teammate, a Wimbledon and U.S. Open doubles champion, and an Olympic gold medalist. Oh, I imagine he'll also have a whiplash forehand." Would the association bigwigs still have said "Sorry, no can do, Mr. Sock?"

It is hard to know the fate of American tennis star Jack Sock had that lighted court been built. Without the court, the Socks traveled another road to support young Jack's tennis. They gravitated to a center of tennis excellence. At first, Jack's mother took him to Kansas City each weekend—a 400-mile round-trip from Lincoln, Nebraska—to train at the Mike Wolf Tennis Academy when he was 10. Jack wrote that "We drove down every weekend of the year for clinics at Mike's academy. We would leave Lincoln Saturday morning early enough to participate in the three-hour clinic that afternoon. We'd stay at a Drury Inn that night. Then we'd wake up go to practice on Sunday for three hours before driving back to Lincoln in time for school on Monday. We did that for a whole year."[25] When Jack was 12, he and his mom and brother (also a tennis player) moved to Kansas City so Jack and his brother could train at the academy full-time. Jack's father remained in Lincoln, where he was a financial adviser. Jack wrote that "My parents decided to sacrifice living together for the sake of our tennis." The rest is tennis history. As radio personality Paul Harvey used to say, "Now you know the rest of the story."

The Socks were not the first Lincoln family to gravitate to a center of tennis excellence. That distinction belonged to the Reckewey family in the late 1990s. Their empty-nest story was unusual for the time and made local headlines. Tennis-playing brothers Joel and Jon Reckewey left Lincoln at ages 16 and 14, respectively, to also train at the Mike Wolf Tennis Academy in Kansas. At first, they drove the 400 round-trip miles on weekends for lessons and clinics. Soon the boys moved to Kansas on their own, attended school there, and trained at the academy year-round. The Reckeweys paid a fee of $2,000 per month for the boys' tennis expenses. On top of that there were lodging, food, and everyday costs. An academy pro lived with and supervised the boys in an apartment paid for by the Reckeweys. Father Kent was a former college basketball player who understood the commitments and pressures of athletics. Kent did not want the fact that the family spent tens of thousands of dollars a year on tennis to put undue pressure on the boys to win matches: "This opportunity is freely given from Mom and Dad. They're welcomed to it with no strings attached. If what you do is measured by wins and losses, the pressure can be tremendous. What we're trying to stress to the boys is performing to the best of their ability and learning the strategy and proper technique. I want them to learn life lessons through tennis such as the value of hard work and discipline."[26]

Mother Nancy frequently made the three-hour drive to Kansas to deliver meals, do laundry, and tidy up the apartment. She said, "The only reason this works is because they're three hours away and easily gotten by car. If they wanted to go to one of those academies on the coast where I'd have to fly, I don't think I'd let them do that."[27] Kent Reckewey added that "I miss them, and I miss seeing their day-to-day growth. You can't give away parenting to a coach or someone else. We want to make sure our values are passed down to them. When we are together now, it's very focused quality time." Finally, Nancy said, "You can't make your kids do something like this. They must want to do it. They make the choice."

What became of the Reckewey brothers? They both played collegiately. Joel was a four-year star at the University of Nebraska, while Jon captured three Big 12 championships and a national championship playing for the Baylor Bears. The brothers later cofounded Reckewey Tennis, a tennis academy in Nebraska, and now serve as professional tennis coaches.

Looking back today on the family's choice to send the brothers to Kansas to live and train, Joel Reckeway said this:

> I am grateful that my parents gave Jon and me the opportunity to train at a high-level tennis academy in another state. The investment they made was priceless because of the commitment, sacrifice, time, travel, and support they provided for us day in and day out. The tennis academy we attended had the most premiere tennis coaches and players in the area and was instrumental to our tennis success and to the tennis professionals we are today. Of course, moving away did not guarantee success. A center of excellence is not enough. Our successes were also the result of our hard work at the academy—training three hours a day, six days a week, for five years. We gave a lot to tennis, and tennis has given back to us. It has given us wonderful experiences and taught us to navigate through life, and we are better people because of it.[28]

Assemble Your Own Center of Excellence

Do you know the plot of the musical *Camelot*? In part it involves King Arthur's attempts, such as formulating a roundtable for knights, to make Camelot the pleasant and just society it was decreed to be. The play's opening lyrics tell of the wonder King Arthur seeks: "The rain may never fall till after sundown. By eight, the morning fog must disappear. In short, there's simply not, a more congenial spot, for happily-ever-aftering than here in Camelot."[29] The play's closing lyrics offer hope that the glory of Camelot might live on: "Ask every person if he's heard the story, and tell it strong and clear if he has not, that once there was a fleeting wisp of glory, called Camelot." King Arthur strived to assemble a center of excellence called Camelot.

In my interviews, I heard several stories about families building a center of excellence to help foster their child's talent development. Sandy Ham, father of Olympic gymnast brothers Morgan and Paul, refused to ship the boys out of town to a gymnastics hotbed. Instead, he joined the local gym's board of directors and from that perch arranged for top-flight Russian coaches to live in their community, often in his home, and train the local gymnasts.

Savannah lived in Kansas City, far from any twirling center of excellence, but her family assembled a center of excellence around her. Mother Sammie took advantage of local coaches to provide initial training. When more advanced coaching was needed, Sammie and Savannah flew to Ohio and Georgia, where Savannah worked with renowned coaches. Savannah's success was a homemade affair. Sammie said, "It takes all of us. It takes strong coaches. It takes my husband helping Savannah approach twirling like a competitive sport. It takes a local seamstress that adores making her costumes. It takes Grandma picking us up at the airport. It takes my oldest son driving her to and from lessons and picking up a costume. It takes all of us. It really does."[30] Sammie and Savannah were also instrumental in building a hometown center of excellence for upstart twirlers. Sammie arranged for Savannah to do a lot of exhibitions to build a local culture for twirling. Sammie said, "My philosophy is to get Savannah out in front of people to keep the baton sport in people's minds. If there is one little girl watching a parade who sees Savannah twirl and says, 'Mom, I want to try that,' then that keeps the sport alive."

Moving to chess, the Troff parents built a center of chess excellence for son Kayden, who was raised near Salt Lake City, Utah, an area with minimal chess resources.[31] Once Kayden learned to play, his father linked him to a local chess club and tournaments. There was not much local competition, though, and five-year-old Kayden would beat kids of all ages and adults too. Dan, Kayden's father, took it upon himself to teach Kayden more even though he himself was just a recreational player. Dan studied chess 10 to 15 hours a week during lunch breaks and at night after the kids went to bed so he could learn chess and teach Kayden what he learned. Dan read books, studied grandmaster games, and watched videos that allowed him to create a chess book with specialized lessons for Kayden that Dan delivered during their nightly training sessions. When Dan could no longer keep pace with Kayden's growth, he hired elite chess coaches to work with Kayden. Lessons were conducted via the Internet, so Kayden reaped the benefits of worldwide grandmaster instruction in his own home. Finally, the Troffs helped make their local community a center of excellence for Kayden and other children by running a weeklong scholastic chess club each summer. Dan spent about 400 hours planning and supervising the camp each year.

When considering how you might assemble a center of excellence, consider the powers of the Internet. The Internet allowed the Troff family to access the best coaching from their home. The Internet has recently made chess progress possible for almost anyone. Lessons with a grandmaster are possible via Skype, recent grandmaster games are available for analysis, tutorials are commonplace, and playing websites are just a click away. It seems that the Internet has also distributed chess talent beyond New York. Earlier, I presented data showing that about 30–40 percent of top 10 scholastic players were from New York during the 1990s. I accessed the most recent top 10 chess rankings for the same age groups and found that just 15 percent were from New York. New York is still a good place to learn chess, but now almost anyone anywhere can use the Internet to make their own home a center of chess excellence. Parents should explore the Internet's instructional powers when parenting talent.

Finally, there is the center-of-excellence–building story of Olympic skier Nick Goepper, at one time the world's top-ranked slope-style skier—a freestyle event that features tricks and jumps along a snow course with ramps and rails. Unlike most top-flight skiers, Nick did not grow up in the mountains of Utah or Colorado. He was raised in pancake-flat Indiana. Rather than flee the Midwest, Nick skied 12 hours a day—100 runs a day—on a nearby hill with a mere 400-foot vertical drop, while the big western ski mountains boasted 5,000-foot drops. Even at home, Nick and his sisters filled garbage cans with snow and distributed it beneath ramps to do some backyard skiing.

To train and cross-train through the summers, Nick and his family were resourceful. They built a skateboarding park in the backyard where Nick could work the rails and practice tricks. They soaped the rails to reduce friction. Nick would ski down the rails for hours and land in an Astroturf pit. Nick and his siblings built steps up a tree to a seven-foot platform so Nick could jump from there onto a trampoline to practice twists and turns. Nick's gymnastic-trained sisters were his first coaches, teaching him the twisting and spinning fundamentals that he would use in slope-style skiing.

After years of home training and steady improvement, Nick eventually left home to train at a skiing academy. But it was those years of home training, in the family-built center of excellence, that taught him to ski and deal with whatever comes his way. Nick said, "It kind of taught me—I mean, it's a cliché—but to never give up. There's always going to be roadblocks. But if you really want to succeed at something, you [find a way]."[32]

CHAPTER SEVEN

Parents' Roles in Establishing Singleness of Purpose

Motivational speaker Les Brown offered this singleness-of-purpose advice to those wanting to reach their potential:

> If you want a thing bad enough to go out and fight for it, to work day and night for it, to give up your time, your peace and sleep for it . . . if all that you dream and scheme is about it, and life seems useless and worthless without it . . . if you gladly sweat for it and fret for it and plan for it and lose all your terror of the opposition for it . . . if you simply go after that thing that you want with all your capacity, strength and sagacity, faith, hope and confidence and stern pertinacity . . . if neither cold, poverty, famine, nor gout, sickness nor pain, of body and brain, can keep you away from the thing that you want . . . if dogged and grim you beseech and beset it, with the help of God, you will get it.[1]

Psychologist Mihaly Csikszentmihalyi studied highly productive individuals to uncover their success secrets and found that most were almost single-minded in pursuit of their work. Here is what one productive individual wrote when invited to participate in the study:

> I hope you will not think me presumptuous or rude if I say that one of the secrets of productivity is to have a VERY BIG waste paper basket to take care of ALL invitations such as yours—productivity in my experience consists of NOT doing anything that helps the work of other people but to spend one's time on the work the Good Lord has fitted one to do, and do it well.[2]

Such single-mindedness is a hallmark characteristic of the talented. They practice daily, practice long, and practice hard for many years and make many sacrifices along the way. They are fully invested in the talent area. Recall some of the singleness-of-purpose accounts in Chapter 2. A chess parent said that his talented and chess-consumed son "doesn't do much outside of chess. He's just dedicated his life to chess. That's all he's done since he was a youngster. . . . He just lives and breathes chess."[3] Musician Jim Brickman said, "Music is a 24-hours a day, constant, constant, constant. It never ends—but in a wonderful way." And wildlife photographer Joel Sartore spoke of his commitment and sacrifice: "My life was marked by *National Geographic* stories. . . . Twenty stories later, though, it's the North Slope I'll remember best: Alaska's loss of wilderness and innocence—and the story during which my wife got cancer."[4]

How is this commitment, this single-mindedness, possible? What ignites it? What fuels it? What sustains it? The simple answer is motivation. Motivation ignites, fuels, and sustains actions. Motivation, though, is not a simple construct. This chapter describes motivation's key elements and what parents might do to foster their child's motivation.

Motivation Arises

People don't practice for hours on end unless they are highly motivated to do so, but what is the source of that motivation? How does motivation arise?

One explanation is that children are motivated to pursue activities that give them an edge in competition for resources—most prominently, the attention and admiration of parents. A child recognized for her ability to jump and tumble—even when that ability is normal and age appropriate—is likely to become interested in gymnastics. A child whose drawings get favorable comments—even though drawing ability is modest and age appropriate—might develop an interest in art.

Psychologist Benjamin Bloom found that families did sometimes distribute attention and resources unevenly among children, favoring a talented child over his or her siblings. Money earmarked for a new family car was spent on piano lessons instead. Family activities and vacations revolved around competitions in the talent area. Families sometimes relocated or split into two household to accommodate the talented child's instructional needs. Special privileges were afforded the talented child. One parent remarked, "We did give him special privileges [that the other children did not get]. We didn't feel that he should have little chores around the house because it cut into his music time. When we realized he did have this talent, we let him have full reign of time and did not force him to do things that other children do. We realized he was special and should not be asked to wash the car."[5] My investigations also uncovered occasional unequal distribution of parent resources among siblings. One parent, speaking about his talented son, said, "We dedicate most of our time to him."[6] Another said, "We didn't really pursue some of our other child's interests because a lot of time was spent on him and chess. If we hadn't been doing chess activities, maybe we would have turned our focus and pursued more of the other child's activities."

Competition for resources motivates some children to seek their own talent area free from sibling competition. Watching an older sister receive attention for performing tricks on a bicycle might spur a younger sibling to a nonbiking niche where attention and resources are more likely available. Psychologists call this sibling differentiation—the process through which children are motivated to pursue domains untapped by siblings. Although my investigations certainly found evidence for sibling differentiation, there was more evidence for sibling unity, or what I call footstep following. For example, there were the Rolfzen volleyball-playing twins, the Mancuso volleyball-playing siblings, the Ruud football-playing brothers, and the Hamm gymnastic brothers. There were speed skaters Bonnie Blair and Dan Jansen, each following a long line of accomplished skating siblings. There are numerous other examples of talented younger siblings following in their sibling's footsteps in swimming, baton twirling, chess, and music.

Such footstep following leads back to a second explanation for why motivation arises: modeling. The old adage "Monkey see, monkey do, monkey do the same as you" describes the nature and power of modeling. Consider this classic experiment by psychologist Albert Bandura.[7] Some children observed an adult model acting aggressively toward a large bottom-weighted Bobo doll that returns to a standing position when knocked down. Children who witnessed the aggression—both physical and verbal assaults—were more likely to repeat those assaults when later placed with the doll than children who did not observe the model. When the model was praised for assaulting the doll, the model's behaviors were even more likely to be copied by children. The combination of modeling and praise was a powerful motivator for children to copy the observed actions.

Many of the talented children I studied had parent or sibling models who motivated them to sample the talent area. Thomas Rudd played in the National Football League (NFL) before sons Bo and Barrett did. Thomas said, "They grew up around NFL players. So, I think they thought that playing football in the NFL was fairly normal."[8] The same was true for volleyball star Lauren Cook, who was raised in a household with volleyball parents—a former college star and a national champion college coach. Olympic speed skater Bonnie Blair was the last child amid a long line of skating siblings. Blair said, "When I was born, it wasn't a matter of when I was going be a skater, it was how quickly could they get me on skates."[9]

Among talented Nebraska youths I studied, Olivia Calegan followed two older brothers into swimming. Olivia said, "It wouldn't have even crossed my mind to start swimming if it weren't for my brothers. They're the reason I got involved in the sport."[10] Olivia's father Robert said, "Olivia's been more successful in the pool than her brothers, but I think a lot of that comes from watching them as she was growing up. Olivia became a natural at swimming because of her exposure to it at such a young age. Her brothers were great role models." Swimmer Caroline Thiel has three swimming siblings, including one younger sibling who is nipping at her heels. Basketball star Aguek Arop hails from a family where several brothers played basketball including an older brother high school teammate and a younger brother star on the rise. Rodeo star Jayde Atkins and her brother learned to rodeo modeling their parents' lifestyle. Jayde's mother said, "Our kids have just kind of grown up around that and been on horseback from the start. Jayde has always had a pony or something to ride since she could walk and it's just always been part of her lifestyle."[11] Softball star McKenzie Steiner also had an older softball-playing sister. McKenzie said, "I watched my older sister play softball for a really long time and thought it would be something really good for me to try. I always looked up to her as a role model."[12]

Modeling family members, especially siblings, certainly does not give one a competitive advantage, but it gives one something maybe more important: group identity, a place to belong. Author Daniel Coyle writes that "Future belonging is a primal cue: a simple, direct signal that activates our built-in motivational triggers, funneling our energy and attention toward a goal."[13] Psychologist Geoff Cohen said, "We're the most social creatures on the planet. Everything depends on collective effort and cooperation. When we get a cue that we ought to connect our identity with a group, it's like a hair trigger, like turning on a light switch. The ability to achieve is already there, but the energy put into that ability goes through the roof."[14]

Observing models also gives people something else: a vision of one's future self—a vision that motivates one to realize that future self. Daniel Coyle writes that "Kids weren't born wanting to be musicians. Their wanting . . . came from a distinct signal, from something in their family . . . that sparked an intense response that manifested itself as an idea: I want to be like them. . . . [I] better get busy."[15]

Coyle conducted an unscientific examination of the past 10 100-meter world record holders and the top 10 football running backs all time. He found that the average birth order among the track stars was fourth in families with an average of 4.6 children. Among the running backs, it was 3.2 in families with an average of 4.4 children. Coyle explains that speed is not a biological gift but instead is something earned through deliberate practice and singleness of purpose and is set off by observing and copying older siblings. The younger siblings saw a vision of their future selves and saw themselves running behind. Their motivation to join the group sent a strong motivating signal: "You're behind. Keep up!"[16]

Motivation to Be Special

Whether a child's motivation to dabble in a talent area first arises from a desire to gain resources or to follow the crowd, the child naturally improves. Gradually the bangs on piano keys become discernable notes, the baton begins to maneuver cleanly through the fingers, and backyard hacks come to resemble golf swings. As the child improves, she becomes special and people recognize this. Not special meaning exceptional but special meaning distinct—ahead of the pack, better than most. Parents I interviewed noticed this specialness:

- "She walked early. She was 10 months old. She crawled for three weeks, walked for a week, and then started running everywhere. She had very keen body awareness and seemed gifted in terms of movement."[17]
- "I played a game of chess with him and couldn't understand what was going on. I had to think about my moves. He had played for just three months and I used to be a master-level player."[18]
- "She took a dance class when she was three and there were batons there. She wanted to take the baton home and would throw fits because she couldn't. By age four, she was putting the baton through her fingers and her teacher said this was special."[19]
- "He's much more intelligent than the two of us and we knew that at an early age, so we had our hands full at age five when he was killing me at Scrabble."[20]
- "I'd hear her singing in the backseat and think, 'Wow, she's really good.'"[21]

The motivation to be special comes largely from external rewards the child receives, primarily attention and praise. The pianists Bloom studied confirmed that parent attention and praise were early motivating factors for them to practice and perform:

- "My mother liked to hear me play. I knew it gave her pleasure. So, when she would come home, I would sometimes run over to the piano as she was coming in the door and play her favorite pieces."[22]
- "[Father] loved to hear us play together. That brought the whole family together."[23]
- "There was an awful lot of praise and an awful lot of attention. Play for the family, play for this one, play for that one. There was so much reward for performing."[24]

Bloom wrote that "The youngsters learned that musical activity was something special in their homes, something worthy of applause. All of the notice meant there was much to be gained from paying attention during lessons and practicing daily, and much to be lost if they did not do these things."[25]

Over time, the pianists recognized that their specialness extended outside the home as they compared themselves to other children. Here is what they said:

- "I think I knew I was special. There wasn't anybody my age who played, that I knew."[26]
- "I became identified with the piano. That was the only way I could stand out and be someone special."[27]
- "I must have liked it, being special."[28]

The pianists eventually received external rewards—attention and praise—from outside the home, which strengthened their feeling of specialness. Their piano teachers told them that they were the favorite student or best pupil. Teachers also gave them extra lesson time, special encouragement, carefully selected material, choice recital program spots, and special opportunities to perform for others locally. The pianists said:

- "I think I became her most promising student. So, she showered a lot of attention on me. I would come in for an hour lesson, but it would always be like an hour and a half."[29]
- "I knew [my teacher] was delighted with me. I got lots of approval from him, and lots of approval from my parents after they talked to him."[30]

The pianists were also recognized for their specialness by peers. The pianists said:

- After performing for schoolmates, "The kids went wild because they had no idea. . . . They just stomped their feet and screamed and howled and hollered."
- "I was a little kid, and here were my parents and all the teachers in my school and the principal of my school . . . telling me that I was going to be great and famous and how unusual I was."[31]

There is an important caveat to the use of praise that parents should heed. Parents should praise effort, not ability. This idea arose in Chapter 5 in the discussion of growth versus fixed mind-set. It is important for learners to have a growth mind-set, one that conveys that talent depends on effort and not inborn abilities. A study by psychologist Carol Dweck revealed that some praise is helpful (that which supports a growth mind-set) and that some praise is damaging (that which supports a fixed mind-set).[32]

In a multiround experiment, Dweck and her colleagues gave fifth grade students a puzzle-solving test in round one that was fairly easy. When students finished, they were given their score and a single line of praise. Through random assignment, half were praised for their intelligence ("You must be smart at this") and half were praised for their effort ("You must have worked really hard"). In round two, students were given their choice of test. They could choose a test more difficult than the first but one they would learn from, or they could choose an easy test just like the first one. Among those praised for their intelligence, most chose the easy test. Among those praised for effort, 90 percent chose the difficult test. Dweck concluded that the children praised for intelligence chose to look smart and not risk making mistakes and appearing unintelligent. In a third round of testing all the children were given a highly difficult test, which everyone failed. Reactions to failure, though, were markedly different. Those praised for effort at the start tried hard, enjoyed the test, and attributed their failure to needing to try harder to acquire new knowledge. Those praised for intelligence at the start found test taking miserable and attributed their poor performance to not being smart. There was one more round of testing—this time simple tests such as those in the first round. Those originally praised for effort improved their first-round score by 30 percent on average. Those originally praised for intelligence lowered their first-round score by 20 percent on average. This study proves that praise is a powerful motivator but only if aimed at effort, which advocates a growth mind-set. Praising one's inherent intelligence or natural ability in talent areas such as music and tennis is debilitating.

Motivation to Be Competent and Passionate

Do you know the story of Dick and Rick Hoyt? Dick was a sedentary man who had never run more than a mile, had never learned to swim, and had not ridden a bicycle since childhood. Dick's teenage son, Rick, was wheelchair bound and could not speak. One day, Rick communicated via computer that he wanted to be part of a five-mile charity run to support a paralyzed classmate: "Dad, I want to do that."[33] With that request, Dick mustered the motivation and strength to push Rick through the race. Rick found the run exhilarating; Dick found it painful. Afterward, Rick communicated "Dad, when we were running, it felt like I wasn't disabled anymore." That sentence became Dick's motivation to push, pull, and carry his son to places few could imagine. Since that first five-mile race, the pair has completed more than 1,000 races, including 72 marathons (26.2 miles) and 7 Ironman triathlons (2.4-mile swim, 112-mile bike ride, and 26.2-mile run). The pair has also scaled mountains, cross-county skied, and biked across America.

Only one thing could make Dick Hoyt do all this: intrinsic motivation. There are two types of motivation: extrinsic and intrinsic. Extrinsic means

that the motivation stems from outside the person. The extrinsically motivated person works to gain external rewards such as attention, praise,
applause, or awards. The intrinsically motivated person works to gain internal rewards such as a sense of competency ("I accomplished or mastered
that") or simply the passion of participation ("That was fun. That felt good.").

In the previous section, we saw that children were motivated to be special
in the eyes of parents, teachers, and peers. This is extrinsic motivation.
Extrinsic motivation is a good and natural brand of motivation for getting
started in an area, but it cannot sustain one's actions long-term. A stronger
and more personal brand of motivation, intrinsic motivation, is needed for
that. Those who develop talent shift motivation from extrinsic to intrinsic.
They become self-motivated to practice long and hard to attain competence
and to stir their passion for the talent area.

The pursuit of competence is in line with human nature according to psychologist Robert White, who posits that humans have an intrinsic need to
explore and influence their environment, to improve themselves, solely to
experience competence.[34] People are motivated to pursue domains where
competence is likely. One of the pianists in Bloom's study reflected on the
importance of attaining competence: "Piano was something I was good at,
and that was important to me. I had to be good at something."[35] Author and
dual-expert Josh Waitzkin emphasizes the importance of pursuing competence, or what he terms "excellence": "The key to pursuing excellence is to
embrace a long-term learning process, and not to live in a shell of static, safe
mediocrity. Growth comes at the expense of previous comfort or safety. . . .
Successful people shoot for the stars, put their hearts on the line in every
battle, and ultimately discover that the lessons learned from the pursuit of
excellence mean much more than the immediate trophies and glory."[36]

Psychologist Ellen Winner takes the human nature angle of pursuing
competence one step further.[37] Winner believes that some humans have a
"rage to master," an innate and sometimes obsessive motivation to master an
area of interest. Others, such as psychologists Bloom[38] and Ericsson,[39] believe
that the rage to master is environmentally driven as the individual's interest,
skills, and intrinsic motivation grow in tandem. Either way, talented people
have a passion for their area and a rage to pursue it. The novelist Naguib
Mahfouz, who participated in Mihaly Csikszentmihalyi's creativity study,
said, "I love my work more than I love what it produces. I am dedicated to
the work regardless of its consequences."[40] When chess parents were asked
why their sons spend so much time studying chess, they responded as
follows:

- "He is passionate about it, just thrilled by it. It gives him a lot of joy and
  satisfaction."
- "He loves it. He loves it. I don't know why. This is the thing that he loves."

- "He loves it. . . . He likes doing something really well. But the main thing is that he has a passion for the game. He just loves it."[41]

Grandmaster Maurice Ashley contends that the joy of chess stems from the challenge of gaining competence or mastery:

> I think the process [of learning chess] is the most delicious part of the struggle. . . . Learning about chess is just fabulous. Relish the moment as you're learning. . . . You have to enjoy the path because otherwise what's the point of what you're doing? It is not about getting to the top of the mountain, it's about the climbing. Because when you're at the top, then suddenly you're standing there like, "Okay, now what?" We don't sit still as humans. We venture and venture and venture. This spirt requires that you enjoy the path as much as you can. . . . For me, the process is the joy.[42]

The juncture between competence and passion might best be realized in a state of mind that talented individuals sometimes experience called flow. "Flow" in this sense is a term coined by psychologist Mihaly Csikszentmihalyi that describes a mental state accessed when a person is fully immersed in an activity.[43] There is hyperfocus, complete absorption. The person is, as some say, in the zone. Perhaps you have experienced flow as you played a competitive game of tennis or assembled a challenging puzzle.

Csikszentmihalyi discovered flow in his attempts to understand why chess players, rock climbers, dancers, composers, and others devoted many hours a week to their talents when participation rarely resulted in money or fame. His interviews with talented people revealed that their motivation to pursue talent came from a joyful feeling they experienced only when engaged in their chosen activity. They felt fully engaged and highly focused. The activity seemed effortless, almost automatic. Things flowed. Here is the key: To obtain this flow state, people had to be working at the edge of competence, where challenge met or slightly exceeded skill. Playing tennis against much better opponents leads to frustration, while playing against much weaker opponents leads to boredom. Playing against opponents of equal or slightly better skill provides the ideal challenge-skill balance likely to produce flow. In the flow state there are no distractions, no worry of failure, and no awareness of self or time. The experience becomes autotelic, which is a Greek-derived term for something that is an end in itself. The reason to participate in chess or rock climbing or dancing is that the experience is often flow-like and joyful, utterly intrinsic.

Here is how poet Mark Strandt described the flow of his poetry writing: "Well, you're right in the work, you lose your sense of time, you're completely enraptured, you're completely caught up in what you're doing . . . so saturated with it that there's no future or past, it's just an extended present."[44]

As a side note, Csikszentmihalyi believes that the pursuit of talent is a noble calling. He contends that much of the world finds pleasure in things that are easy such as watching television or in things long programmed into our genes such as hunting, eating, and mating. It is more difficult to enjoy things recently discovered in our evolution such as math, music, or poetry. What Plato wrote 25 centuries ago is still true today: The most important task for a society is to teach the young to find pleasure in the right things. In this sense, those pursuing talent lead exemplary lives as they seek and find pleasure in honorable things.

Motivation to Fulfill Identity

It is hard enough to find the motivation to practice many hours a day and dedicate oneself to a talent domain for a few days or months, so how is it possible to sustain such motivation for many years? It's not easy. Look what happens with New Years' resolutions. Eighty percent are eventually broken, and one-third don't last a month. I bet that many are broken before confetti hits the floor. People pledge to lose weight—several times a year—because they can't sustain motivation to diet and exercise. People swear off smoking and drinking for a while but relapse when motivation wanes even though they're "just a puff away from a pack" or fighting "one drink, one drunk" status. It is hard to sustain motivation, but that's exactly what talent seekers do.

Sustained motivation, persistence, comes largely from having established a sense of identity. After years of toiling in a domain, the talented person realizes his or her identity—"I am a musician," "I am a swimmer," "I am a writer"—and that realization sustains motivation.

Most of the pianists Bloom studied developed personal identities as musicians by the time they reached high school. Over a period of years, they had been given attention and special treatment for their musical abilities, developed competence through top-flight instruction and deliberate practice, and found passion for music. After all that, Bloom wrote, "It became impossible for the pianists to separate what they did at the piano from who they were. They thought of themselves as belonging to a special group of people—musicians."[45] One pianist said, "I think there's a tremendous force. The psychological effect that operates when you've done something for so long. You feel that it must have incredible value to you simply by virtue of spending so much time." Music was their identity.

Part of one's identification with a domain such as music is the lack of an identity elsewhere. Bloom argues that the pianists were so ingrained in music that it would have been difficult for them to shift interests, to stop studying music and pursue something else. They felt that there wasn't anything else they could do, even if they wanted to, as well as playing the piano. Moreover, the large time investment to music and the many personal and family sacrifices made essentially closed the door to other potential interests or talent options. While they were choosing music, they were not choosing science or athletics. The choice was made, and an identity was formed. One pianist commented that "There was nothing to take equal interest with music, which I had been doing so much longer than anything else."[46] Another said, "It's what I know how to do. It's what I've been trained for. I don't know how to do anything else as well."

Even with a firmly established identity, sustaining motivation is not easy in the face of failure and success. Let's start with the less obvious success. Writer Matthew Syed writes about the dangers of anticlimax—the odd feeling of loss that comes with winning.[47] Recall what chess grandmaster Maurice Ashley said about winning: "It is not about getting to the top of the mountain, it's about the climbing. Because when you're at the top, then suddenly you're standing there like, 'Okay, now what?'"[48] Consider too what British track cyclist Victoria Pendleton said after training arduously for the 2008 Olympics and then winning. "People think it's hard when you lose. But it's almost easier to come in second because you have something to aim for when you finish. When you win, you suddenly feel lost. You have all this buildup for one day, and when it's over, it's, 'Oh, is that it?'"[49] Poet Shel Silverstein wonderfully captured the anticlimax effect in his poem *The Search*. A near lifetime of searching finally culminates in a pot of gold at rainbow's end, and the weary searcher exclaims "It's mine at last. . . . What do I search for now?"[50] As writer Robert Louis Stevenson once quipped, "To travel hopefully is a better thing than to arrive."[51]

Writer Josh Waitzkin agrees that we should not dawdle after victories but set out to meet the next goal: "When we have worked hard and succeeded at something, we should be allowed to smell the roses. The key is to recognize that the beauty of those roses lies in their transience. It is drifting away even as we inhale. We enjoy the win fully while taking a deep breath, then we exhale, note the lesson learned, and move on to the next adventure."[52] New England Patriots coach Bill Belichick has never been one to smell the roses too long. After capturing his fifth Super Bowl trophy in 2017, his immediate reaction was that the team's Super Bowl run put the Patriots five weeks behind other teams in preparing for next season. There was little time to celebrate. It was time to get back to work and move on to next season.

Failure is a more obvious threat to motivation and persistence because everyone fails and fails a lot, as already described in Chapter 4. There was Ty Cobb, baseball's greatest hitter, making an out two of every three at bats; Abraham Lincoln's long line of failures before becoming president; F. Scott Fitzgerald's rejection slip–filled walls; and Michael Jordan being cut from his high school basketball team. Psychologist Howard Gardner investigated creative individuals and found that even the most extraordinary had more flops than hits and often endured long dry spells before attaining success.[53] Consider artist Vincent van Gogh. He was a flop during his lifetime, selling only

1 painting. But failure did not squelch his painting identity and motivation. He painted more than 900 paintings in his lifetime and was only recognized as a brilliant artist after his death.

Another example of failure and redemption involved four-time Olympic speed skater Dan Jansen, who did not capture gold until his fourth and final Olympics. Jansen was a smooth and powerful speed skater who won two world championships and set eight world records. Yet he repeatedly came up short at the Olympics. There were slips, stumbles, and illnesses, and there was the death of his sister, Jane, on the day of an Olympic race. To Jansen's family, friends, and competitors and to Jansen himself, it seemed that he would never capture Olympic gold. But then came redemption, and sportswriter Lisette Hilton captured it:

> Skating in the fourth pair, Jansen was on a record-setting pace after 600 meters. He experienced a heart-stopping slip but quickly regained his balance, barely touching the ice. He finished in 1:12.43, beating the world record by .11 seconds. None of the other skaters could hit his mark. . . . Competing in his last Olympics, the skating gods finally smiled on Jansen and watched as he won the 1,000-meter race at Lillehammer, Norway. . . . He waved to the sky in memory of his sister and took the victory lap with eight-month-old daughter Jane in his arms. Jansen didn't know what to think when he realized he had won gold. "I was shaking," he said. "I guess the first thought was, 'Finally, it's happened for me.'"[54]

What those with strong identities do, psychologist Howard Gardner claims, is frame defeats and setbacks in positive ways.[55] They perceive failure as the price of improvement. Failure identifies what went wrong and what must be done to fix it. It does not dim motivation but intensifies it. Dual-talent competitor and writer Josh Waitzkin agrees and says that talented people embody the investment-in-loss principle. They recognize that they must lose to win. Waitzkin writes that some people "don't learn from their mistakes and practice with a desperate need to win, to be right, to have everything under control. This cripples growth."[56] Basketball star Michael Jordan was not one to cripple growth; he kept shooting. Jordan said, "I've missed more than 9,000 shots in my career. I've lost almost 300 games. Twenty-six times, I've been trusted to take the game winning shot and missed. I've failed over and over and over again in my life. And, that is why I succeed."[57]

Elaine Maxwell, educational consultant, nicely summed up how the talented, even in the face of failure, maintain motivation and their hard-earned identity: "My will shall shape my future. Whether I fail or succeed shall be no one's doing but my own. I am the force; I can clear any obstacle before me or be lost in the maze. My choice; my responsibility; win or lose, only I hold the key to my destiny."[58]

Two related motivational concepts, self-efficacy and attributions, especially allow one to persist and maintain identity in the face of failure. Self-efficacy is the brainchild of psychologist Albert Bandura.[59] It is the belief that one is capable in an area such as basketball or music. Bandura believes that high self-efficacy for a task leads individuals to persist in the face of difficulty and rebound quickly from failure. He believes too that talented individuals are high in self-efficacy within their talent domain. In a study that included expert, nonexpert, and novice volleyball players, experts rated their self-efficacy for serving higher than nonexperts and novices. After serves were missed, experts' self-efficacy ratings remained unchanged, while those for nonexperts and novices declined. Experts maintained the belief that they could succeed even in the face of failure, while failure plagued the others with doubt.[60]

Attributions are one's explanations for success or failure. We have seen already that attributing success or failure to inborn ability is counterproductive. If outcomes are the result of inborn ability, then increasing motivation and practicing longer or better are not viable avenues for success. Another dead-end attribution is blaming others. If something is the teacher's fault or the judge's fault, then there is no recourse one can take to succeed. The "somebody did me wrong" blame game is not functional. Another sorry attribution is luck. If good luck propelled you or bad luck doomed you, there is no reason to change because luck is outside of your control. The best and most correct attributions pertain to skill and will: "I failed because I lacked the necessary skills to complete that jump" or "I failed because I did not put forth enough effort in practice or competition." Either way, the responsibility and power to improve rests where it belongs, squarely on one's own shoulders.

As a college professor, I witness students making faulty attributions all the time. They blame their troubles on things that they believe are outside of their control and therefore do nothing to overcome the perceived barrier. Here are some sample faulty attributions and my *"you need to take control"* response.

- "The class is too large." *"Sit in the front and it will seem like it's just you and me."*
- "I get bored in class." *"Take a detailed set of notes. Recording complete notes is incompatible with boredom."*
- "I don't feel well and must miss class." *"Attend if possible. Would you miss your wedding if it was today? If you must miss, get someone to record the lecture."*

Faulty attributions are commonplace in sports too. When a team loses, the officials are often blamed. Consider this situation. With five minutes remaining in a game, the star player fouls out with his team trailing by one point.

Replay following the game shows that the call was wrong. The team goes on to lose by three points. Afterward, the coach is livid and blames the loss on the official for the bad call. Now examine the stats for the losing team: 21 turnovers, 32 percent shooting from the field, 8 of 16 from the foul line, and outrebounded by 7. Was the bad call the reason for the loss? Remember too that the star player had accumulated four fouls previously and that the team trailed when the blown call was made. To attribute the loss to bad officiating is counterproductive. Doing so ignores the team's many self-inflicted problems and negates any attempt to fix those problems. We must be careful about who we blame. A true expert blames himself but keeps his identity intact. His motivation to improve is unwavering.

Here are some parent recommendations based on chapter content and on other motivational ideas for fueling motivation and establishing singleness of purpose.

Provide Early Attention

Children hunger and compete for parental attention. Someone once told me the two keys to child rearing: (1) find out what they want and (2) give it to them. One of the most important things any parent can do is interact with their young child. But let your child take the lead. Watch what she chooses to do and join in. Notice what he enjoys and do more of it. Smile, laugh, talk, have fun—play. Toss in plenty of positive comments. Through early play and attention, your child might just discover a path that she wants to pursue further—perhaps a path laid down by parents or siblings, perhaps a new path all her own.

Be or Provide a Role Model

Children seek identity, membership in a group. Provide them with role models they might come to identify with. Expose them to your interests, avocations, and talents and those of their siblings. Provide opportunities to meet new role models in a variety of domains through books, movies, and live events. Nebraska high school diving champion Austin Alexander was at a public pool as a child watching divers practice. That single experience jump-started a life of diving. Several twirlers discovered their eventual element watching older children twirl and perform routines. Models are powerful motivators.

Provide External Rewards and Occasional Practice Nudge

Early on, external rewards such as ribbons and praise are powerful signals telling children an important message: You're special. And feeling special is a powerful early motivator for pursuing a domain. Now, here's an interesting caveat: Feeling special, even when you're not all that special, can impact how hard you try and how much you accomplish down the road. Here's why: People come to do what they believe, even what others believe, is possible. Harvard psychologist Robert Rosenthal was the first to prove this.

Rosenthal administered IQ tests to many elementary school children early in the school year.[61] When results were in, he told teachers that some students were special. They had performed remarkably well on the test and were poised to bloom academically. And bloom they did, increasing their year-end scores far more than students not identified as special. Here's the thing: the students Rosenthal identified to teachers as special were not special at all. He had selected them randomly. And yet, they prospered. Teachers' expectations and beliefs became students' expectations and beliefs. Teachers made certain children feel special, and special they became. Parents need to do the same.

When parents reward children, they should especially reward them for their efforts or acquired skill. It is vital that children attribute success or failure to skill ("You've become really good using your left hand to shoot") or will ("All your effort practicing that passage is really paying off")—things under their control—and not to ability ("I'm lousy at math") or bad luck ("I just had a bad day"), which rests beyond their control.

Parents might also need to provide an occasional practice nudge, as music teacher Anne Nagosky indicated when interviewed:

> There is not one kid out there who will always practice without being reminded. The most successful students see that if they do something regularly and in a thoughtful manner, they make progress. Little kids don't get that. That's why they need an occasional push from parents until they get older and things begin to click. They eventually realize, "Hey, if I work hard and practice what my teacher tells me, I get better and make more progress."[62]

Brenda Brenner, one of the top national violinists and music instructors, was certainly nudged to practice by her parents when growing up. Brenda remembers her mother saying "If you want to take lessons, then you have to practice. Otherwise, you have to call your teacher and tell her you're canceling your lesson. I'm not paying for lessons you're not practicing for."[63]

Navigate

The talent journey usually involves a motivation shift from extrinsic to intrinsic. External rewards and praise lose their luster as the budding star becomes motivated by an internal desire to achieve competence and by a passion-filled rage to master. This stretch of track is long and difficult, and parents can no longer supply the steam. That must come from within the child. No amount of parents wanting, cajoling, or insisting is going to make children practice two to four hours a day and is certainly not going to make them love it. Either the child powers the train or the train doesn't move.

While parents can't take the wheel, they can help clear the tracks and navigate. As you have seen throughout this book, there is much parents can do to help. For example, they can hire qualified teachers, monitor lessons and practices, and manage and finance their child's talent life. They can make concessions such as missing school for competitions and make sacrifices such as changing jobs, quitting jobs, or taking second jobs. They can do extraordinary things such as relocating family, flying for weekly lessons, or building a great room onto the house to accommodate practice. Or they can do simple yet vital things such as attending lessons and helping their child practice.

There are other ways parents can help children maintain singleness of purpose. One is by providing emotional support. One chess parent remarked, "I don't advise on chess. There's no advice I can give him really. I guide him emotionally."[64] Another chess parent said, "I don't understand the game of chess very well but I understand the psyche of winning and losing and pressure. I just try to keep him upbeat and let him know I'm there for him. They are just young kids and they need a lot of support. We're not over the point yet where when he loses he might be fighting back the tears as hard as he can, so he needs mom or dad there for him."[65] Another chess parent commented, "I would say my biggest role is providing his emotional support. I travel with him everywhere he goes. We talk a lot; I'm his anchor." Finally, a skating parent said, "You have to help them deal with the emotions in some way. You don't want it to be all internalized because that's the wrong response. It will chew them up and destroy them. So, you have to find a way to let them have a proper outlet for disappointments and criticism."[66]

Another way parents can help is by advocating rest to recharge motivational batteries. Several parents I interviewed encouraged their talented children to take time away from their domain to keep fresh or to jump-start waning motivation. A skating parent said, "If we're taking a family vacation or if we're having a family dinner, or it's somebody's birthday, I make sure that we say, you're not skating now, these breaks are important."[67] A twirling mother said, "You have to take a mental break. You can't have a kid be intense her whole life, they can't do it. You've got to know when to back off and take a break." Another twirling mother said, "She takes August off from competition and we go to the beach. She still twirls everyday but just for fun." Finally, Josh Waitzkin describes how his family handled things when he lost the national chess title game: "How could I have lost? One of the problems with being too high is that there is a long way to fall. . . . An eight-year-old is hardly prepared to deal with such loaded issues, and I was very fortunate to have a family with the ability to keep, or at least regain, a bit of perspective in times of extreme intensity. We went fishing."[68]

Parents can also provide a well-timed kick. Although parents overwhelmingly described their talent-seeking children as self-motivated, they admitted that they sometimes need a motivational boost. The parent of a National Spelling Bee champion described her motivational intervention: "They are children and when they have time, they tend to waste it so I remind them and say, 'You know I don't like you watching TV. It makes you happy, I can see, but you know you have to read. When you watch TV, you are losing out on your dream."[69] A chess parent said that his son was motivated about chess competitions but was not always sufficiently motivated about completing homework his coach assigned. The father said his son "lacked the discipline to do the homework, and we, his parents, have definitely filled that role." Another chess parent said this to her son: "Sometimes mom's job is to be your cheerleader, to cheer you on, to tell you, you can do it. Sometimes my job is to be the listening ear and let you talk and work things out, and sometimes my job is to give you a kick in the pants. And that's what you're getting right now."[70] The parent went on to say that "Because we know his dream, because we know what he wants to do, sometimes we have to say 'no, you need to do this.' But in a loving and supporting way." When children's motivation waned, parents also reminded them that parent support was contingent on children's effort. Parents in effect said that developing talent has to be your choice and your dream. If that is your choice, we'll help you however we can. If you commit, we'll commit. However, if you are not fully committed, we won't be either.

Temper Practice

As described in Chapter 4, deliberate practice in the learning zone is focused on small incremental improvements and is challenging. For this reason, experts curtail practice sessions to maximize concentration and performance. Across talent disciplines, most experts practice a maximum of four to five hours a day and do so over two to three segments a day, each lasting an hour to 90 minutes. To do more in a day or a session is not helpful and even counterproductive. It is too much of a good thing. Parents should therefore monitor practice schedules to be sure children are benefiting from practice and are not becoming stale or fatigued.

Monitoring and tempering practice is especially important when the talent domain is athletic. Dr. Tommy John, the son of former major league pitcher Tommy John, is a chiropractor and wellness coach who has written a book titled *Minimize Injury, Maximize Performance*. Tommy John the pitcher suffered an overuse elbow injury in 1974 that was repaired by a miraculous new surgery that would be aptly named Tommy John surgery. Today, a staggering 25 percent of active major league players have undergone Tommy John surgery. Even more alarming, 57 percent of Tommy John surgeries are done on athletes 15 to 19 years old, and the surgery rate for this population is increasing 6 percent a year. Dr. John contends that this growing baseball overuse injury reflects a wider youth sports problem whereby injuries have skyrocketed in the past 20 years.

Drs. Randolph Cohen and Eric Eisner have observed the youth sports injury uprising in their sports medicine practice in Hollywood, Florida. They attribute the rise to children specializing in a single sport from a young age and throughout their childhood. Cohen said, "They just can't take that repetitive type of consistent pounding on their bones, joints, and ligaments without developing an inordinately high rate of injury that ends up curtailing their career and curtailing what they are capable of doing."[71]

One key to avoiding overuse injuries is to avoid early specialization. A study of 1,200 youth athletes conducted by Dr. Neeru Jayanthi of Loyola University found that early specialization in a single sport is a strong predictor of eventual injury. Athletes who specialized were 70–93 percent more likely to be injured than were those playing multiple sports.[72]

Multisport diversification need not keep your child from developing expertise. In fact, Ohio State football coach Urban Meyer has a strong preference for recruiting multisport athletes. Meyer is not alone in this; 71 percent of Division 1 football players were multisport athletes. Consider too that 29 of 32 first-round NFL picks from a recent draft were multisport athletes growing up.[73]

The benefits of early sports diversification, relative to specialization, are not restricted to injury prevention. Other benefits include less pressure to succeed, less emotional burnout, greater long-term success, and greater overall athletic ability in terms of hand-eye coordination, balance, endurance, explosion, and agility. Given these data, it appears that athletic singleness of purpose should include training in sports outside the target sport, at least early on.

Still, most Division 1 college athletes did specialize by age 12. This includes 87 percent of women gymnasts, 68 percent of men's soccer players, and 66 percent of men's tennis players.[74]

So, what's a parent to do? The recommendation is to expose children to multiple sports and to encourage participation in a variety of sports early on until the time is right for specialization should the child choose to specialize. Also, consider the sport. In sports such as gymnastics and swimming, peak performance is reached in adolescence, so earlier specialization is likely warranted.

Provide Identity Protection

If you and your child take the full talent development journey, a time will come when identity is revealed: he is a French hornist or a dancer; she is a swimmer or a writer. You should accept and protect this precious identity. One parent said, "Well, I knew he had talent and I didn't want to see it whither. If you're really good at one thing, you're very, very fortunate so I just wanted to encourage that in him. I was proud of his skill. I just knew it gave him joy."[75] Another parent said, "He's my son and I love him and I want him to be whatever he can be. And, if it happens to be chess, then that's what I want for him. I want him to be happy."[76]

Parents can help children protect their identities by helping them counter obstacles such as distractions, doubt, defeat, and winning. Regarding distractions, author Henry Emerson Fosdick cautioned that "No steam or gas drives anything unless it is focused, dedicated, disciplined."[77] Help children stay talent focused by providing managerial assistance—travel arrangements, correspondence, paperwork. Guide children to put their time where their goals are and not be afraid to say "no," just like the creative person at the beginning of the chapter who opted out of the creativity study. Motivational speaker Les Brown reminds us that "When not pursuing your goal, you are literally committing spiritual suicide."[78]

Doubt is a dangerous talent enemy. If you believe that you can, you can; if you doubt that you can, you can't. Doubt stems from past experiences and misguided beliefs. I doubt that I can fix a car because I never have before. Moreover, I believe that I'm not mechanically inclined because of the subtle automotive messages my father conveyed when I was a kid: "You're putting wiper fluid in the radiator, you lunkhead. Get away from the car before you ruin it." As a parent, help your children build strong self-efficacy—the confidence that they can achieve goals in their talent area. Remind them about the hard work, acquired skills, and successes that have taken them this far. Remind them that abilities do not come naturally through genes but through hard work. Remind them that their potential rests in their hands—no doubt about it.

Regarding defeat, bring it on. Help children frame failure as the gateway to success. Tell them that losing breeds learning. Tell them the stories of Michael Jordan, Abraham Lincoln, Ty Cobb, and the rest. Tell them not to shun defeat but to welcome it and all the knowledge it brings. Tell them to keep working, practicing, and competing at the edge of competence where failure runs rampart but growth awaits. President Woodrow Wilson advised "Nurse your dreams and protect them through the bad times and tough times that always come."[79]

Regarding winning, help children celebrate and smell victory's fragrance. Remind them, though, that victory's sweet odor, like that of the rose, is transient. Talent development depends on setting increasingly challenging goals and meeting them one after the other. Following victory, help children set off on the next challenge that awaits. After all, as grandmaster Maurice Ashley said, "It is not about getting to the top of the mountain, it's about the climbing."[80]

CHAPTER EIGHT

Parents as Managers

In the movie *Rocky*, Mickey said to Rocky "Well, what you need is a manager. A manager, listen to me. . . . I got all this knowledge, I got it up here now, I wanna give it you. . . . I wanna take care of ya. . . . You can't buy what I'm gonna give ya." Having a manager was central to Rocky's success, just as managers today are central to the success of major corporations, small businesses, movie and rock stars, and everyday people depending on life managers.

This chapter focuses on the management roles that parents play for their talented children. It departs from previous chapters because its two-pronged message is simple: (1) kids can't manage their own talent development because they are too young or too busy, and (2) parents can provide necessary management.

This chapter begins with a couple of accounts in which parents took on formal managing roles and then describes the everyday roles most parents assume as they manage their child's talent. I revisit my personal management experience after that.

Adora Svitak, Writer and Speaker

Adora Svitak was a writing prodigy. She began reading at age three and made a quick progression from simple books to chapter books. Adora was not satisfied with just reading, though; she wanted to write for others. Her mother, Joyce, said, "Adora's thinking was natural, 'This book was written by someone, and I want to write books too. And, after I write them, I want other people to read them.'"[1]

And write she did. Adora began writing short stories at age 4. Joyce said, "I knew she had some kind of writing talent when she was five because she would write pages after pages, even though it was childish type of writing, but I knew kids that age don't just keep writing. . . . The progress was exponential. She would write a five-page story one week and then a twenty or thirty page story the next week." The stories also became increasingly sophisticated, Joyce said, to the point where Adora published her first book when she turned 8. The book, *Flying Fingers: Master the Tools of Learning through the Joy of Writing*, offers tips on how to teach children to write. Her second book, *Dancing Fingers*, was published when Adora was age 11. This is a collection of poems and poetry writing ideas for schools and families.

Adora's first book sparked a public speaking career that began with presentations on literacy and writing at local elementary schools when she was 8 years old and expanded to hundreds of worldwide presentations at schools, corporations, and conferences on three continents. At age 13, Adora delivered her most famous speech, "What Adults Can Learn from Kids," at TED. The speech received more than 3 million views on TED.com and has been translated into more than 40 languages.

Of course, Adora could not manage all of this. That is the role Joyce played. She was Adora's manager. In a sense, that management began by providing a stimulating early environment. Joyce said, "The environment we provide for her is limitless in what she can learn and experience. There is no impossible goal. It's an encouraging environment where we never say 'no' to any reasonable request." Joyce said that she and her husband stressed reading when Adora was young: "Reading really helped shape Adora's love for learning and writing. My husband has been especially devoted. He would read books to her, more than an hour a night, that were not children's books. They were interesting, fascinating." Joyce also managed Adora's child care so that learning was involved: "When I hired baby sitters, I would teach them how to teach my children. For instance, I'd say, 'I'm not good at drawing and you are so I want you to teach my children to draw.' . . . I told them not to passively spend time watching TV but to work on things that involved language or math."

Joyce quit her job to manage Adora's writing and speaking engagements. "Managing Adora's career is my full-time job," Joyce said. That began with making sure Adora received a good education. Adora is homeschooled and takes most classes online. Joyce manages all the school interactions and makes sure Adora is progressing. A homeschool arrangement makes sense given Adora's writing focus and heavy travel schedule. Motivation is not something Joyce needs to manage. Joyce said, "She is very motivated, the challenge is time. If she has time, she will write every day. She sets writing goals for herself every month and usually meets them, sometimes writing a short story a day."

Managing Adora's publishing and speaking engagements is Joyce's primary focus. Joyce said, "As Adora's career path has moved from writing to publishing, to teaching in local schools, to public speaking worldwide, my time commitment has naturally grown." Joyce said that shepherding Adora's first book through the publication process was time-consuming, but now the bulk of Joyce's managerial time is spent arranging Adora's many speaking engagements. This involves all the scheduling, travel arrangements, and client correspondence. It also involves helping Adora practice her speeches and providing feedback that she can "take or leave." Travel is extensive. Joyce said, "We are not only traveling throughout the United States but pretty much all over the world. Adora has spoken in England, Canada, China, Vietnam, Hong Kong, Dubai, Costa Rica. . . . We next go to the University of Huston and then on to Toronto, Mexico, France, Switzerland, and India." After presentations, Joyce helps Adora reflect on her speeches "to make sure Adora is doing a good job and giving clients what they want."

At one point, Joyce considered hiring a professional manager:

> It is a full-time job and sometimes even more than full-time and it can be hard. But the reason I keep doing it is that I don't just manage somebody. The person I manage is my daughter. At one point I said to my daughter, "This is so much work for me, would you rather I hire some kind of professional? Someone who can do a better job?" And she said, "But who will rub my tummy when I have a tummy ache?" We just don't see how anyone else could take on my role. . . . It's a working relationship but you also have this mother-daughter relationship which is very loving and fulfilling—we just don't see a reason to have anyone else manage her or work with her because it has been working out so well.

McKenzie Steiner, Softball Player and Musician

McKenzie Steiner is a father-managed softball and music double play. As a high school freshman, she started for her Class A team and garnered attention from Division 1 college coaches. As a musician, she's been lead singer for the McKenzie JaLynn and the Renegades Band since age 14. McKenzie is a Nebraska Country Music Foundation Junior Hall of Fame inductee and a three-time NCMF Top Youth Vocalist. She has twice been invited to audition for the television series *The Voice* but declined both invitations to focus on school. She and her band have cut an album in Nashville and have opened for Grammy Award–winning bands.

McKenzie's father, Scott, has not played the typical on-the-sidelines managerial role that most parents play. Instead, he served as softball and band manger. Regarding softball, McKenzie was raised in a softball home and followed her older sister into the world of travel team softball in which teams travel their region and often beyond playing about 100 games a year. Scott said,

I've been one of her team coaches ever since she started playing when she was six years old. It's club softball, so we practice year-round and travel and play about 100 games a year. In addition, McKenzie and I practice her pitching in the backyard all the time. And, for ninety percent of her career, I've called pitches for her in games. It was only when she started playing high school ball that I stepped back from that role. I also arranged for McKenzie to work with a local pitching coach in the off-season, but I continue to practice with her year-round.[2]

McKenzie's high school coach, Mark Watt, reported that Scott has served important managerial roles by coaching her team, developing her pitching skills, and calling pitches. He guided McKenzie's older sister, who was also a pitcher, in the same way. Coach Watt said, "Her father started that music group and found very talented people to be in it. I've heard her band play and it's highly impressive that a 14-year old can perform with adults professionally. There are not many kids that can do that successfully."[3]

Regarding that band, it was Scott who hatched the idea and largely assembled the four-piece band. "The band took two years to build, and I built it around McKenzie as lead singer," Scott said.[4] His first thought was to form a youth band, so he placed ads for youth musicians on Craig's List but eventually decided to form a more conventional and professional band after hearing from Eric Toombs, a talented 25-year-old drummer who loved music and wanted to join McKenzie as a way of giving back to younger musicians the way older musicians once mentored him. Together, Scott, McKenzie, and Eric interviewed and auditioned prospective members until the McKenzie JaLynn and the Renegades Band was formed when McKenzie was just 14 years old.

Since its formation, the band has performed regularly in local and regional venues mostly because of Scott's managerial work. He maintains a website showcasing McKenzie and the band's experiences, seeks donations for the band, and works to book new shows. Eric said, "Scott's biggest role now is booking shows for us and he's really good at it. He gets nothing for doing this and it's so much work. But, he loves and believes in the band and wants to hear us play. What I like best about Scott, as a promoter, is that he is a dreamer. He wants us to play the Pinnacle Bank Arena and other big arenas. I love that because such optimism keeps you looking ahead."[5]

Scott handles the band's managerial role because he loves McKenzie and her music. Eric said, "We've not had to hire a manager to manage our band. Scott's doing that because he loves it and he really wants McKenzie to play. After a show, he's so positive: 'I loved it, it was perfect.' Which is great because when he loves it, he does all this from love."[6] On his managerial role, Scott said, "I'm more of a 'dadanger' than manager; managers get paid. I'm more of an encourager than anything else but if encouraging McKenzie and bragging about her is managing, then I guess I'm a manager."[7]

Parents' Everyday Managerial Roles

We have already seen the helpful, selfless, and sometimes heroic things that parents do to provide an optimal early experience, assist with practice, hire and support mentors, create a center of excellence, and help children develop and maintain a singleness of purpose. Here we view a few snapshots of other things that parents I interviewed do behind the scenes as they manage their children's talent growth.

Parents Recognize the Scope and Importance of the Managerial Role

The parent of a pianist said, "My work, especially before age twelve, was critical in his development. I was intensely involved managing him."[8] A chess parent warned that "You have to be willing to pay the price. If you're not, it won't happen. It's a huge burden. Absolutely. It's not overstating that our life is entirely structured around his chess. I spend several hours a week managing his chess career. It's a part-time job."[9] Another chess parent said that managing his son's chess career was a lot like running his company at work. He keeps a chess calendar showing tournaments, lessons, and payments. He talks to coaches about lesson goals and plans and sits in on lessons to take notes and review those with his son throughout the week. The parent of an Olympic figure skater remarked, "I'm his personal secretary. I'm his assistant. It's work. I have an office. I go there and use the computer, fax machine, and copier to do skating work. For half the day, all I do is skating work. . . . I feel like a parent's role is crucial in the development of a kid's talent. They can't do it without parent involvement."[10]

Parents Commit Time and Resources

Two things are needed for good management: time and resources. Some parents cut back on work to afford more time. One skating mother cut her work hours and then retired when she was just 47 years old to manage her daughter's skating career. She said, "I had to go part-time at work to be there to drive her from school to lessons each day. Eventually, I just retired because all the travel for skating competitions was not possible with my job."[11] A chess parent said that she chose to work part-time so she could manage her son's chess career. And what she made went toward his chess expenditures. Another chess parent took less prestigious and less prosperous jobs in academia so he could spend more time managing his son's chess career. He said, "As much as I loved my students, the job was less important to me than my son and his development."[12]

Some parents work one or more jobs to afford more talent resources. Some twirling parents remarked that the coaching and judging they do goes right back into coaching, competition, and costume fees for their children. The parent of a figure skater worked two jobs when her son was younger to finance skating costs. Years later, she quit those jobs and managed her son's skating corporation. She said, "I had to wear some new hats. I was no longer mom advising him on finances, I was the secretary of his corporation."[13] The parents of a chess player worked second and third jobs to generate chess management resources. The parents worked as custodians for years at nearby office buildings and ran an annual summer chess camp requiring 400 hours of their personal time.

Parents Preserve and Accrue Resources

Speaking of resources, some managerial activities were carried out to preserve or accrue resources. One twirling parent and her daughter do fundraisers to offset twirling costs. The mother said, "My mother owns a quilt store so a couple Saturdays a month my daughter performs for the quilters out on the sidewalk while I sell cookies we baked. It's a way to raise a little money for twirling."[14] She also said, "We're in a financial situation where we just have to do our best. I'm a penny pincher, budget person, I'm always looking for a deal to save us money."

One chess parent created and manages a website to promote her son's chess accomplishments and seek donations. She also manages her son's writing of a weekly chess column for which he is compensated. She said that this is no easy task:

> He's writing a chess blog that is a trade-off for sponsorship. They are paying for some chess lessons with a grandmaster. All these people who read the blog are saying to him, "You're the most amazing, incredible writer ever," and I just have to laugh. He's twelve. Yes, he's writing his thoughts and ideas, but only because I'm sitting there every minute saying, "Okay, what do you want to say? What do you think? What idea are you trying to get across here and how do you want to say it? And, that doesn't sound quite right, can you say it in a different way? Or, your grammar's not quite right here." So, every time he writes it takes him hours because it's his work and he's twelve. But it takes me that long too.[15]

Parents Act as Travel Agents and Companions

Examining the travel schedules of talented youngsters leaves you hoping that they are earning frequent flyer miles. Twirlers are usually competing in multiple national competitions and one world competition per year. Chess players are usually competing in multiple national and world events per year. One chess father owns a company, and his assistant makes the family's travel arrangements for three or four international events and two or three national events per year. The player's mother usually accompanies him for these two-day to two-week events because she teaches piano and has a flexible schedule. Another chess parent remarked, "My son calls me his agent. That's kind of what I feel like. I do all the planning and everything else and he just gets on the plane or in the car and we go."[16] One twirling parent and her daughter arrive five days early for world competitions so the daughter can be rested and acclimated to the time change and her new surroundings.

Some students and parents jet around the country a few times a year for instruction or fly instructors to their hometowns. One twirling mother said, "My daughter and I fly from Missouri to Ohio for lessons so we have airline, hotel, and rental car costs, plus the cost of the lesson. We try to maximize our time there by having a four-hour lesson, going for dinner, and then coming back and reviewing for another hour. I want to make sure that our time is well spent."[17] One music student and his mother fly from Utah every week for lessons at a California conservatory. His mother said, "I'm a pretty good travel agent at this point. I buy a lot of plane tickets and arrange a lot of cars and hotels. I'm also the one packing all his things and making sure things get where they're supposed to be. Kind of a porter." Some parents and children also make long road trips for lessons. Several drive an hour or more each way. A twirler and her mother drive three hours each way for lessons.

Parents Do Competition Preparation

Across all talent areas, there is paperwork that parents must complete: membership applications, registration forms, and documentation. The world of competitive figure skating, though, raises paperwork to a world-class level. One skating parent remarked, "As a parent, you need to stay on top of other elements that go along with skating. There is all sorts of paperwork and deadlines. There's registrations, membership renewals, ordering equipment, and all the drug testing paperwork."[18] Speaking of drug testing paperwork, another skating parent said, "Nobody realizes how much paperwork there is. It's ridiculous. We have to document where he is and when he's there for drug testing purposes." Another skating parent added "I don't know if anybody understands the amount of paperwork elite athletes have for drug testing. It's unbelievable. Every three months, we must document where she is every day. And, if something changes, we need to call in that day and tell them where she is. If you're out of compliance more than a couple times, they could keep you out of the Olympics. Managing all this is much more than everybody thinks."

Skating and twirling parents arrange for costumes and music and do some last-minute grooming before competitions. One skating parent said, "There is a lot to do around competitions. I'm involved with music selection and costume design. I'll say to her, here's a stack of music, let's listen to stuff and see if there's something you find interesting. We'll flip through magazines together trying to find inspiration for dress or costume designs. I try to provide options and help channel her decisions without making them for her."[19]

A twirling mother is heavily involved in costume design and manufacturing. Twirlers ordinarily need three costumes per year, with each costume commonly costing around $500 minus the rhinestones, which are attached later. The mother said,

> I have a local gal here that lives fifteen minutes down the road. She sews and makes costumes for a lot of dance companies. I come up with the idea and she makes them out of her home and charges me about $75 per costume. And then I buy the stones. I shop around for the rhinestones and buy them in bulk at a discounted rate. I attach them all myself. This way, most of our costumes run under $300. They look like a million bucks though.[20]

Regarding competition grooming, one skating mother said, "I did her hair for competitions. I had to sew it in because she didn't want bobby pins on the ice."[21] A twirling parent remarked, "My job was to put her hair up and help get her costume on. Then my job was to sit there and be supportive and have a hair pin and bottle of water ready to go." Another twirling parent said that it was vital for her to attend competitions instead of her husband because he would never be able to handle "the hair challenge."

Parents Endure Competition

Once competitions begin, some parents are relaxed, while others are basket cases. One twirling parent assumes a calm and assured approach. She said, "When we arrive at competitions, the job is already done. She has prepared herself and there is no need for me fretting. We try to have a normal routine. Our philosophy is to have a fun day. I tell her, 'You have learned, worked hard, and practiced. There is nothing that can be done at this point to change the outcome. Just do your routine and whatever happens, happens.'"[22]

Another twirling parent is not so calm. She said, "We start in the morning and try to be positive and hope we can get the hair done without going, 'you're hurting me.' And, if we can get started off good, I'm happy. I'm just trying to keep things positive for her. Trying to make sure she gets there on time and that she practices and stretches. But at the same time, I'm stressed out. I have butterflies in my stomach. And by the end of the week I have a headache. And I barely eat. I try, but my stomach is in knots—I'm nervous for her."[23] Another twirling mother described her competition anxiety, saying that there have been times when "I actually missed her performance because I had to run to the bathroom and throw up. But, I didn't tell her and she asks, 'Did you see me?' And, I'm like, 'You were great, wonderful.'"[24]

Chess parents are equally nervous when attending tournaments. One parent said, "Watching his games is emotionally draining. I'll come down to the tournament room to look at his position for a while and then go back to my hotel room to read. I always take a book along to a tournament thinking I'll read a lot. But, I maybe read two pages during a four-hour game. And, I don't remember what I read."[25] Another chess parent said,

> During any given round, I stand as if on a perch, hawk-like in various positions about the room eyeing my chess child. I cannot read or write while the game is on. Even if I remained outside the playing hall, my thoughts would be too locked on the battle inside to allow me to concentrate on anything else. . . . I shut down bodily functions and remain standing motionless and expressionless watching my child's game for hours. . . . I become unaware of the passage of time. . . . I do not eat, I do not drink, I do not go to the bathroom. . . . I simply cannot do anything else.[26]

Parents Provide Life Management

Parents provide all sorts of life guidance and assistance to keep children on their talent development track. One way pertains to schooling. You have already seen that some parents homeschool their children to allow greater focus on the talent area and increased opportunity for travel. Those who don't homeschool work closely with schools to arrange for ongoing instruction while traveling for competitions, which could span more than two weeks. One chess parent said that he has had to educate school personnel about what his son has accomplished and why it is so important that he travel for long periods for chess. When they travel his son misses a lot of school work, and it is sometimes hard to catch up. The parent said, "Keeping up with school is sometimes a complete nightmare." The parent speaks to teachers before they leave and gathers work. He said, "I set up email correspondence with teachers for submitting work and copy pages from about 10 big books before we go. It's a lot of heavy lifting."[27]

Much is also said and done regarding time management. One parent said, "My wife's role is organization, time management, and nagging. She makes sure things get done."[28] Another parent said that she teaches time management indirectly: "You don't say to a kid, 'I'm teaching you time management right now.' Instead, it's, 'We can't go to the gym until your homework is finished.' I think a huge factor in building talent is learning time management because if you can't manage time, you can't succeed." Parents preserve time as well. One parent picks her daughter up for school rather than have her take the bus home because it affords the daughter more time to practice. Another parent prompts her daughter to eat and do homework on car trips to spend that time efficiently.

Parents do a lot of reminding. They remind their talented children to schedule appointments, confer with teachers, complete homework, and write thank-you notes. One parent said that he often reminds his son about survival skills when he's competing in chess over several days. He reminds his son to eat, drink, and take exercise breaks to quiet his mind.

Parents take steps to keep their talented children healthy and well. Many stressed the importance of a healthy diet, plenty of sleep, and regular exercise. Some of the children have serious medical conditions—diabetes, asthma, or latex allergy—and those parents stay close to their children to monitor their health. One skating parent said, "I lived at the rink for quite a few years and watched him while he was skating because he has asthma. I was always afraid that if he had an asthma attack no one would know what to do. There were a few times he had an attack and I was relieved I was there."[29] Similarly, another skating parent said, "My daughter has a latex allergy so I always went to her practices and events in case there was a problem." Another parent took her baton twirling daughter to a sports psychologist to help her better perform under pressure and ease up on herself. The parent said, "A bunch of times, she'd come off the floor and fall apart. She was overly critical about her performances, which I thought were really good, and beat herself up. She'd say I had too many drops or was not smiling enough. So, I took her to a sports psychologist to help relieve the pressure." Finally, one parent told the recurring story of trying to keep her figure skating son well fed and strong during competitions. "I want to be sure he eats so I order food at the ice skating rink, but he doesn't eat it, and then I eat it. Then I order him something else and the same thing happens, he doesn't eat it and I do. Then at the end, he's starved because he hasn't eaten anything, but I'm feeling sick and stuffed. I've eaten everything because I don't want to waste food."

Parents Provide a Protective Buffer

In a few cases, parents felt that they needed to protect children from others. One chess parent spoke about protecting his son from those who approach him after a game:

It is very important to protect his psychological environment. A lot of people don't understand this at all—how emotionally drained one can be after a game. So, you want to be very careful. You don't want to be rude to other people. They are well-wishers. They want to make sure he is okay, but what they are doing is making him feel worse. So, to find a careful line in protecting him is important. It is very important. Especially after a loss.[30]

Another chess parent spoke about protecting her son from the press:

> I'm the go-between for him and the press and that has been a major managerial role. I try to protect him. He gets bombarded by reporters who want to talk to him. The week he became the first child to win the State Championship, we literally had one reporter coming in while the other was leaving for days. I finally had to intervene because it's important that he have the chance to still be a kid. So, I try to achieve a balance for him where he can be a champion and represent America and still be a kid, where chess commitments don't take over his life. So, I manage the requests for his time, and we built a website so people can get information there.[31]

The mother of an Olympic figure skater said that she needed to protect her daughter from a zealous press:

> When we were at the Olympics, we didn't anticipate how the media can be completely overwhelming even though we were warned about it. It's crazy, it's invasive—the whole paparazzi sort of thing. . . . Now that the Olympic cycle is over for another four years, we're happy things are returning to normal and we have our family time. We like to do things in the background. We don't need or appreciate the notoriety of what our family does being publicized. It's just not who we are.[32]

Managing Talent: My Personal Experience Revisited

In Chapter 1, I chronicled my own story raising a chess champion—a story heavy on parent management. Here is a quick recap. I introduced my son, Keaton, to chess and fed his early interest with lots of play and instruction. I didn't know much about chess, so I purchased materials and studied them so I could teach him. I began researching tournaments and clubs and taking him to those. Soon I located and hired an instructor and then another. I joined in on lessons and reinforced lesson points as we studied together most days. Keaton competed in progressively more tournaments—two or three a month in nearby cities or remote Nebraska towns plus two or three national tournaments a year. Local events ate up a weekend, while national events lasted 5 to 10 days. As Keaton's playing strength grew, I hired a grandmaster coach in New York and arranged and monitored telephone lessons. I also arranged for Keaton to attend weeklong camps throughout the United States. I persuaded the school district to allow him to be mentored in chess five hours a week and receive academic credit. I established a local chess culture. I spoke with principals and persuaded several to offer chess clubs. I taught chess at four elementary schools, and Keaton was my coinstructor before instructing one on his own. I also organized dozens of chess festivals, tournaments, and camps where Keaton could participate, teach, or showcase his skills. I wrote a weekly chess column for the local paper and worked with local media, which did stories about Keaton. I handled all travel arrangements, attended all events, and paid all bills.

Here I highlight three of the managerial roles I played: advocate, competition shield, and career mentor.

Advocate

At first, Keaton's chess career flew under the national radar. He was from Nebraska, a chess wasteland, while most strong players were from New York or other coastal cities. His location limited competition opportunities, which kept his profile and rating depressed. Each summer, there was a prestigious camp for just six elite junior players sponsored by a national organization. Keaton's position on national rating lists was not high enough to merit an invitation to the weeklong camp. I contacted the instructor, a world-renowned grandmaster, and asked if there was any chance Keaton could participate. He said that the camp was full and that there was a list of alternates should one be needed. I politely pressed on and told him about Keaton's accomplishments and unbridled passion for chess. Finally, the instructor told me to send an application letter and some of Keaton's game moves. The instructor must have liked what he saw. When one of the invitees dropped out a week before the camp, Keaton was the first replacement choice. We flew to New York, and Keaton seized the opportunity. The instructor told me later that Keaton was a delight and easily as strong as the players who outrated him. Keaton was invited back the following year.

Although Keaton captured six National Scholastic Championships, he never won any of the occasional events that guaranteed a full-ride scholarship offered by the University of Texas–Dallas and a spot on its national championship chess team. In those events, Keaton came heartbreakingly close a few times. When it was time to apply for colleges, his heart was set on the University of Texas–Dallas or another university on the East Coast that was also a chess powerhouse. The problem was that these schools only recruited a handful of students to compete on their chess teams, and most of them were chess grandmasters or international masters from other countries. Again, I advocated. I wrote a letter to each chess coach detailing Keaton's credentials and describing what he could bring to the team and the university. In addition, I joined him on campus visits and in coach meetings and delicately advocated. He was offered a spot on the team and a full scholarship at both schools.

Competition Shield

A scholastic national tournament is stressful. Forget about personal space. Five thousand players might compete in various sections, with all of them cramped into one room the size of an airport hangar. Throw in one or two parents and a couple of siblings per player milling about, and you have a rock concert crowd and a resource-strapped venue. Just try merging onto an elevator or finding an eatery without a winding line. There's more. Rounds are long, and there is little break between them. Four-hour rounds begin at 2:00 and 7:00 p.m. on Friday; 9:00 a.m., 2:00 p.m., and 7:00 p.m. on Saturday; and 8:00 a.m. and 1:00 p.m. on Sundays. That's crazy; why not just run seven marathons in three days? And did I mention that it was nearly impossible to find food between rounds? Then there is the competition. Although most players are there for the fun of it, a couple dozen in each section are all business and are competing for a coveted national championship. Their chess ratings jump off the charts, they're battle tested, and they wear scornful looks that shout "I got this!" Moreover, many top players don team jackets from their chess-enriched New York City school. And they don't come alone; joining them is a team of grandmaster coaches with Russian accents. It's all quite intimidating.

Like *Star Trek*'s Starship Enterprise, I raise my shields to protect Keaton from this insanity and help him play his best. First, we arrive a day early to get the lay of the land, scout out remote eateries, and relax. Months before, I book a hotel a few blocks from the main venue and request a quiet room: top floor, end of the hall, and away from the elevator and ice machine. I have earplugs should we need them. The morning of the first round, we visit the playing hall, check out the chess sets, and locate the bathrooms. We reexamine his own equipment: clock, fresh batteries, water bottle, granola bars, score pad, and sharpened pencils. We take a long walk outside away from the hum and grab the ritualistic pretournament meal—pancakes—not too early and not too late but just at the right time for optimal digestion.

At the tournament venue, I have Keaton wait in a quiet area while I join the 10-deep crowd pushing to view first-round pairings. I report back to Keaton, and we wait for the commotion to die down before entering the tournament room and finding his place. I linger a bit as he sets up for his game, and then I lean in and give him the parting advice I offer each time: "Everything you need to play great chess is in your heart and in your head. Trust it." While he battles, I find food that he can eat between rounds, knowing that time won't allow a restaurant excursion should his game go long. Plus, we would rather find a quiet out-of-the-way bench or grassy area to eat our food.

Between rounds, the New York City kids in the matching jackets cram into side rooms their schools rented to analyze their tournament games with their grandmaster coaches. To me, this approach is all wrong. In my view, there is nothing a coach can see in that last game or offer before the next game that can help. The die is cast. Instead, Keaton and I use the time to eat, relax, toss a football, and recharge emotional batteries before the next game.

It is Saturday night, and Keaton is exhausted. Three games in one day against strong players does that. We find some pizza for his postgame meal and take a brisk evening walk. At my urging, he showers away some stress. Lights off early for maximal rest. I lay stock still in bed even though I cannot sleep—my mind is filled with chess—hoping that Keaton finds sleep soon. I wake early and sneak from the room, leaving him to get his last bit of rest before the championship rounds. I return with bagels and muffins just as his alarm sounds. He picks at his food, but I give him time and space and remind him that he needs to bank energy. We take the stairs down and make a few turns around a small park away from the chaos before the battle renews. Shields are up, and Keaton is ready to fire.

Career Mentor

Chess is not like professional golf. There are no big endorsements, nor is there big prize money. Moreover, outside the world champion, few chess competitors are well recognized or well compensated. Few people get rich playing chess. I knew this from the start, but I supported Keaton's chess development because the process was so delicious and enriching. He loved chess, and I loved him and his chess. Still, I began to wonder what he might do with chess someday beyond competing, how he might remain in the game should he choose to. With that thought, I introduced Keaton to chess mentoring.

It began when he was in second grade, the year he started playing. I started a chess club at his school, and 100 students joined. I had parent helpers distribute chess sets and snacks, but I needed instructional help too. Enter Keaton. I had him deliver short lessons to small groups and work with individuals honing skills such as checkmating with a king and rook. Keaton enjoyed teaching and took it in stride. He was simply reenacting what I and his own chess mentors had done for him.

Over the years I taught several after-school chess clubs, and Keaton joined me for each. We were coinstructors. Together, we readied the room, delivered short lessons, and assisted children as they played. Keaton certainly knew his chess and was enthusiastic and animated in his delivery. Being an educational psychologist, I offered occasional feedback during car rides home: "Plan some activity to capture their attention." "Move the pieces more slowly on the demonstration board. Be sure they're following each move and understanding its purpose." "Wait longer after questioning them. Chess is a thinking game. Let them think." I also addressed issues pertaining to management: "We need to welcome parents when they come to visit." "We can't let children leave until we see them with a parent." "We need to make sure students demonstrate respect for the equipment, classroom, and each other. Let's talk about how we make sure that happens."

When Keaton was in ninth grade, I helped him fly solo by helping him land his own chess club teaching position at a local elementary school. A parent volunteer was present to provide adult supervision. Keaton instructed this club for four years before leaving for college. Also while in high school, Keaton gained additional teaching experience at chess festivals and camps I organized. There, he presented chess lectures to hundreds of kids and hob-nobbed with seasoned chess instructors I recruited from New York. Keaton also directed a chess class for children with special needs, gave blindfolded exhibitions, and gave simultaneous exhibitions playing 50 players at one time.

Mentor training paid off. After college, Keaton built a business teaching chess at several schools. Today he teaches dozens of private students, some national champions, through his online chess mentoring.

CHAPTER NINE

Beyond Talent Development

Fostering Academic Success

My mom planted the seeds of my life as educator. While my older brother and sister were at school, Mom and I played school at home before preschools and homeschools were fashionable. Each day we read, wrote, and drew. Science took place in the woods across the street, where we collected bugs and leaves for examination. Physical education was playing catch or stickball in the backyard. I still cherish the tattered report card Mom gave me because I wanted one just like my older siblings. Mom assigned me an A in writing, spelling, reading, arithmetic, and science. My only B was in conduct. Mom wrote, "Kenneth should try harder to play more nicely with his brother and sister." Mom was a great teacher and, in retrospect, a fair evaluator. If I wanted straight A's, I would have to earn them.

Not all of my subsequent teachers were as good as Mom. My fifth grade teacher was among the pedagogically challenged. He showed two or three movies a day on an old reel-to-reel projector. Before a movie started, he sent a student to the cafeteria to fetch a couple of cartons of milk. He had students get the milk because they paid just 5 cents per carton, while teachers paid 10 cents. When you have a four- to six-cartons-a-day habit, I suppose those few cents saved add up quickly. He chugged the milks and then slept through the movie and never stirred until the film spun and snapped in the take-up reel. After a film, there was no class discussion or reflection, just a short intermission before the next flick.

Then there was my ninth grade science teacher, who used an alarming musical chairs–like practice for handing back graded tests. First, she had all students stand in the side row. Then, she announced the name and score of the highest scorer and had that student take the first seat in the front row.

She followed this procedure until all students were reseated from front to back in descending test score order. I still wake up in a cold sweat some nights recalling these haunting words: "And, finally, Kenneth got a 63 percent. Ken, it looks like we're out of chairs. Please go next door and see if they have an extra one."

Of course, there were excellent teachers too, such as Professor DuBois, whom I credited in Chapter 6 for sending me on an educational psychology rampage. Professor DuBois was so effective that students could not help but learn. Before a lesson, he provided objectives that informed students what they must learn. During a lesson, he provided cues that alerted students to what was important and what they needed to note. Cues such as "This is absolutely critical" and "This will be on the test" had us scribing notes at a feverish pitch. After the lesson, he guided test review by providing practice test questions like those students would see on the test. The first day of class Professor DuBois said, "Educational psychologists, by definition, should be the best instructors on a college campus. After all, they are experts in how students should learn and how teachers should teach." He was such an expert.

Students too can be ineffective or effective learners. Consider how Abe and Zada prepare for a science exam on genetics. Abe begins studying the night before the exam after watching several reruns of *The Simpsons*. Lying on his bed and listening to music, he reads and rereads his scant lecture notes that are nothing more than a few scattered terms with some half-baked definitions. He mindlessly recites the partial definitions of terms such as "mitosis," "meiosis," "genotype," and "phenotype" until he nods off to sleep. A morning alarm finally buzzes, jarring him from a DNA nightmare. Test score: 47 percent, thanks to some nifty guessing.

Zada meanwhile began daily test preparation a week before the exam. She sat at a desk in a study area free from distractions. She did more than review her recorded notes, which were stocked with lesson terms, complete definitions, examples, and elaborations. She organized her notes. She created a chart comparing mitosis and meiosis and another comparing genotype and phenotype. She drew associations among ideas such as the differing number of divisions and daughter cells for mitosis and meiosis. And she tested herself before the teacher did, making sure she could define terms and generate Punnett squares to predict genotype. If something confused her, she sought answers from the text or the teacher well before the exam. Test score: 100 percent, thanks to some nifty study strategies.

I tell these stories because not all is well in education. There are many weak teachers and students among the strong. When teachers are ineffective, it is difficult for students to learn. When both teachers and students are ineffective, learning is nearly impossible. When teachers are effective, students are likely to learn. And when both teachers and students are effective, students are likely to flourish. That is what we want in education: effective teachers and effective students.

Just as parents can help develop athletic and artistic talent, parents are in an ideal position to help develop academic talent. After all, parents hold the talent factor keys in academic domains too. Parents can provide enriched early experiences, facilitate practice, provide or secure mentoring, create a center of excellence, and foster motivation to establish singleness of purpose in math or science as readily as in tennis or art. Parents can steer children to learn like Zada instead of Abe. This chapter describes a teaching and learning method called SOAR that parents can use to develop academic talent and foster academic success.

Soar to Success

The foundation of learning is the same for any domain—be it music, history, political science, or golf. For learning to occur, the learner must *select* the important information to be learned, *organize* it, *associate* it, and *regulate* learning. The first letters of these four processes spell "SOAR." When learners do these four things, they soar to success. SOAR is a teaching and learning system I developed, researched,[1] wrote about,[2] and taught to thousands of teachers and students. Parents can help their children soar and teach them how to soar so they can soar to success in any academic area.

Let's see how SOAR works for learning scientific information about symbiosis[3] when presented as a series of terms and definitions (Figure 9.1). First, the learner must select critical information, which involves there being two organisms in a nutritional relationship and whether those organisms are benefited, harmed, or unaffected (Figure 9.2). Next, the selected information should be organized in a graphic form—such as a matrix (Figure 9.3)—so that associations among selected ideas appear readily (Figure 9.4). Last, the learner should regulate learning to be certain she has learned the material. A good way to do this is self-testing (Figure 9.5).

The problem is that most students don't use SOAR strategies and are grounded when left to their own devices. When they should select critical lesson information, they instead are inattentive and fail to note critical ideas for later study. When they should organize ideas graphically, they instead organize them linearly in lists or outlines or do not organize them at all. When they should associate ideas, they instead study them in a piecemeal fashion—one idea at a time—as if the ideas have no connection. When they should regulate, they instead use redundant strategies such as rereading, recopying, reciting, and regurgitating. Ridiculous.

Symbiosis

Symbiosis - *A situation in which two living organisms live together in a close nutritional relationship.*

Commensalism - *A type of symbiosis where one organism benefits and the other is unaffected.*

Mutualism - *A type of symbiosis where both organisms benefit.*

Parasitism - *A type of symbiosis where one organism benefits and the other is harmed.*

Figure 9.1

Select

Symbiosis - *Two organisms in nutritional relationship*

Commensalism - *Benefited and unaffected*

Mutualism - *Both benefited*

Parasitism - *Benefited and harmed*

Figure 9.2

That students use ineffective strategies is not really their fault. After all, most students are never taught how to learn. This sounds crazy, but reflect on your own academic training. Were you taught how to record a complete and high-quality set of notes, how to organize them, how to create associations, and how to self-test? Not likely. Schools focus on the products of learning and ignore the processes. They teach math and science but not how to learn math and science. They present information about the First Amendment to the U.S. Constitution and how to add mixed fractions but never address how to learn such information. Schools focus on what is to be learned but not how to learn it. If schools shirk that responsibility, then parents must step in and teach their children how to learn, how to soar to success.

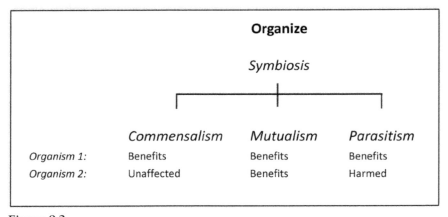

Figure 9.3

Associate	**Regulate**
• There are 3 types of symbiosis involving 2 organisms in a nutritional relationship	• In what type(s) is an organism harmed?
• Organism 1 always benefits	• In what type(s) is an organism benefited?
• Organism 2 is unaffected, benefited, or harmed	• In what type(s) is an organism unaffected?
	• A tapeworm eats from the host and the host is weakened. What type is this?

Figure 9.4

Figure 9.5

Let's take a closer look at SOAR processes and how to maximize them.

Select

Learning begins with attention. If students don't attend class or pay attention during class, they don't learn. Game over. Youngsters need to employ active listening strategies to aid information selection. They might track the speaker—eyes glued to him all times—as if he were a wild bear. They could predict what the speaker might say next and raise questions in their minds. They could relate lesson ideas to one another and to background knowledge. They could sit in front, where distractions are less likely and things are better seen and heard.

Older students should record notes to aid selection.[4] The more notes students record, the higher their achievement. Here's why. First, the act of note taking relieves boredom and aids attention. Someone recording notes pays greater attention than someone who listens but does not take notes. Second, notes are needed for review. Students need a complete external record of the lesson to review because memory is fallible. Without review, students remember little from yesterday's lesson, let alone one from weeks ago. Here's the problem: Most students are sketchy note takers, recording just one-third of important lesson ideas. That's crazy, like writing down just three digits from a 10-digit phone number you want saved.

Look at the two sets of notes about the solar system's first two planets (Figures 9.6 and 9.7).[5] The first set is complete; the second contains about a third of important information. Imagine having those sketchy notes for review. They're not so helpful. There is a lot of missing information, such as Venus's distance from the sun, and incomplete information, such as the figure 3,000 without its reference to diameter. Students need a complete set of notes to review.

Complete Notes	**Incomplete Notes**
Mercury	*Mercury*
Miles from sun: 36 million	*36 million miles*
Revolution time: 3 months	*from sun*
Orbit speed: 30 m/sec	*3,000*
Diameter: 3,000	*Rocky surface*
Surface: rocky	*Rotation time:*
Moons: 0	*59 days*
Rotation time: 59 days	*Venus*
Venus	*22 m/sec orbit speed*
Miles from sun: 67 million	*8,000*
Revolution time: 8 months	*Rotation time:*
Orbit speed: 22 m/sec	*243 days*
Diameter: 8,000	
Surface: rocky	Figure 9.7
Moons: 0	
Rotation time: 243 days	

Figure 9.6

Organize

A good memory is an organized memory. Just as we have difficulty retrieving things from a messy closet where things are tossed in haphazardly and strewn about, such is the case with memory. Good memory storage and retrieval depends on creating and maintaining an organized filing system. "This food experience belongs with cooking show recipes gone awry." "This information fits with presidential gaffes."

Our memory operates best when organized in graphic patterns such as images of faces or chairs, hierarchies showing the chain of military command or bird types and subtypes, sequences for executing a tennis serve or adding mixed fractions, and matrices for comparing political candidates or comparing car models. Let's see some examples of ineffective versus effective organization.

In the first example, there is a list of states in alphabetical order and their respective medical marijuana legislation (Figure 9.8).[6] Then, we see the same

---

List for Medical Marijuana in U.S.

Legal (Yes)

Illegal (No)

Only CBD Oil Legal (C)

Alabama (C), Alaska (Yes), Arizona (Yes), Arkansas (No), California (Yes), Colorado (Yes), Connecticut (Yes), Delaware (Yes), Florida (C), Georgia (C), Hawaii (Yes), Idaho (No), Illinois (Yes), Indiana (No), Iowa (C), Kansas (No), Kentucky (C), Louisiana (No), Maine (Yes), Maryland (Yes), Massachusetts (Yes), Michigan (Yes), Minnesota (Yes), Mississippi (C), Missouri (C), Montana (Yes), Nebraska (No), Nevada (Yes), New Hampshire (Yes), New Jersey (Yes), New Mexico (Yes), New York (Yes), North Carolina (C), North Dakota (No), Ohio (No), Oklahoma (C), Oregon (Yes), Pennsylvania (No), Rhode Island (Yes), South Carolina (C), South Dakota (No), Tennessee (C), Texas (C), Utah (C), Vermont (Yes), Virginia (C), Washington (Yes), West Virginia (No), Wisconsin (C), Wyoming (C)

Figure 9.8

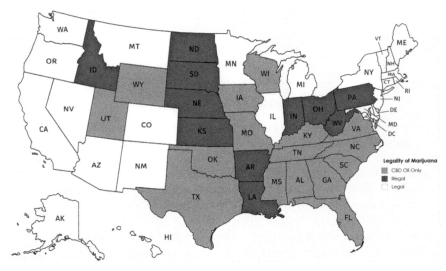

Figure 9.9

information in visual form (Figure 9.9). Big difference. The visual image is more efficient and is easier to store in memory.

In the second example, there is a list of musical instruments (Figure 9.10).[7] After that, there is a hierarchy organizer showing those same instruments (Figure 9.11). It is easy to see that the hierarchy is better organized and a more efficient way to store information than the list.

List of Musical Instruments

Saxophone	Triangle
French horn	Trombone
Flute	Cello
Bass drum	Violin
Trumpet	Clarinet

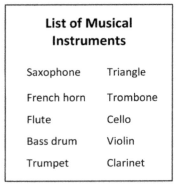

Figure 9.10

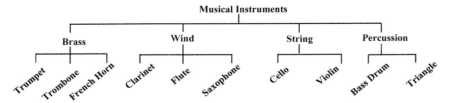

Figure 9.11

Experimental Procedure Paragraph

Students viewed a lecture and took notes one of three ways. They either recorded notes in their conventional format, on a skeletal outline, or within a matrix framework. Following the lecture, students studied for twenty-five minutes and did so by either reviewing notes or using their notes to write an essay. Students were tested immediately after, and there were three tests: a five-minute synthesis test, a ten-minute application test, and a five-minute factual recognition test. The tests were administered in that order. Finally, students took a delayed test. It was a recall test and students had fifteen-minutes to complete it.

Figure 9.12

In the third example, there is a brief paragraph describing an experimental procedure (Figure 9.12).[8] Then, there is a sequence organizer showing the procedure (Figure 9.13). Again, it is easy to see that the sequence is better organized and more efficient for memory storage than the paragraph.

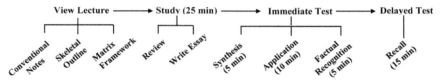

Figure 9.13

Planet Outline	In the final example, we see the start of an outline of planet characteristics (Figure 9.14). Then, there is a matrix organizer showing the planets (Figure 9.15). The matrix is well designed and better for comparing planets. The matrix organizer is more efficient and more easily stored than the outline.

Planet Outline

Mercury

Miles from sun: 36 million

Revolution time: 3 months

Orbit speed: 30 m/sec

Diameter: 3,000

Surface: rocky

Moons: 0

Rotation time: 59 days

Venus

Miles from sun: 67 million

Revolution time: 8 months

Orbit speed: 22 m/sec

Diameter: 8,000

Surface: rocky

Moons: 0

Rotation time: 243 days

Figure 9.14

In the final example, we see the start of an outline of planet characteristics (Figure 9.14). Then, there is a matrix organizer showing the planets (Figure 9.15). The matrix is well designed and better for comparing planets. The matrix organizer is more efficient and more easily stored than the outline.

Students should create graphic organizers when they want to see and store information efficiently. We will next see that there is another benefit to graphic displays: They reveal important relationships.

Associate

Piecemeal learning is ineffective. Here's some proof. Suppose I dumped jigsaw puzzle pieces on a table and asked you what the final puzzle revealed. To answer, would you pick up one piece and say "This is a violet-colored piece" then pick up another and say "This one is a light green color?" Of course not. You would assemble the puzzle and see what the connected pieces reveal. The same is true for learning. Little is gained from a piecemeal approach. Students must assemble lesson pieces and see the big picture (Figures 9.16 and 9.17).

To appreciate the power of associations, let's return to a couple of organization examples just presented. First is the list versus image organizers for medical marijuana. The list does not easily reveal patterns among states. The visual organizer quickly reveals several patterns: western states and northeastern states tend to make medical marijuana legal, southeastern states tend to allow CBD oil products only, and the midwestern states, stretching from

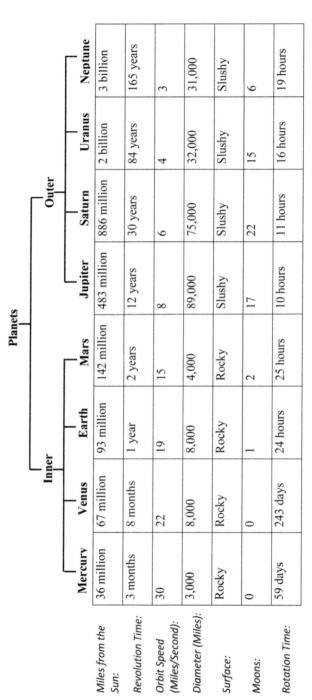

Planets

		Inner				Outer		
	Mercury	**Venus**	**Earth**	**Mars**	**Jupiter**	**Saturn**	**Uranus**	**Neptune**
Miles from the Sun:	36 million	67 million	93 million	142 million	483 million	886 million	2 billion	3 billion
Revolution Time:	3 months	8 months	1 year	2 years	12 years	30 years	84 years	165 years
Orbit Speed (Miles/Second):	30	22	19	15	8	6	4	3
Diameter (Miles):	3,000	8,000	8,000	4,000	89,000	75,000	32,000	31,000
Surface:	Rocky	Rocky	Rocky	Rocky	Slushy	Slushy	Slushy	Slushy
Moons:	0	0	1	2	17	22	15	6
Rotation Time:	59 days	243 days	24 hours	25 hours	10 hours	11 hours	16 hours	19 hours

Figure 9.15

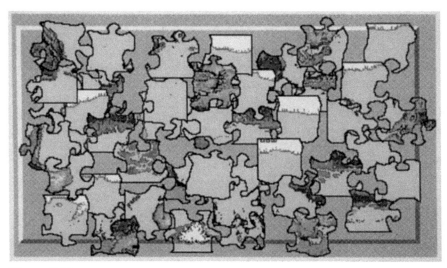

Figure 9.16

Figure 9.17

north to south and across to the mid-Atlantic region, tend to allow no forms of medical marijuana.

Next, let's revisit the outline and matrix organizers for planets. The matrix quickly reveals several planet relationships. As planets' distance from the sun increases, their revolution time increases and their orbit speed decreases. Inner planets have rockier surfaces, smaller diameters, fewer moons, and

longer rotation times compared to outer planets. These across-planet relationships are obscured in an outline.

All of the associations mentioned so far are internal associations because
they occur within lesson material. There is another equally important type:
external associations. These are associations that extend outside lesson
material. They link lesson material to one's prior knowledge and experiences, making new information more relevant and memorable. Returning
to marijuana legislation, an external association might be "Western and
northeastern states are most liberal, so it's no surprise that they favor comprehensive programs." And "States that outlaw medical marijuana are con-
servative Bible Belt states, so it makes sense that they outlaw medical
marijuana." Returning to planets, external associations might include
"Slushy planets remind me of a snow cone" and "I would be twice my age
on Mars."

Students need to make associations among ideas rather than learn in a
piecemeal fashion. A graphic organizer facilitates association making because
it shows the big picture, the intended message, with just a glance.

Regulate

Students should regulate learning—monitor whether they are learning
effectively, monitor whether they know their stuff. To do so, students should
self-test. Students should never let the instructor be the first to test them.
They should test themselves thoroughly before the test so there is nothing
the instructor can ask them that they haven't already asked themselves.

But students rarely self-test. Instead, they use redundant strategies such as
rereading, recopying, and rehearsal that don't really work. Need some proof?
Which way is George Washington facing on the dollar bill? Try sketching the
face of a telephone calling pad.[9]

Figure 9.18
(U.S. Treasury)

How did you do? Probably not so good. Even though you've looked ol' George in the face thousands of times, you probably did not know that he faced left (Figure 9.18). You say that you failed on the money task because you're strictly credit cards these days? Okay, what's your credit card number? How about your three-digit security code? With all the repetition typing those numbers into websites or reciting them over the phone, you would think you'd know them by now. Speaking of phones, you probably dropped that call too, misplacing or forgetting the various letters and symbols (Figure 9.19). Here's

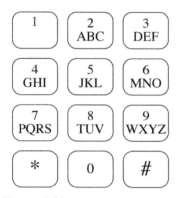

Figure 9.19

the problem: Repeated exposure to information does not move information into memory. For that, you need to regulate along with selection, organization, and association, of course.

Returning to self-testing, students studying the experimental procedure material might ask themselves, among other things,

- What were the experiment's four main steps?
- What were the three types of notes students recorded?

Students studying the planet material might ask themselves among, other things,

- How far is Earth from the sun?
- What is the relationship between revolution time and orbit speed?
- What is the range of planet sizes?
- What two types of surfaces do planets have?
- How old would I be on Mercury and on Mars?

Another SOAR Example in Psychology

Here is another SOAR example pertaining to a topic covered in psychology: reinforcement schedules. As in most cases, information is presented in paragraphs, or blocks of information. Read these paragraphs now and see how much you learn (Figure 9.20).

Reading this probably got a bit confusing, and it is unlikely that you noticed the patterns among the schedules. Let's try SOAR. First, we select

---

Schedules of Reinforcement

Okay, class, we've just covered reinforcement. Now, we'll see that there are different schedules one might use in delivering reinforcement.

Suppose you have a pigeon and you want to train it to peck a key. To train the pigeon, you give it food pellets for pecking the correct keys. There are four main schedules you can use to deliver the reinforcement. The type of schedule used determines several things about the animal's behavior.

Fixed-interval schedules deliver reinforcement following the first response after a fixed time interval. The pigeon, for example, might receive food for its first peck after a 10-second interval. Fixed-interval schedules produce slow response rates that contain pauses in responding. The animal tends to pause after it's reinforced and then increase responding as the interval ends, because reinforcement is again anticipated. It is relatively easy to extinguish (eliminate) behaviors learned on this schedule.

Variable-interval schedules deliver reinforcement following the first response after a predetermined but variable time interval. The pigeon, for example, might receive food following intervals of 5, 15, 2, and 18 seconds for an average interval of 10 seconds. Variable-interval schedules produce slow but steady response rates. It is difficult to extinguish behaviors learned on this schedule.

Fixed-ratio schedules deliver reinforcement following a fixed number of responses. The pigeon, for example, might receive food following every 10 key pecks. Fixed-ratio schedules produce rapid responding, although the animal pauses briefly following reinforcement. It is relatively easy to extinguish behaviors learned on this schedule.

Variable-ratio schedules deliver reinforcement after a predetermined but variable number of responses. The pigeon, for example, might receive food after making 5, 15, 2, and 18 pecks for an average ratio of 10 pecks. Variable-ratio schedules produce rapid and steady responding. It is difficult to extinguish behaviors learned on this schedule.

Figure 9.20

and note critical information. We construct a complete set of notes (Figure 9.21). Don't worry that these notes are linear; we'll handle that in the next SOAR step.

Next, we organize these notes. We begin with a hierarchy showing that there are two main schedules—interval and ratio—and two subschedules for each—fixed and variable. Then we extend this hierarchy into a matrix by adding the categories for comparison down the left side—definition, example, response rate, and extinction—and then inputting details in the matrix cells (Figure 9.22).

Complete Notes

Schedules of Reinforcement

<u>Fixed Interval</u>

Definition - reinforce first response after a fixed time
  interval

Example - food for first key peck after 10 s

Response rate - slow, pauses

Extinction - relatively easy

<u>Variable Interval</u>

Definition - reinforce first response after predetermined
  but variable interval

Example - food for first key peck after 5, 15, 2, and 18 s

Response rate - slow, steady

Extinction - difficult

<u>Fixed Ratio</u>

Definition - reinforce after fixed number of responses

Example - food after every 10 key pecks

Response Rate - rapid, pauses

Extinction - relatively easy

<u>Variable Ratio</u>

Definition - reinforce after predetermined but variable
  number of responses

Example - food after 5, 15, 2, and 18 key pecks

Response rate - rapid, steady

Extinction - difficult

Figure 9.21

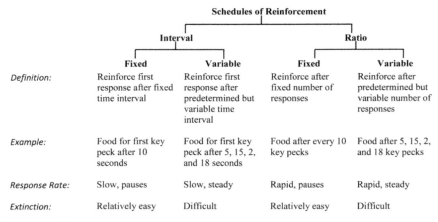

Figure 9.22

The matrix is efficient and looks great, but its real purpose is to divulge associations, such as these internal associations:

- Interval schedules are based on time; ratio schedules are based on number.
- In fixed schedules, the reinforcement pattern remains constant; in variable schedules, the reinforcement pattern changes.
- Interval schedules produce slow responding; ratio schedules produce rapid responding.
- Fixed schedules produce pauses in responding; variable schedules produce steady responding.
- Fixed schedules are easy to extinguish; variable schedules are difficult to extinguish.

Here are some external associations we might create:

- A salesperson who receives a commission for every five products sold is reinforced on a fixed-ratio schedule.
- Slot machines pay off on a variable-ratio schedule.

We are not done yet. We must regulate if learning is occurring. Here are some practice test items we might construct and answer before we face the real test:

- What is the definition of variable interval schedule?
- Which schedules involve steady responding?
- Which schedules are difficult to extinguish?

- A teacher uses pop quizzes to assess students at any time. What kind of student study behavior is likely to occur?

A SOAR Example in Chess

Although this chapter is about nurturing academic talent, SOAR can also be used to nurture traditionally nonacademic talents such as chess, music, and soccer. Let's see how SOAR can boost chess talent.

Chess is in some ways a simple game. One can learn how the six unique pieces move and play a simple game with perhaps an hour of instruction. In most other ways, chess is complex. Even former world champion Garry Kasparov called chess a black and white jungle (reflective of the board's black and white squares). And why not? After each player makes just 1 move, more than 400 different positions are possible. After just 3 moves, 9 million possible positions. After just 4 moves, 288 billion possible positions, yep billion. Moreover, there are more than 1,000 established opening sequences, each going about 10 moves deep, that players try to memorize. On top of that, each new position requires players to calculate several possible move options in their heads, each option several moves deep.

One aspect of chess that players must learn is tactics. Tactics are established ways to attack and win material. There are usually seven tactics commonly taught in chess books. These are often taught one at a time as if each tactic has no link to another. Instruction fails to organize the tactics in useful or memorable ways or to draw associations among tactics to aid understanding and memory. Instruction also fails to test players' tactic skills effectively. Here is how tactics might be taught and learned using SOAR.

Select and Organize

The Chess Tactics organizer in Figure 9.23 shows tactic relationships. It shows that two tactics involve a double attack, two involve a line attack, and three involve a guard attack. No chess book I have seen groups the tactics in this helpful manner.

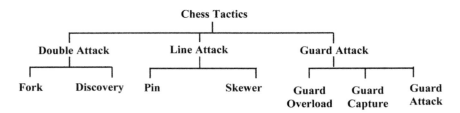

Figure 9.23

Chess Tactics Matrix

FORK	DISCOVERY	PIN	SKEWER	GUARD OVERLOAD	GUARD CAPTURE	GUARD ATTACK
One piece attacks 2 or more enemy pieces.	One piece moves exposing 2 enemy pieces to attack.	One piece attacks enemy piece and more valuable piece in line behind it.	One piece attacks enemy piece and less valuable piece in line behind it.	Enemy piece guards 2 pieces under attack. Capture 1 and then the other.	Enemy piece guards a piece under attack. Capture guard and then the other.	Enemy piece guards a piece under attack. Attack guard and capture other piece when guard moves.
Knight attacks king and queen.	Knight moves to check king and expose enemy queen to rook attack.	Bishop attacks rook and king in line behind rook.	Bishop attacks king and rook in line behind king.	Knight guards bishop and pawn. Capture knight with bishop and then capture pawn with rook.	Knight guards bishop under attack. Capture knight with bishop and then bishop with rook.	Knight guards bishop under attack. Attack knight with pawn and then capture knight or bishop.

Figure 9.24

The Chess Tactics Matrix (Figure 9.24) organizer provides each tactic's description and example so that each tactic can be learned separately and, more importantly, in conjunction with other tactics so that vital tactic associations such as the following can be made.

Associate

- All six tactics actually involve a form of double attack.
- Forks, pins, and skewers involve one piece attacking two pieces.
- Discovery, guard overload, guard capture, and guard attack involve two pieces attacking two pieces.
- There are two straight-line attacks: pins and skewers.
- There are three attacks involving guards: guard overload, guard capture, and guard attack.
- With a pin, the more important piece is second; with a skewer, the more important piece is first.
- In guard overload, the guard is neither attacked nor captured. The guard is captured in guard capture and attacked in guard attack in a two-for-one trade.
- To remember fork, think about how a fork has multiple prongs and each can attack a different pea.
- To remember discovery, think about how a new attack is discovered when something moves out of the way. Think about how you only discover what is on a computer screen when the pop-up ad is removed.
- To remember pin; think about pinning something to your clothing. It cannot move.
- To remember skewer, think about skewering vegetables on a barbeque skewer.
- To remember guard overload, think about how a bodyguard can only defend one person at a time.
- To remember guard capture, think about football. If you knock down the guard, you can get to the quarterback.
- To remember guard attack, think about an old western. If the guard is fired upon, he cannot guard his buddy trying to run behind the wagon.

Regulate

Too often, practice testing is done on a topic-by-topic basis. In math, for example, students might learn about perimeter and then are given perimeter problems to solve. Next, they might learn about area and then are given area problems to solve. This one-topic-at-a-time approach is faulty because real life does not work that way. In life, no one tells you that you have a perimeter or area problem to solve. Instead, you are confronted with unidentified problems that must be identified before solved. For example, you need to paint four walls each measuring 10 by 14 feet. Is this a perimeter problem or an area problem?

The same is true in chess, most books teach a tactic and then provide practice problems germane to just that tactic. But in a chess game, no one stands over you and says "Hey, this is a great time to use a pin tactic. See if you can find the pin." Instead, any position might invite any tactic. A player must examine all positions with those seven tactics in mind. That is why these SOAR items in Figure 9.25 assess all the possible tactics at once.

For each diagram in Figure 9.25, name the tactic opportunity shown. The first one is done for you.

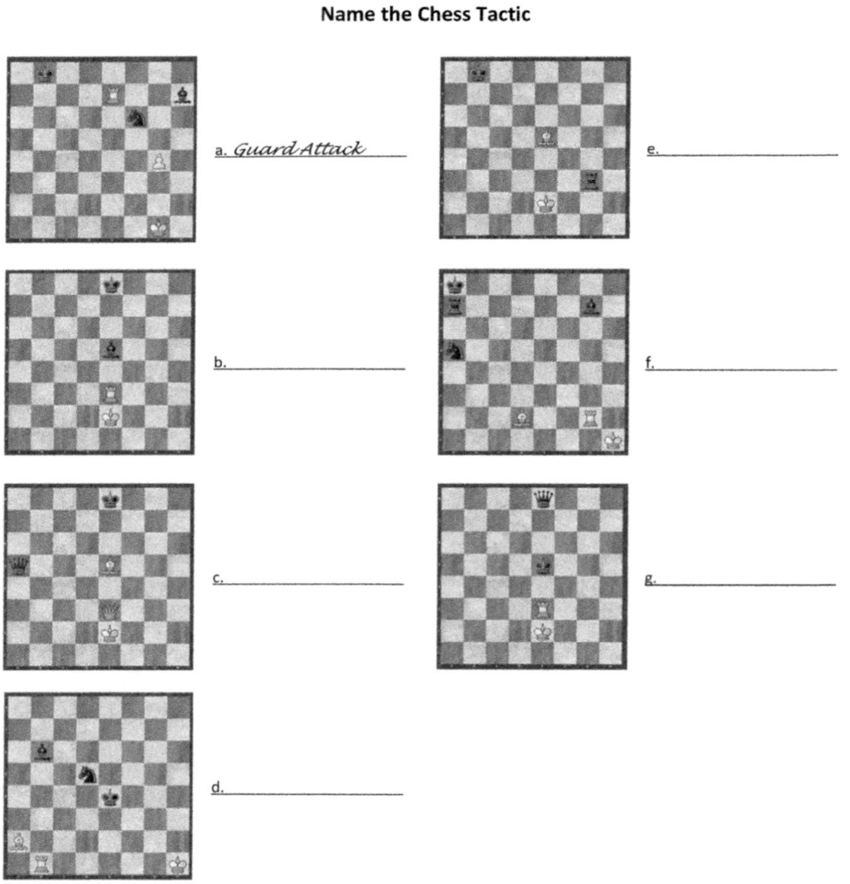

Name the Chess Tactic

a. *Guard Attack*

b. _____

c. _____

d. _____

e. _____

f. _____

g. _____

Figure 9.25

SOAR Works

Four research experiments that colleagues and I conducted prove that SOAR works.[10] In all four experiments, college students either used SOAR strategies to learn information or used their preferred strategies or the SQ3R (survey, question, read, recite, and review) study method. In some cases, SOAR materials were provided; in one case, students were trained to use SOAR in just 30 minutes. Across the four studies, SOAR students outperformed others on fact-based items (e.g., How far is Earth from the sun?) 74 percent to 60 percent, about one and a half letter grades. On relationship items (e.g., What is the relationship between revolution time and orbit speed?), SOAR students outperformed others 80 percent to 39 percent, a whopping 41 percent SOAR advantage.

How to Teach SOAR

There are two possible roads to teaching SOAR strategies and improving student learning. The first road involves teacher improvement. Make teachers so effective that students learn almost in spite of themselves. Teach teachers to teach in SOAR-compatible ways. I call this educator Teacher A. When presenting a lesson on reinforcement schedules, Teacher A might help students select information by providing prequestions that direct student's attention while reading such as "What is the difference between a fixed and variable schedule?," "Which schedule involves slow and steady responding?," or "What types of schedules are easy to extinguish?" Teacher A might also provide a set of skeletal notes that guide note taking by providing the lesson's main ideas, the bones, with spaces to fill in the lesson's details, the flesh between the bones (Figure 9.26).

Teacher A might help students organize by providing a completed matrix or a skeletal matrix that reveals the lesson's main topics, the schedules, and the categories for comparison: definition, example, response rate, and extinction (Figure 9.27). Students complete the empty cells.

Teacher A might facilitate association by providing students with associations or by prompting students to create them: Interval schedules produce _____ responding; ratio schedules produce _____ responding. _____ schedules are easy to extinguish; _____ schedules are difficult to extinguish.

Teacher A might facilitate regulation by providing students with practice questions or prompting students to construct practice questions this way: Write a question that covers the two schedules that involve pauses. Write a question that covers schedules that produce steady responding.

This road to student success is indirect because student learning depends on teacher effectiveness. The student learns well when instruction is good

Skeletal Notes

Fixed Interval
Definition _____
_____

Example _____
_____

Response rate _____
Extinction _____

Variable Interval
Definition _____
_____

Example _____
_____

Response rate _____
Extinction _____

Fixed Ratio
Definition _____
_____

Example _____
_____

Response Rate _____
Extinction _____

Variable Ratio
Definition _____
_____

Example _____
_____

Response rate _____
Extinction _____

Figure 9.26

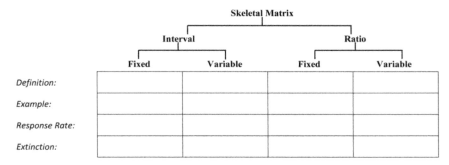

Figure 9.27

but learns little when instruction is poor. There is another problem even when instruction is good: students still do not learn how to learn on their own. For that we need a second more direct road and Teacher A+.

Teacher A+ is Teacher A plus something more. Teacher A+ teaches effectively, in SOAR-compatible ways just like Teacher A, but does one more thing: Teacher A+ teaches students how to learn. Here's how. While presenting content effectively like Teacher A, Teacher A+ also embeds strategy instruction, such as how to create a matrix, in the content lesson. While teaching math or science or history or music, Teacher A+ has the opportunity, if not the obligation, to also teach students useful strategies that they can use now and for a lifetime.

Here's an example. I was at a scholastic chess camp in Omaha, Nebraska, and attending a session taught by a New York City chess master. He stood in the front of the room beside a large demonstration board where he could make game moves for all to see. His presentation was captivating and informative. He described a game during which a battle raged in the board's center. Suddenly, the White pieces attacked along the right flank, sacrificing pawns in the hunt for bigger prey. Bishops and rooks rushed in behind their fallen comrades and knocked down the Black king's protective castle, drawing the frightened monarch into the board's center where his army afforded little protection. Suddenly the instructor turned toward a student off to one side and asked, "Can you see?" The boy sheepishly responded, "Not really, you're kind of in the way." Undaunted, the instructor calmly replied, "Well, let me teach you a little strategy." He paused for effect and then bellowed "MOVE!" as he gently escorted the student to an unoccupied center seat in the front row. "That's the strategy." He continued:

> You love chess. You want to learn chess. Your parents want you to learn chess and are paying a lot of money for you to learn chess. So, don't let this important learning opportunity escape you. When something hinders

learning, do something about it. That's really the strategy, people. Don't let learning pass you by. Take control. Do whatever you need to do to learn in that moment, including changing your seat or politely asking your teacher to move. That take-control-of-learning strategy can serve you well in chess today or in any aspect of your education down the road.

Do you see what happened? In the context of teaching chess, the instructor slipped in some needed strategy instruction germane to that moment. It was quick and seamless and could yield positive effects for a lifetime.

For the record, good strategy instruction includes five components: (1) Name the strategy. Strategies should have names so they are easy to remember and call upon. (2) Model the strategy. Strategies are skills, and skills, such as a topspin backhand in tennis, are best learned when modeled. (3) Sell the strategy. Tell the learner why it is effective and worth using. Why would a tennis player use topspin if she doesn't know it controls a shot? Why would a student take notes if he doesn't know the benefit? (4) Practice the strategy. Again, skills are never learned without practice. Provide an opportunity to practice the topspin stroke and practice recording notes. (5) Generalize the strategy. The real benefit of a strategy is that it has utility at other times in other places. Tell the learner when and where else the strategy might prove useful.

Let's see how strategy instruction might go when presenting the planets matrix (that was shown Figure 9.15) to students:

- Name: Class, I'm teaching you the matrix strategy.
- Model: Look how I created this matrix. I put the topics, the planet names, on top, categories such as moons on the side, and details in the matrix cells. For example, Mars has 2 moons.
- Sell: Isn't this matrix great? It helps you easily see relationships, such as "As revolution time increases, orbit speed decreases." We see that relationship by looking across two adjacent rows. Look at this outline covering the same planet facts. We need to look in 16 different places to potentially see that same relationship. Matrices are better than outlines for comparison.
- Practice: We also want to compare the six moons that circle Neptune. Here is information about each. Try practicing the matrix strategy with that information.
- Generalize: Of course, you don't need to be in outer space to use the matrix strategy. It is appropriate whenever there are things to compare such as rational and irrational numbers in math or the two world wars in history.

Perhaps the two roads to student success are really the same road. Ideally, teachers should emulate Teacher A by being so effective that students learn almost in spite of themselves and should also emulate Teacher A+ by embedding strategy instruction in content instruction so that students learn how to learn and can soar to success even when instruction is poor.

How are things going in schools? Are Teacher A and Teacher A+ teaching our children? Unfortunately, not so much. Instructors often teach in ways that limit learning—failing to aid SOAR strategies. My own investigation into teacher training suggests that prospective teachers are not taught in their preservice training how to design instruction that ensures student learning.[11] They are not prepared to be Teacher A. When it comes to Teacher A+, things are no better. Teachers rarely teach strategies, rarely teach students how to learn. As mentioned earlier, teachers focus on the products of learning and largely ignore the processes.

Why are teachers not teaching students how to learn? One reason is that many educators have the false belief that strategy instruction is remedial. They believe that students develop good learning strategies as naturally as they develop height and weight and that educators need not teach learning strategies. That's wrong. Learning strategies are not developed naturally. They are developed through instruction and practice just like musical and swimming talent. A second reason that teachers do not teach students how to learn is that many were not taught how to learn when they were students either. Therefore, teachers ignore strategy instruction or advocate the weak strategies they grew up on such as outlining and rehearsal.

Weak instruction and failure to teach students how to learn certainly leave students in a bad place, with weak academic skills. I have read about students' weak learning practices in research reports and seen them first-hand in college classes: students recording incomplete notes, failing to organize material, studying in a piecemeal fashion, and employing redundant strategies. These were students who learned a bit of math and science along the way but not much about learning.

What This Means for Parents

We saw in Chapter 2 that schools rarely or adequately address talent domains such as dancing, singing, and running, instead focusing on the child from the shoulders up and slightly to the brain's left side. If such talents are to grow, it is parents who must sow talent seeds and nurture talent crops. Parents have ample time and can influence talent factors. Schools meanwhile focus on academics such as math, science, English, and history. But we see in this chapter that some teachers do not make the grade teaching academic subjects. They are not Teacher A or Teacher A+, and students pay the price. So, just as talent development falls to parents, academic success to some extent does too. Parents have the opportunity, if not the obligation, to help children learn and learn how to learn. Parents can and should help children soar to success.

The opportunities are plentiful. Your youngster is interested in sea creatures or dinosaurs or fishing or cooking; the time is ripe to teach about these things and teach him how to learn. Your school child is studying art or Roman history; the time is ripe to assist in her learning and teach her how to learn. Your student struggles in math or biology. The time is ripe to remediate and teach him how to learn.

Let's look at three examples of how a parent might take on Teacher A and A+ qualities. The first involves reading to a young child. See how the parent reads the story *but also teaches strategies*. In this example, the question strategy aids regulation, the prediction strategy aids selection, and the what-I-know strategy aids association:

> For months, the weasels and the mice had been at war. *I'm going to use my question strategy here. Why have they been at war? I'm going to also use my prediction and what-I-know strategies now. I bet the weasels have won these wars, because I know that weasels are far bigger than mice.* The weasels were bigger and stronger than the mice, they won battle after battle. *See, my prediction was right.* The surviving mice called a meeting. *Hmm, I have another question: Why are they calling a meeting? I predict that they are going to discuss making peace with the weasels. Now I'll use my what-I-know strategy: That's what I'd do, because I don't believe in fighting.*
>
> "I have a plan," said one mouse. "We have lost all our battles because we do not have any leaders. I vote that we choose four mice to be our generals and lead us into battle." *Oops, my prediction was wrong. Silly mice.*
>
> The other mice agreed that this was a good idea. They chose four of their number to be generals and lead them into war. *Kaylee, why don't you use your what-I-know strategy here? What famous military generals do you know?* To show that they were generals, the four mice were given large helmets with great feathers called plumes in them. They also had large heavy badges dangling from ribbons from their necks. *Kaylee, let's have you use the prediction strategy now. What do you predict will happen in a war when these mice wear all these heavy things?*

Here is a second example that involves helping a child learn about the nervous and endocrine systems:[12]

> *Here's why you're having trouble with this material. The text presents all the information about the nervous system in one paragraph and all the information about the endocrine system in a second paragraph as if these two systems have nothing in common. That's silly. They both regulate stuff in the body. They share similarities and have differences, but the text kind of hides that stuff. Let me show you a good strategy that helps you to compare these systems. It's called the matrix strategy. We build the matrix like this (Figure 9.28) by putting the two systems on top, the categories for comparing them down the left side, and the key information in the intersecting matrix cells. . . .*

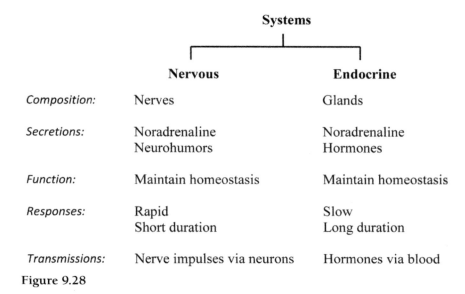

Systems

	Nervous	**Endocrine**
Composition:	Nerves	Glands
Secretions:	Noradrenaline Neurohumors	Noradrenaline Hormones
Function:	Maintain homeostasis	Maintain homeostasis
Responses:	Rapid Short duration	Slow Long duration
Transmissions:	Nerve impulses via neurons	Hormones via blood

Figure 9.28

Now that we built this matrix, we certainly don't want to try memorizing each fact separately by rehearsing each one over and over. That doesn't work. Instead, we'll use an association strategy. We'll try to associate information within the matrix—those are called internal associations—and try to associate matrix information with things we know outside the matrix—those are called external associations. Here are a few internal associations I see. Let's have you add more.

- *Both systems secrete noradrenaline. Nerves also secrete neurohumors; glands also secrete hormones.*
- *Nerves and glands maintain homeostasis.*
- *Nerves act rapidly with short duration; glands act slowly with long duration.*

Here are a few external associations I might develop. Let's have you add more.

- *Nerves are like light switches turning on and off quickly.*
- *The pain of touching a hot stove travels through nerves.*
- *In boxing, nerves are quick little jabs, and glands are big slow upper-cuts producing lasting effects.*

Here is a third example that involves a parent helping a child learn Spanish vocabulary using an association strategy called keyword:

I know a good strategy for learning language words and their meaning called the keyword strategy. It's an effective strategy because it combines two powerful things: association and imagery. Let me model it for you and then you can try.

You need to know that trigo means "wheat." Here's what we do. First, we create a keyword for trigo by associating it with a familiar English word like "tree."

Next, we associate the keyword, "tree," with the language word's definition, "wheat." We do this by creating an image that combines the two—perhaps a wheat tree. Now, when you hear or see the word trigo, *you think tree, see the wheat tree, and know that* trigo *means "wheat." Let's have you practice the keyword strategy for the next Spanish word,* carte, *which means "letter."*

Of course, the keyword strategy is effective for more than learning Spanish. For example, you can use it in your anatomy unit for learning about bones and their location. Scapula *is the shoulder blade. "Scapula" sounds like "spatula." I imagine a spatula scraping something off my shoulder blade. You can even use it in your art history class. Tchaikovsky painted Swan Lake. "Tchaikovsky" sounds like "cough-ski." I imagine a man coughing as he skies across a swan-filled lake.*

Fishing for Academic Success

Let me sum up and speak about fishing. In education, we need instructors like Teacher A who teach in ways that help students soar to success. But we need more. Recall the old adage "if you give a man a fish you feed him for a day, but if you teach him how to fish you feed him for a lifetime." Teacher A is a fish giver. And that's good; we need fish giving. We also need Teacher A+, who is a fishing teacher, teaching students how to learn so they can learn for a lifetime. Our hope is that teachers step up and assume these roles. But whether they do or not, there is plenty of room on the boat for parents to catch fish and teach fishing so their children soar to academic success.

CHAPTER TEN

Conclusion

Nurturing Children's Talents

This concluding chapter raises and answers nine talent questions and offers parting thoughts.

What Is Talent?

Some think that talent is a starting point. People are born with talent or special abilities. That's silly. No one is born playing a horn concerto or with golfing genes. Some think talent is an endpoint. People practice hard and one day become talented. This makes more sense but is limiting. What happens if you never reach talent? Did you fail? What happens when you do reach it? Does the pursuit of talent end? I think that talent is a continuum, a process of increasing growth. This process viewpoint means that all people can be somewhere on that talent continuum and that talent can grow indefinitely. There are no winners and losers, only developers. Talent is a pursuit available to all, and nothing is wasted in the pursuit of talent.

Is Talent Born or Made?

Talent is largely made. Richard Williams set out to raise tennis stars, Lazlo Polgar set out to raise chess champions, and Earl Woods set out to raise a golf-devouring Tiger. And each did just that. Psychologist John Watson famously proclaimed "Give me a dozen healthy infants, well-formed, and my own specified world to bring them up in and I'll guarantee to take any one at random and train him to become any type of specialist I might select—doctor, lawyer, artist, merchant-chief, and, yes, even beggar man and thief."[1]

Talent likely has a biological component too. Psychologist Howard Gardner contends that people have biological proclivities that favor talent growth in certain broad areas such as musical, spatial, logical, and kinesthetic. Chess champion Bobby Fischer was likely born with logical and spatial leanings, while Wolfgang Mozart was likely born with musical leanings. It is unlikely that Fischer could have been Mozart or that Mozart could have been Fischer.

But none of the famously talented people you know and that I studied could have been who they became without a constellation of environmental factors—such as good coaching and deliberate practice—firing in sync. Whatever biological hand we are dealt can be enhanced as we draw new environmental cards that support or even override biology. With the right environment, we can alter our bodies and our brains. We can make talent.

Do Environmental Factors Foster Talent?

Psychologist Benjamin Bloom, who studied 120 eminently talented individuals, concluded that "What any person in the world can learn, almost all persons can learn if provided with the appropriate conditions of learning."[2] Bloom's investigation and those since point to the six talent factors described throughout this book as being the appropriate, if not necessary, conditions of learning: (1) an enriched early environment to set one on the talent path, (2) strong mentors, (3) a long and arduous deliberate practice routine, (4) a center-of-excellence training ground, (5) a singleness-of-purpose rage to learn and achieve, and (6) a talent manager.

Most parents unfortunately don't know about these talent factors—even those who raised talented children. Several parents I interviewed said they were uncertain about how to help their increasingly talented children and consequently sort of muddled through the process. The parent of a baton twirler said, "It's all trial and error. You don't really know how it's going to turn out. Are you doing the right thing? You don't ever really know."[3] The parent of a musician said, "It's been a big fat accident. We wish we had known more. Did we get in the way? Did we hold him back? We didn't know enough." The parent of a figure skater added, "I wish there had been a manual about what was going to happen to us and what to do." Hopefully, this book can relieve uncertainty, reduce misguided trials and errors, and be that missing guide or manual that parents seek for developing children's talents.

Who Can Nurture Talent?

Children cannot nurture their own talent. They have neither the capacity nor the resources necessary to create an enriched early environment, seek and hire mentors, provide a center of talent excellence training ground, stimulate and maintain motivation, regulate practice, and manage and finance the talent enterprise. Schools, as presently arranged, cannot really do so either. They are strapped helping all students meet basic academic standards heavy on verbal and mathematical skills. Schools can help nurture academic talent in domains such as science and mathematics and can offer limited support in talent domains such as music and chess but largely ignore many talent domains such as figure skating and rodeo.

Parents are in the optimal position to nurture talent. They can provide an enriched early environment, secure mentors, regulate practice, locate or build a center of talent excellence, spur motivation, and manage all aspects of talent development. Doing all of this is no easy task. In fact, it can be life altering and require extraordinary actions and sacrifices. But the parents I interviewed often went to extraordinary lengths to fulfill these myriad roles. Parents did so because their children displayed talent development needs begging to be met and because parents loved their children and wanted them to be happy and fulfilled.

Is Talent Development for All Families?

Guiding children along the talent development continuum—in music, soccer, or academics—is a natural goal for all families. Guiding children to pursue talent at its highest levels is not for all families. If the child is not passionate about the talent domain and not committed to pursuing talent, it's game over at least for now. My son, Keaton, was not interested in chess when first introduced to it. When reintroduced later, he fell head over heels for chess. Talent development at high levels only works when the child has a single-minded passion to pursue the talent area and is willing to practice hard over an extended period. Parents cannot drive the talent train; they can only climb aboard and help guide the train. That is why so many parents told their children "We are willing to fully commit to supporting your talent adventure so long as you fully commit. Our commitment and can only match your commitment. This is your show."

Some families might have a child who wants to pursue a talent domain full bore but wonder if the child is better served being well rounded. This is a value judgment left to each family. Here, though, are some considerations. First, most talented children I studied were happy and well adapted. Most were strong students and had friends. Some participated in activities outside their talent domain. Even though they had singleness of purpose, their lives were not one-dimensional. Second, psychologist Howard Gardner, who studies extraordinary people, believes—and I concur—that it is better to spend time leveraging strengths than shoring up weaknesses.[4] The world is fast becoming a technical place where specific strengths trump general competence. Third, not pursuing one's talent might be destructive. Motivational speaker Les Brown said, "When you are not pursuing your goal, you are committing spiritual suicide."[5] Recall the chess player who was so passionate about chess that when his parents removed chess as a brief punishment, they lamented that "It was like yanking out the soul."[6]

The pursuit of supreme talent can be derailed when faint-of-heart families believe that the journey is too long. If you are in this camp, know that you are correct. The journey is long and hard for child and parents alike. Also know, however, that it is not as far as it looks. I interviewed highly productive educational psychologist Michael Pressley, who told this story: A child comes before a tribal leader for his initiation into adulthood. The boy must jump from a cliff. The leader nudges the boy toward the edge; the child peers downward and recoils in fear. The sage leader calmly says, "Go ahead and jump. It's not as far as it looks."[7]

Pressley told this story because it mirrored his own this-is-too-far thoughts as a graduate student long before becoming a top educational psychologist. Pressley said, "If anybody had told me when I was in graduate school that I'd be sitting where I am right now, I probably wouldn't have believed it, but in retrospect it isn't as far from there to here as I would have thought at the time."[8] The talent road is long but passable.

As for whether pursuing talent is right for your family, you might only realize that there is a decision to be made after the train has left the station. Many families are unaware early on that their child is on a talent track. Psychologist Benjamin Bloom wrote that only a few of the 120 talented people he studied were child prodigies, and none of them displayed talents at young ages predictive of their eventual talent status.[9] Bloom estimated that just 10 percent of the talented individuals he studied had progressed far enough by age 12 for anyone to confidently predict that they would eventually rise among the top in their talent fields. In my own investigations a figure skating parent said, "If someone had told me ten years ago that we would be where we are today, I'd have not believed it."[10] Another figure skating parent added, "When he started skating, we didn't know he was going to be this good. And, we weren't even hoping he'd be this good. It just wasn't on our radar." The parent of a twirler remarked, "I would never in a million years have thought this is what I would be doing in my lifetime."

What Are the Talent Upsides?

Talent pursuit and fulfillment has myriad benefits. First, there are enjoyment and employment. Talented people enjoy their talent domain and enjoy pursuing talent. Recall what chess parents said when asked why their sons spend so much time studying chess:

- "He is passionate about it . . . just thrilled by it. . . . . It gives him a lot of joy and satisfaction."
- "He loves it. He loves it. This is the thing he loves."
- "He loves it. He just loves it."[11]

And parents love being on the talent journey too. The parent of a figure skater said, "Skating has brought us the greatest joy. It has made the family united. Skating competitions have allowed us to see the world, learn so much, and join together. Skating has helped make us what we are as a family."[12] A chess parent wrote this about his talent development involvement: "I have no regrets because everything I did in the past has brought [my son] into my life. Everything that seemed to be a mistake or a hardship or a sacrifice was the right thing done at the right time. . . . I feel lucky to share this with my son."[13]

Many talented people turn talent enjoyment into talent employment. My own investigations have shown talented children emerging as professional musicians, coaches, photographers, writers, chess players, and volleyball, football, baseball, basketball, and skating athletes. In these ongoing roles, enjoyment continues. Fiction writer Stephen King said, "Yes, I've made a great deal of dough from my fiction, but I never set a single word down on paper with the thought of being paid for it. . . . I have written because it fulfilled me. . . . I did it for the buzz. I did it for the pure joy of the thing. And if you can do it for joy, you can do it forever."[14]

Another benefit is self-growth—not just in the talent domain but as a person. Motivational speaker Zig Ziglar said, "What you get by achieving your goals is not as important as what you become by achieving your goals."[15] Talented people become winners who are confident that they can accomplish anything they set their mind to in the same way they tamed their talent domain. They know how to achieve great things. They know how to pursue talent. Olympic speed skater Dave Cruikshank said that he brought his Olympic drive and know-how to his post-Olympic challenges developing a performance training center for ice hockey players and developing a company that produces performance apparel and gear. One chess coach remarked, "Because I was a chess master, I felt I had the confidence and knowledge to master difficult college subjects like calculus. If I could master chess, I knew I could master calculus."[16] A figure skating parent said, "[My son's] skating path put him on a path to much more. There is confidence, a strong identity, and pride—so many things other than skating success." And collegiate tennis star Joel Reckeway said that he and his brother "gave a lot to tennis, and tennis has given back to us. It has given us wonderful experiences and taught us to navigate through life, and we are better people because of it."

Talent development yields more than personal benefits; it also yields universal benefits. It yields highly talented individuals such as Wolfgang Mozart, Pablo Picasso, Charles Darwin, the Polgar sisters, and the Williams sisters, inspiring models who show the rest of us that talent is within our reach. All people can glean tips from their talent stories. They teach us, for example, to leverage our strengths and to frame our failures as opportunities for growth. Talent development yields life-altering scientific discoveries, classic literature, and inspiring Olympic performances. The world is a better and more enjoyable and inspiring place because talented people walk among us and disperse their gifts.

What Are the Talent Downsides?

There are a few potential downsides to talent development. Let me report up front, though, that I have yet to hear a talented child or parent regret pursuing talent. All embraced the opportunity and were grateful for it.

The most obvious downside is the sacrifices that children and families make. For children, there were scattered reports about missing celebrations or sleepovers or limiting other interests because of rigorous practice and competition schedules. One chess parent remarked, "The extraordinary time we put toward this one activity takes him out of a lot of fun and games. The kid gives up an enormous amount to dedicate himself to the sport the way he does."[17] That said, there were chess players participating in band or on the high school football team. A rodeo star was also the point guard on her high school basketball team. A talented violinist was also a talented baseball player. And one Nebraska student split her talent training between softball and music. Parents seem in tune with their children's heavy talent schedules and take steps to relieve pressure. One parent insists her daughter take the entire month of August off from baton twirling and go to the beach. The parent of a figure skater said, "If we're taking a family vacation or having a family dinner, or it's somebody's birthday, I make sure that we say, 'you're not skating now.' These breaks are important."[18]

For parents, there are untold sacrifices and heavy financial costs. Some families relocated, split the family in half, or sent children off on their own to talent academies. Some parents took on second and third jobs to finance talent development; others quit jobs or cut back on work to dedicate more time to coaching, managing, or homeschooling their talented offspring. Some flew or drove long distances for lessons, and others flew coaches to their homes. Most spent thousands or tens of thousands of dollars annually to finance talent development. But all parents reported that sacrifices were made willingly and lovingly for the betterment of their talented children. One parent whose teenage sons lived and trained at a tennis academy several hours from home said, "This opportunity is freely given from Mom and Dad. They're welcomed to it with no strings attached."[19]

Another downside is that sometimes the talented child's siblings receive less parental attention and resources than the talented child. One chess parent admitted that "We didn't really pursue some of our other child's interests because a lot of time was spent on him and chess. If we hadn't been doing chess activities, maybe we would have turned our focus and pursued more of [the other child's] activities."[20] The parent of a writer and public speaker also said that it was difficult to treat her two children equally. Because the parent spent so much time managing and traveling with the writer, the writer's sibling sometimes felt slighted. The parent said that if she had it to do over, she would try to provide greater balance raising her two daughters. Several families avoided sibling imbalance by one parent primarily managing one child and the other parent managing a second child. Such was the case for a Missouri family in which mom managed the daughter's twirling development and dad managed the son's baseball development. Most parents, though, strived to support all their children's inclinations, much like this chess parent: "We try to shine the spotlight on all our children. We try to make each child the star in their moment, but they also have to learn that not every moment is theirs."

The last potential downside to talent development is not letting children be children—replacing natural play with the regimented practices and competitions that often permeate talent development. Author Rachel Garlinghouse wrote that revisiting her carefree childhood—a tree house where she and her siblings played restaurant and served up birdseed soup and mud pies, a red barn for hide-and-seek, a tire swing where made-up songs were shouted, a screened-in porch where stories filled notebooks, a hill for bike riding, a water pump to quench thirst, apple trees for a snack, a moss-strewn front yard that tickled feet, and the end-of-day smell of dirt, grass-stained clothes, and sun reddened cheeks—reinforced her commitment to let her kids be kids.[21] She wrote that her kids do not need to be in a sport to learn teamwork. The three children are a team. They do not need to be in classrooms or gyms or on manicured sports fields to socialize and play. They can do that naturally and need not rely on trophies and ribbons or coaches to tell them they are fantastic. And they do not need to find their gifts at ages six, four, and two. They are free to explore myriad experiences, places, people, and things for a lifetime.

I agree with Ms. Garlinghouse, *Last Child in the Woods* author Richard Louv,[22] and others who speak for the importance of children's natural play, especially in nature's classroom. I concur too with developmental psychologists who posit that early learning should be developmentally appropriate and play based. Teaching numbers and letters outside some meaningful context is inappropriate; the aim should be enriched and fun experiences. In fact, I called for this early experience approach in Chapter 3 when I recommended offering young children a talent menu stocked with a wide array of experiences and opportunities for natural and playful interactions.

This natural approach, though, does not preclude parent interaction and can be the gateway to talent development. As a child plays and shows interest in barn swallows or harmonicas, the time is ripe for parents to feed those interests in appropriate ways. Regarding barn swallows, a parent can draw attention to the bird's forked tail and tell the legendary story of how an angry god threw fire at the bird and singed its central tail feathers, search for its cup-shaped mud nest, examine a map to chart its migration pattern, discuss how older swallow siblings help with feedings, and search for the beetles, ants, and other creatures that comprise its diet. Regarding harmonicas, a parent can join the child in a harmonica duet, share some spirited harmonica playing from the Internet, jointly experiment with different blowing and hand-cupping methods to produce different sounds, find photos of different harmonica types, and break open a cheap harmonica to explore its gadgetry. In all cases, parents should follow their children's lead and help fuel their interests. This type of interaction might be short-lived as the child loses interest in barn swallows and harmonicas in favor of medieval swords and black holes. No problem. Parents shift gears with their child, join in, and satisfy or fuel those new interests. Eventually the child might develop a thirst for something, such as baton twirling or chess, that is not quickly quenched. The child might ask more and more questions, seek materials, and seek help learning more. Before you know it, the talent train is pulling away from the station, and parents must decide whether to hop aboard or call it back to the station.

Is It Too Late to Develop Talent?

It can never be too late to board the talent train when the talent track is a begin-anywhere never-ending continuum. Although Olympic or rock star talent might take years to develop, the talent journey is the prize whether the journey lasts 10 years or 10 days and whether it begins at age 4 or age 40. The take-home message is to find your passion today and pursue it, perhaps to the winner's circle, perhaps to a personal record. As author Cathy Better wrote, "Each day that we awake is a new start, another chance. . . . Roll that day around on your tongue, relish the taste of its freedom. Breathe deeply of the morning air, savor the fragrance of opportunity. Run your hands along the spine of those precious twenty-four hours and feel the strength in that sinew and bone. Life is raw material. We are artisans. We can sculpt our existence into something beautiful or debase it into ugliness."[23] Win, lose, or draw, the pursuit of talent at any age is something beautiful.

Any Final Advice?

This is the final question I asked parents of talented children. Here is some of the advice they offered:

- Character building comes before talent building. When character is in place, talent can follow.
- Set high expectations that children will rise to.
- Have a child-centered home.
- Expose your kids to different things and see what they love, what they grab onto, what makes their heart sing.
- Do all you can to provide opportunities for your kids if they show an interest.
- The best thing you can do for children is spend time with them.
- Be sure it is really the child's vision and not yours that is guiding things.
- Remember that it is about the kids, not the parents.
- It is all about helping the child achieve to the best of his or her ability.
- Their talent needs to be expressed. It needs a platform. Parents must help with that expression and supply that platform.
- The key is surrounding them with the right people. People they can admire and look up to.
- Seek the help of people more experienced and knowledgeable. You can't be your child's only guide.
- Help them get good coaching even when they are young. Good fundamentals learned early will translate to better performance when they are older.
- Talent must be nurtured, encouraged, supported, and motivated. Behind every great athlete, there are people in the past who made a difference in the path they took and how far they went.
- Greatness requires sacrifice. Children and parents must be willing to pay the price. None of this just happens.
- It's about the process, not about winning.
- The experience of pursuing talent is what is most rewarding.
- There is always going to be someone better. You can't always win.
- There is always something to be gained from a bad experience.
- When they fall, let them learn to pick themselves up.
- Support them in the good times and in the bad times. There will be bad times.
- A parent must know when to push and when to back off.
- Keep it fun. They must want to do it. Be involved in whatever your children are involved in. Support their passion. If you don't understand the area, get educated right along with them. Be involved. Don't just hand them off to someone else and sit on the sidelines. Know the people they are working with and learning from. Live their lives with them.
- Make every moment with your kids count. Nothing beyond this moment is promised.

- Understand that talent is a vehicle for achieving other things. It opens doors to other opportunities.
- Talent is not solely for one's own good. It is for the good of humanity, the good of the world.

Parting Thoughts for Parents

I watch the play *Hamilton*, read the *Harry Potter* series, listen to a Garth Brooks song, or watch Tom Brady dice up the opposition's secondary, and I know there is greatness among us. We might believe that such greatness is god given and for the chosen, not the masses. Psychologist Benjamin Bloom concluded otherwise: What any person in the world can do, almost all can do if presented with the right conditions for learning—a constellation of important conditions such as practice, mentoring, and singleness of purpose in alignment.[24] Poet Ralph Waldo Emerson simply said, "Every artist is first an amateur."[25] Children start as a lump of clay that becomes art with skillful molding. And this is where parents come in. You are the molders. Your children's talents rest largely in your hands.

Parents as molders comes with great responsibility—a responsibility to help children find their unique element and realize their full potential. But parents and children are sometimes thrown off course by a society peddling and rewarding false ambitions. A cacophony of societal messages tells families that success comes in trophies and ribbons, in honor rolls and honor societies, and in Ivy League educations and top corporate rungs—standards based on looking good more than being good. I urge parents to ignore these commercial messages and reject meaningless races up makeshift mountains. Instead, parents should provide the footholds that raise children on their personal and joyful climbs.

Parting Thoughts for All

Parents play a central role in talent development, but must it be that way? Not all parents are equipped to play this role. They might be poor or poorly educated and content to raise children who are simply fed, safe, and good citizens—important accomplishments indeed but accomplishments light years from Carnegie Hall. Is there another way, another path, to talent development that does not rely so heavily on parents?

Let's consider a *60 Minutes* news story about how chess talent blossomed in a desolate and impoverished place where talent would not be expected to grow. The place is Franklin County, Mississippi, where "half the county is covered by national forest, the other half it seems by churches. This is the buckle of the Bible belt. Seven thousand people live here and no one's in a hurry. There are only two stop lights in the entire county and one elementary school."[26]

The Franklin County talent transformation began with a wealthy and anonymous benefactor who had seen how chess instruction bore champions and bettered lives in poverty-stricken inner-city Memphis, Tennessee. The benefactor wondered if similar results were possible in the country "where a chess board was as out of place in the county as a skyscraper."[27]

To find out, the benefactor hired Dr. Jeff Bulington, known as Dr. B, to attempt the transformation. Dr. B had a track record for success. He was the knowledgeable and charismatic teacher who brought chess to inner-city kids in Memphis. Dr. B signed a 10-year contract, signaling his commitment to work his chess-teaching magic in the county. When asked why he would teach chess in the middle of nowhere, Dr. B responded, "If there are people there, it's not nowhere. This is somewhere. It's just a somewhere that doesn't get a lot of attention."[28] Perhaps that was true when Dr. B started, but thanks to the chess Renaissance he helped create, it is not true now.

Dr. B did not do it alone; he did not teach chess on a street corner. Chess became part of the school curriculum just like math, science, and English. In fact, chess became a vehicle for teaching other subjects. As Dr. B introduced a famous game played in Paris, the chess lesson smoothly turned into a brief lesson about Paris before turning back to the game. Bobby Poole, a part-time preacher and Dr. B's full-time chess assistant, said, "We teach history. We teach geography. We teach science. We teach math. We teach it all using the chess board."[29] Consequently, chess instruction fostered personal and academic growth. One chess child remarked, "Chess is something that I'm really good at for once." Another player reported that his grades rose from low B's to high B's and A's because of chess. Before chess came to Franklin County, only 7 of 93 graduates went to college; now every player interviewed plans to attend college.

Chess lessons also extend outside the school day to an after-school chess club frequented by many chess-enthused students. The benefactor had originally thought that maybe a dozen kids would take up chess, but Dr. B reports that a couple hundred kids are involved. And when the boards and pieces are finally tucked away at day's end, chess does not end for the Franklin County kids. "They've become so immersed in the game, with its infinite number of possible moves, that when these students finish playing chess, they go home—and play more chess."[30]

At home, parents support their children's chess and see its benefits beyond winning games and trophies. One chess parent runs a café in town but believes that her son will do more than flip burgers for a living. She posited, "Is it fun to see your kids dream a little bigger than the county line?"[31] Another chess parent said, "You always want to see your kids go further. And I think chess can be a vehicle to take 'em there, you know? This gives them a window at a young age, that, 'Hey, there's a whole world out there. I don't need to set my goals at making $8 an hour, I need to set my goals at whatever I want 'em to be.'"

That chess kids and parents now envision lifetime goals that once seemed unimaginable is understandable, given that chess talent blossomed in the unlikeliest of places and in less than two years. Franklin County dominated the Mississippi state championships held in Starkville. Mitch Ham was among the many Franklin County parents there supporting the team. His assessment: "What happened is a bunch of hillbillies beat the snot out of a bunch of really highly educated, sophisticated people."[32] Regarding the winning effect on the Franklin County players, Mr. Ham added, "That was very sobering for them to suddenly realize, 'Wow, we are good.' So, them having that realization of their own potential was a beautiful moment."

After dominating the state competition, 33 chess players and their parents made the 10-hour bus trip from Franklin County to Nashville, Tennessee, for the national championships to see how they stacked up against 1,500 scholastic players from 644 schools. Results were staggering. The fifth grade team finished 8th in the country, and the sixth grade team placed 10th. Asked what the Franklin County players are capable of down the road, Dr. B confidently replied "In the top three at least."[33] When four players were asked if the world chess champion might someday emerge from Franklin County, they optimistically responded "Maybe. Absolutely. Absolutely. It's super possible."

There was another vital player in the Franklin County success story: the community. Buoyed by Franklin County's newfound chess enthusiasm and success, the community built a new chess center in the middle of Meadville, the county seat. Now each day after school, kids flock there to meet their chess friends and get more instruction from Dr. B. But the new center is more than a boost to chess; it is a boost to the community. "Chess has filled a social void and given Main Street a pulse. . . . The chess center has become a beacon in the county."[34] Asked if chess has made the community at large more hopeful, Dr. B answered, "Certainly parts of it. I mean this flower hasn't blossomed yet. It's just starting to, right? There's a lot yet to come."

The Franklin County story lays out an alternative less parent-oriented talent development path than the parent-centered stories told throughout this book. The Franklin County story does not negate or minimize the vital roles that parents have played; it offers a promising new blueprint whereby talent guidance is shared by many for the betterment of all.

The Franklin County success story is shared by a generous and insightful benefactor who sees an educational need and provides a creative solution. Much the same thing happened in New York City, where dozens of private and corporate benefactors launched and supported the Chess in Schools program, which supplies chess instruction to many schools as part of the school curriculum. An example in the arts is Mr. Holland's Opus Foundation, inspired by the motion picture *Mr. Holland's Opus* about a dedicated music teacher. The foundation donates musical instruments to underfunded music programs nationwide.

The Franklin County success story is shared by Franklin County school administrators and teachers who welcomed chess into their schools. They recognized that much was to be gained by educating children in more than math and science. Talent writer Ken Robinson admonished schools for failing to educate the whole child, instead focusing instruction from the shoulders up and slightly to the brain's academic left side.[35] I agree that schools need to widen their instructional focus beyond language, math, science, and history and help children pursue diverse interests and talents.

The Franklin County success story is shared by a community that supports its children because such support raises children to new heights and makes the community a better place for all. When communities give, communities receive.

And the Franklin County success story is shared by parents who accompany their children on chess trips, sing their praises, and help them envision a better life knowing that if they can make strong chess moves, they can make strong moves in all life's challenges.

Notes

Preface

1. M. Levine, "Raising Successful Children," *New York Times Sunday Review,* August 5, 2012, https://www.nytimes.com/2012/08/05/opinion/sunday/raising-successful-children.html.

2. K. A. Kiewra, T. O'Connor, M. McCrudden, and X. Liu, "Developing Young Chess Masters: A Collective Case Study," in *Chess in Education: Selected Essays from the Koltanowski Conference,* ed. T. Redman (Richardson: Chess Program at the University of Texas at Dallas, 2006), 104.

Chapter 1

1. Z. Ziglar, *Biscuits, Fleas, and Pump Handles* (Dallas, TX: Crescendo Publications, 1974), 171.

Chapter 2

1. H. Gardner, *Creating Minds* (New York: Basic Books, 1993), 140.

2. P. Evans, *It's Not about the Tapas* (New York: Bantam Dell, 2006), 127.

3. J. R. Hayes, "Three Problems in Teaching General Skills," in *Thinking and Learning Skills,* Vol. 2, *Research and Open Questions,* ed. J. W. Chipman, J. W. Segal, and R. Glaser (Hillsdale, NJ: Erlbaum, 1985), 391–405.

4. N. Charness, R. Krampe, and U. Mary, "The Role of Practice and Coaching in Entrepreneurial Skill Domains: An International Comparison of Life Span Chess Skill Acquisition," in *The Road to Excellence: The Acquisition of Expert Performance in the Arts and Sciences, Sports and Games,* ed. K. A. Ericsson (Mahwah, NJ: Lawrence Erlbaum, 1996), 51–80.

5. R. W. Weisberg, *Creativity: Beyond the Myth of Genius* (New York: W. H. Freeman), 1993.

6. H. Gardner, *Extraordinary Minds* (New York: Basic Books, 1997), 48.

7. J. B. Watson, *Behaviorism* (New York: People's Institute Publishing, 1924), 104.

8. A. Polgar and J. Shutzman, *Queen of the Kings Game* (New York: Comp Chess, 1997).

9. Ibid., 17.

10. B. Bloom, *Developing Talent in Young People* (New York: Ballantine Books, 1985).

11. Ibid., 4.

12. R. W. Emerson, *Letters and Social Aims* (Boston: Houghton Mifflin, 1904).

13. A. Witte, K. A. Kiewra, S. C. Kasson, and K. Perry, "Parenting Talent: A Qualitative Investigation of the Roles Parents Play in Talent Development," *Roeper Review* 37 (2015): 84–96.

14. Bloom, *Developing Talent in Young People,* 447.

15. Witte et al., "Parenting Talent."

16. Ibid., 87.

17. Ibid., 87.

18. C. L. Ott Schacht and K. A. Kiewra, "The Fastest Humans on Earth: Environmental Surroundings and Family Influences That Spark Talent Development in Olympic Speed Skaters," *Roeper Review* 40 (2018): 28.

19. Ibid., 29.

20. K. A. Kiewra, T. O'Connor, M. McCrudden, and X. Liu, "Developing Young Chess Masters: A Collective Case Study," in *Chess in Education: Selected Essays from the Koltanowski Conference,* ed. T. Redman, 98–108 (Richardson: Chess Program at the University of Texas at Dallas, 2006).

21. Witte et al., "Parenting Talent," 88.

22. Hayes, "Three Problems in Teaching General Skills."

23. Kiewra et al., "Developing Young Chess Masters."

24. K. A. Kiewra and A. Witte, "Prodigies of the Prairie: The Talent Development Stories of Four Elite Nebraska Youth Performers," *Roeper Review* 40(3) (2018): 180.

25. Bloom, *Developing Talent in Young People.*

26. A. Ericsson and R. Pool, *Peak: Secrets from the New Science of Expertise* (New York: Houghton Mifflin Harcourt, 2016).

27. K. A. Ericsson, R. T. Krampe, and C. Tesch-Romer, "The Role of Deliberate Practice in the Acquisition of Expert Performance," *Psychological Review* 100 (1993): 363–406.

28. A. Ericsson and N. Charness, "Expert Performance: It's Structure and Acquisition," *American Psychologist* 49 (1994): 744.

29. D. Coyle, *The Talent Code* (New York: Bantam Books, 2009), 52.

30. Unpublished interview.

31. S. L. Bengtsson, Z. Nagy, S. Skare, L. Forsman, H. Forssberg, and F. Ullen, "Extensive Piano Practicing Has Regionally Specific Effects on White Matter Development," *Nature Neuroscience* 66 (2005): 339–343.

32. Coyle, *The Talent Code,* 33, 44.

33. Ibid., 32–33.

34. Bloom, *Developing Talent in Young People.*

35. Kiewra et al., "Developing Young Chess Masters," 101.

36. Ibid.; K. A. Kiewra and A. Witte, "How to Parent Chess Talent: Classic and Modern Stories," in *The Nurturing of Talent, Skills and Abilities,* ed. M. Shaughnessy, 139–162 (Hauppauge, NY: NOVA Science Publishers, 2013).

37. Witte et al., "Parenting Talent," 89.

38. Unpublished interview.

39. Ibid.

40. Gardner, *Creating Minds,* 140.

41. Witte et al., "Parenting Talent."

42. Ott Schacht and Kiewra, "The Fastest Humans on Earth."

43. Kiewra and Witte, "Prodigies of the Prairie."

44. Kiewra and Witte, "How to Parent Chess Talent"; K. A. Kiewra and A. Witte, "How to Parent Baton Twirling Talent: Four Success Stories," *Talent Development and Excellence* 7 (2015): 13–27.

45. Kiewra et al., "Developing Young Chess Masters," 102.

46. Ibid.

47. Ibid., 103.

48. Ibid.

49. Unpublished interview.

50. Unpublished interview.

51. Joel Sartore, "Has Your Wife, Kathy, Recovered from Breast Cancer?," Joel Sartore: National Geographic Photographer and Speaker, https://www.joelsartore.com/about-joel/common-questions/has-your-wife-kathy-recovered-from-breast-cancer/.

52. E. Winner, "The Rage to Master: The Decisive Role of Talent in the Visual Arts," in *The Road to Excellence,* ed. K. A. Ericsson, 271–301 (Mahwah, NJ: Lawrence Erlbaum, 1996).

53. Kiewra et al., "Developing Young Chess Masters," 103.

54. Witte et al., "Parenting Talent," 90.

55. Ibid., 92.

56. Witte et al., "Parenting Talent," 90.

57. Bloom, *Developing Talent in Young People,* 474.

58. Kiewra et al., "Developing Young Chess Masters," 104.

59. Ibid., 105.

60. Witte et al., "Parenting Talent," 91.

61. K. Robinson, "Do Schools Kill Creativity," YouTube, January 6, 2007, https://www.youtube.com/watch?v=iG9CE55wbtY.

62. K. Robinson, *The Element* (New York: Viking, 2009).

63. Ibid., 3.

64. Ibid., 14.

65. J. Duggan, "Not Just Any 7-Year Old," *Lincoln Journal Star,* March 8, 1998, 1D–2D.

66. Ericsson and Pool, *Peak*, 234–235.

67. Gardner, *Creating Minds*.

68. L. M. Terman and M. Oden, *The Gifted Group at Mid-Life: Thirty-Five Years' Follow-Up of the Superior Child*. Genetic Studies of Genius, Vol. 5 (Stanford, CA: Stanford University Press, 1947).

69. H. Gardner, *Frames of Mind: The Theory of Multiple Intelligences* (New York: Basic Books, 2011).

70. H. Gardner, *Creativity & Leadership: In Depth* (n.p.: Into the Classroom Media, 1998).

71. Unpublished interview.

72. Kiewra and Witte, "Prodigies of the Prairie," 182.

73. Kiewra and Witte, "How to Parent Chess Talent," 146.

Chapter 3

1. K. A. Kiewra and A. Witte, "How to Parent Chess Talent: Classic and Modern Stories," in *The Nurturing of Talent, Skills and Abilities*, ed. M. Shaughnessy, 139–162 (Hauppauge, NY: NOVA Science Publishers, 2013).

2. K. A. Kiewra and A. Witte, "How to Parent Baton Twirling Talent: Four Success Stories," *Talent Development and Excellence* 7 (2015): 13–27.

3. R. Merton, "The Matthew Effect in Science," *Science* 159 (1968): 56–63.

4. B. Bloom, *Developing Talent in Young People* (New York: Ballantine Books, 1985).

5. D. Coyle, *The Talent Code* (New York: Bantam Books, 2009), 45.

6. Kiewra and Witte, "How to Parent Baton Twirling Talent."

7. K. A. Kiewra and A. Witte, "Prodigies of the Prairie: The Talent Development Stories of Four Elite Nebraska Youth Performers," *Roeper Review* 40(3) (2018): 176–190.

8. Kiewra and Witte, "How to Parent Baton Twirling Talent," 16.

9. Ibid., 18.

10. Kiewra and Witte, "How to Parent Chess Talent."

11. Kiewra and Witte, "Prodigies of the Prairie," 184.

12. Ibid., 185.

13. Ibid., 183.

14. C. L. Ott Schacht and K. A. Kiewra, "The Fastest Humans on Earth: Environmental Surroundings and Family Influences That Spark Talent Development in Olympic Speed Skaters," *Roeper Review* 40 (2018): 28–29.

15. J. B. Watson, *Behaviorism* (New York: People's Institute Publishing, 1924), 104.

16. H. Gardner, *Creativity & Leadership: In Depth* (n.p.: Into the Classroom Media, 1998).

17. Unpublished interview.

18. Ibid.

19. Joel Sartore, "How Did You Get Interested in Nature and the Environment?," Joel Sartore: National Geographic Photographer and Speaker, https://

www.joelsartore.com/about-joel/common-questions/how-did-you-get-interested
-in-nature-and-the-environment/.

20. Unpublished interview.

21. Robert J. R. Graham, "The Expert Mind—A Method to Mastery," Robert JR Graham, August 30, 2015, http://robertjrgraham.com/the-expert-mind-a-method -to-mastery/.

22. H. Gardner, *Frames of Mind: The Theory of Multiple Intelligences* (New York: Basic Books, 2011).

23. Gardner, *Creativity & Leadership.*

24. K. Robinson, *The Element* (New York: Viking, 2009).

25. Unpublished interview.

26. A. Witte, K. A. Kiewra, S. C. Kasson, and K. Perry, "Parenting Talent: A Qualitative Investigation of the Roles Parents Play in Talent Development," *Roeper Review* 37 (2015): 87.

27. Ibid.

28. Bloom, *Developing Talent in Young People.*

29. F. Waitzkin, *Searching for Bobby Fischer* (New York: Penguin, 1988), 123.

30. Ibid., 104.

31. Ibid., 4.

32. G. Robson, *Chess Child: The Story of Ray Robson, America's Youngest Grandmaster* (Seminole, FL: Nipa Hut, 2010).

33. Ibid., 125.

34. Ibid., 224.

35. Ibid., 132.

36. Kiewra and Witte, "Prodigies of the Prairie," 181.

37. Ibid., 181–182.

38. Bloom, *Developing Talent in Young People,* 474.

39. Witte et al., "Parenting Talent," 91.

40. Bloom, *Developing Talent in Young People.*

41. Witte et al., "Parenting Talent," 92–93.

42. Ott Schacht and Kiewra, "The Fastest Humans on Earth," 31.

43. M. Patterson-Hazley and K. A. Kiewra, "Conversations with Four Highly Productive Educational Psychologists: Patricia Alexander, Richard Mayer, Dale Schunk, and Barry Zimmerman," *Educational Psychology Review* 25 (2013): 28.

44. Ibid.

45. A. Lareau, *Unequal Childhoods* (Berkeley: University of California Press, 2003).

46. J. Waitzkin, *The Art of Learning* (New York: Free Press, 2007), 9–10.

47. M. Gladwell, *Outliers* (New York: Little, Brown, 2008).

48. Ibid., 28.

49. D. Whitmore Schanzenbach and S. Howard Larson, "Is Your Child Ready for Kindergarten? 'Redshirting' May Do More Harm Than Good," *Education Next* (Summer 2017): 24.

50. J. Spelman, "Redshirting: Should We Give Kids the 'Gift of Time' in Youth Sports?," Land O' Moms, June 25, 2015, http://www.landomoms.com/parenting/ redshirting-should-we-give-kids-the-gift-of-time-in-youth-sports-2.

51. "Probability of Competing beyond High School," NCAA, http://www.ncaa.org/about/resources/research/probability-competing-beyond-high-school.

52. K. A. Kiewra, T. O'Connor, M. McCrudden, and X. Liu, "Developing Young Chess Masters: A Collective Case Study," in *Chess in Education: Selected Essays from the Koltanowski Conference,* ed. T. Redman, 98–108 (Richardson: Chess Program at the University of Texas at Dallas, 2006).

53. Bloom, *Developing Talent in Young People.*

54. Robinson, *The Element.*

55. H. Gardner, *Extraordinary Minds* (New York: Basic Books, 1997).

Chapter 4

1. The epigraph is from Goodreads, https://www.goodreads.com/quotes/156646-practice-makes-the-master.

2. M. Syed, *Bounce: Mozart, Federer, Picasso, Beckham, and the Science of Success* (New York: HarperCollins, 2010), 61–62.

3. Ibid., 62.

4. Ibid.

5. G. Colvin, *Talent Is Overrated: What Really Separates World-Class Performers from Everybody Else* (New York: Penguin, 2008), 103.

6. W. G. Chase and H. A. Simon, "Perception in Chess," *Cognitive Psychology* 4 (1973): 55–81.

7. Ibid.

8. Syed, *Bounce,* 50.

9. J. Waitzkin, *The Art of Learning* (New York: Free Press, 2007).

10. Ibid., 145–146.

11. Ibid., 148.

12. "Jim Ryun Quotes," Brainy Quote, https://www.brainyquote.com/quotes/jim_ryun_127356.

13. B. Bloom, *Developing Talent in Young People* (New York: Ballantine Books, 1985), 485.

14. "Jascha Heifetz Quotes," Brainy Quote, https://www.brainyquote.com/quotes/jascha_heifetz_114403.

15. A. Witte, K. A. Kiewra, S. C. Kasson, and K. Perry, "Parenting Talent: A Qualitative Investigation of the Roles Parents Play in Talent Development," *Roeper Review* 37 (2015): 91.

16. K. A. Kiewra and A. Witte, "Prodigies of the Prairie: The Talent Development Stories of Four Elite Nebraska Youth Performers," *Roeper Review* 40(3) (2018): 181.

17. Witte et al., "Parenting Talent," 91.

18. Kiewra and Witte, "Prodigies of the Prairie," 180.

19. K. A. Kiewra and A. Witte, "How to Parent Baton Twirling Talent: Four Success Stories," *Talent Development and Excellence* 7 (2015): 21.

20. Ibid., 24.

21. Ibid., 19.

22. Kiewra and Witte, "Prodigies of the Prairie," 184.

23. Witte et al., "Parenting Talent," 90.

24. Colvin, *Talent Is Overrated,* 3.

25. D. Coyle, *The Talent Code* (New York: Bantam Books, 2009), 102–106.

26. Colvin, *Talent Is Overrated,* 71.

27. Waitzkin, *The Art of Learning,* 47.

28. Ibid., 110–111.

29. Ibid., 111.

30. G. Robson, *Chess Child: The Story of Ray Robson, America's Youngest Grandmaster* (Seminole, FL: Nipa Hut, 2010), 20.

31. Waitzkin, *The Art of Learning,* 226.

32. Ibid., 228.

33. Unpublished interview.

34. "Colin Powell Quotes," Brainy Quote, https://www.brainyquote.com /quotes/colin_powell_121363.

35. "James A. Michener Quotes," Brainy Quote, https://www.brainyquote .com/quotes/james_a_michener_116031.

Chapter 5

1. C. Dweck, *Mindset: The New Psychology of Success* (New York: Random House, 2016).

2. Unpublished interview.

3. D. Coyle, *The Talent Code* (New York: Bantam Books, 2009), 165.

4. Ibid., 166–170.

5. D. Chatelain, "Mad Chatter: Are Huskers Tired of the 3-Stripe Life?; Feedback on Aguek Arop; Tom Osborne's Psychology Lesson," *Omaha World Herald,* August 26, 2016, http://www.omaha.com/huskers/blogs/bigred/mad-chatter -are-huskers-tired-of-the—stripe-life/article_abcb3778-6ba8-11e6-b66e -0fbae975ba82.html.

6. Ibid.

7. Coyle, *The Talent Code,* 186–187.

8. K. A. Kiewra and A. Witte, "Prodigies of the Prairie: The Talent Development Stories of Four Elite Nebraska Youth Performers," *Roeper Review* 40(3) (2018): 181.

9. Ibid.

10. B. Bloom, *Developing Talent in Young People* (New York: Ballantine Books, 1985).

11. A. Witte, K. A. Kiewra, S. C. Kasson, and K. Perry, "Parenting Talent: A Qualitative Investigation of the Roles Parents Play in Talent Development," *Roeper Review* 37 (2015): 88.

12. G. Robson, *Chess Child: The Story of Ray Robson, America's Youngest Grandmaster* (Seminole, FL: Nipa Hut, 2010), 15.

13. K. A. Kiewra and A. Witte, "How to Parent Chess Talent: Classic and Modern Stories," in *The Nurturing of Talent, Skills and Abilities,* ed. M. Shaughnessy (Hauppauge, NY: NOVA Science Publishers, 2013), 147–148.

14. Witte et al., "Parenting Talent," 89.

15. Unpublished interview.

16. Witte et al., "Parenting Talent," 89.

17. J. Waitzkin, *The Art of Learning* (New York: Free Press, 2007), 81.

18. Ibid., 83.

19. Unpublished interview.

20. Witte et al., "Parenting Talent," 89.

21. K. A. Kiewra and A. Witte, "How to Parent Baton Twirling Talent: Four Success Stories," *Talent Development and Excellence* 7 (2015): 13–27.

22. Unpublished interview.

23. Witte et al., "Parenting Talent," 89.

24. Ibid.

25. Unpublished interview.

26. Ibid.

27. Ibid.

28. Ibid.

29. Kiewra and Witte, "Prodigies of the Prairie," 180.

30. Ibid., 181.

31. Ibid., 180.

32. Witte et al., "Parenting Talent," 89–90.

33. Ibid., 90.

34. F. Waitzkin, *Searching for Bobby Fischer* (New York: Penguin, 1988), 123.

35. Witte et al., "Parenting Talent," 89.

36. Kiewra and Witte, "How to Parent Baton Twirling Talent."

37. Ibid., 23.

38. Ibid.

39. Kiewra and Witte, "How to Parent Chess Talent," 151.

40. Witte et al., "Parenting Talent," 90.

41. Robson, *Chess Child*, 199.

42. Ibid., 149.

43. K. A. Kiewra, T. O'Connor, M. McCrudden, and X. Liu, "Developing Young Chess Masters: A Collective Case Study," in *Chess in Education: Selected Essays from the Koltanowski Conference,* ed. T. Redman (Richardson: Chess Program at the University of Texas at Dallas, 2006), 104.

Chapter 6

1. K. A. Kiewra and J. W. Creswell, "Conversations with Three Highly Productive Educational Psychologists: Richard Anderson, Richard Mayer, and Michael Pressley," *Educational Psychology Review* 12 (2000): 135–161.

2. Ibid.

3. A. Flanigan, K. A. Kiewra, and L. Luo, "Conversations with Four Highly Productive German Educational Psychologists: Frank Fischer, Hans Gruber, Heinz Mandl, and Alexander Renkl," *Educational Psychology Review* 30 (2018): 303–330.

4. Ibid., 316.

5. C. L. Ott Schacht and K. A. Kiewra, "The Fastest Humans on Earth: Environmental Surroundings and Family Influences That Spark Talent Development in Olympic Speed Skaters," *Roeper Review* 40 (2018): 21–35.

6. Ibid., 26.

7. Ibid.

8. Ibid., 27.

9. Ibid.

10. Ibid.

11. Ibid., 28.

12. Ibid.

13. M. Syed, *Bounce: Mozart, Federer, Picasso, Beckham, and the Science of Success* (New York: HarperCollins, 2010), 15.

14. D. Coyle, *The Talent Code* (New York: Bantam Books, 2009).

15. F. Waitzkin, *Searching for Bobby Fischer* (New York: Penguin, 1988), 14.

16. "About IMG Academy," IMG Academy, https://www.imgacademy.com/about-img-academy.

17. Unpublished interview.

18. "Nebraska Volleyball History & Records," Huskers, http://www.huskers.com/ViewArticle.dbml?&DB_OEM_ID=100&ATCLID=211516229.

19. K. A. Kiewra, T. O'Connor, M. McCrudden, and X. Liu, "Developing Young Chess Masters: A Collective Case Study," in *Chess in Education: Selected Essays from the Koltanowski Conference,* ed. T. Redman, 98–108 (Richardson: Chess Program at the University of Texas at Dallas, 2006); K. A. Kiewra and A. Witte, "How to Parent Chess Talent: Classic and Modern Stories," in *The Nurturing of Talent, Skills and Abilities,* ed. M. Shaughnessy, 139–162 (Hauppauge, NY: NOVA Science Publishers, 2013).

20. F. Brady, *Bobby Fischer: Profile of a Prodigy* (New York: Dover, 1973), 3.

21. J. Waitzkin, *The Art of Learning* (New York: Free Press, 2007), 5.

22. Kiewra et al., "Developing Young Chess Masters," 99.

23. Kiewra and Witte, "How to Parent Chess Talent," 146.

24. Ibid., 147.

25. J. Sock, "Family over Everything," The Players' Tribune, January 13, 2017, https://www.theplayerstribune.com/en-us/articles/family-over-everything.

26. R. Powell, "Empty Nest: Reckeweys Leave Home for Tennis," *Lincoln Journal Star,* June 28, 1998, 1C, 3C.

27. Ibid.

28. Unpublished interview.

29. "Camelot: Frederick Loewe," Genius Lyrics, https://genius.com/Frederick-loewe-camelot-lyrics.

30. K. A. Kiewra and A. Witte, "How to Parent Baton Twirling Talent: Four Success Stories," *Talent Development and Excellence* 7 (2015): 24.

31. Kiewra and Witte, "How to Parent Chess Talent."

32. D. Woods, "Olympic Skiing Favorite Nick Goepper Got His Start in Indiana," *IndyStar,* January 16, 2014, https://www.indystar.com/story/sports/2014/01/16 /olympic-skier-nick-goepper-got-his-start-in-indiana/4541159/.

Chapter 7

1. "If You Want a Thing Bad Enough . . .—Les Brown," LinkedIn, January 15, 2016, https://www.linkedin.com/pulse/you-want-thing-bad-enough-les-brown -andre-rynhardt-barnard.

2. M. Csikszentmihalyi, *Creativity: Flow and the Psychology of Discovery and Invention* (New York: Harper, 1996), 14.

3. K. A. Kiewra, T. O'Connor, M. McCrudden, and X. Liu, "Developing Young Chess Masters: A Collective Case Study," in *Chess in Education: Selected Essays from the Koltanowski Conference,* ed. T. Redman (Richardson: Chess Program at the University of Texas at Dallas, 2006), 102.

4. Joel Sartore, "Has Your Wife, Kathy, Recovered from Breast Cancer?," Joel Sartore: National Geographic Photographer and Speaker, https://www.joelsartore.com /about-joel/common-questions/has-your-wife-kathy-recovered-from-breast-cancer/.

5. B. Bloom, *Developing Talent in Young People* (New York: Ballantine Books, 1985), 484.

6. Kiewra et al., "Developing Young Chess Masters," 104.

7. A. Bandura, "Influence of Models' Reinforcement Contingencies on the Acquisition of Imitative Responses," *Journal of Personality and Social Psychology* 1 (1965): 589–595.

8. Unpublished interview.

9. C. L. Ott Schacht and K. A. Kiewra, "The Fastest Humans on Earth: Environmental Surroundings and Family Influences That Spark Talent Development in Olympic Speed Skaters," *Roeper Review* 40 (2018): 28.

10. K. A. Kiewra and A. Witte, "Prodigies of the Prairie: The Talent Development Stories of Four Elite Nebraska Youth Performers," *Roeper Review* 40(3) (2018): 181.

11. Ibid., 183.

12. Ibid., 184.

13. D. Coyle, *The Talent Code* (New York: Bantam Books, 2009), 108.

14. Ibid., 109.

15. Ibid., 105–106, 111.

16. Ibid., 116.

17. Unpublished interview.

18. A. Witte, K. A. Kiewra, S. C. Kasson, and K. Perry, "Parenting Talent: A Qualitative Investigation of the Roles Parents Play in Talent Development," *Roeper Review* 37 (2015), 88.

19. K. A. Kiewra and A. Witte, "How to Parent Baton Twirling Talent: Four Success Stories," *Talent Development and Excellence* 7 (2015), 23.

20. Kiewra et al., "Developing Young Chess Masters," 100.

21. Kiewra and Witte, "Prodigies of the Prairie," 185.

22. Bloom, *Developing Talent in Young People,* 37.

23. Ibid., 73.

24. Ibid., 37.

25. Ibid., 481.

26. Ibid., 38.

27. Ibid., 481.

28. Ibid.

29. Ibid., 482.

30. Ibid., 38.

31. Ibid., 483.

32. C. Dweck, "The Perils and Promises of Praise," *Educational Leadership* 65 (2007): 34–39.

33. R. Riley, "Strongest Dad in the World," *Sports Illustrated,* June 20, 2005, 88.

34. R. W. White, "Motivation Reconsidered: The Concept of Competence," *Psychological Review* 66 (1959): 297–333.

35. Bloom, *Developing Talent in Young People,* 485.

36. J. Waitzkin, *The Art of Learning* (New York: Free Press, 2007), 33.

37. E. Winner, "The Rage to Master: The Decisive Role of Talent in the Visual Arts," in *The Road to Excellence,* ed. K. A. Ericsson, 271–301 (Mahwah, NJ: Lawrence Erlbaum, 1996).

38. Bloom, *Developing Talent in Young People.*

39. A. Ericsson and R. Pool, *Peak: Secrets from the New Science of Expertise* (New York: Houghton Mifflin Harcourt, 2016).

40. Csikszentmihalyi, *Creativity,* 107.

41. Kiewra et al., "Developing Young Chess Masters," 103.

42. B. Killigrew, "Player of the Month: Maurice Ashley," *Chess Life* 54(5) (May 1999): 340–342.

43. M. Csikszentmihalyi, *Flow: The Psychology of Optimal Experience* (New York: HarperCollins, 1990).

44. Csikszentmihalyi, *Creativity,* 121.

45. Bloom, *Developing Talent in Young People,* 55.

46. Ibid., 65.

47. M. Syed, *Bounce: Mozart, Federer, Picasso, Beckham, and the Science of Success* (New York: HarperCollins, 2010).

48. Killigrew, "Player of the Month," 342.

49. Syed, *Bounce,* 209.

50. S. Silverstein, *Where the Sidewalk Ends* (New York: HarperCollins, 1974), 64.

51. "The Meaning and Origin of the Expression: To Travel Hopefully Is a Better Thing Than to Arrive," Phrase Finder, https://www.phrases.org.uk/meanings/387450.html.

52. Waitzkin, *The Art of Learning,* 46.

53. H. Gardner, *Creating Minds* (New York: Basic Books, 1993).

54. Lisette Hilton, "Jansen Persevered Despite Olympic Disappointments," ESPN Classic, http://www.espn.com/classic/biography/s/Jansen_Dan.html.

55. H. Gardner, *Extraordinary Minds* (New York: Basic Books, 1997).

56. Waitzkin, *The Art of Learning,* 108.

57. "Michael Jordan Quotes," Brainy Quote, https://www.brainyquote.com /quotes/michael_jordan_127660.

58. "Quotes for Positive Living," The Daily Motivator, http://greatday.com /q/?q=2020.

59. A. Bandura, "Perceived Self-Efficacy in Cognitive Development and Functioning," *Educational Psychologist* 28 (1993): 117–148.

60. A. Kitsantas and B. J. Zimmerman, "Comparing Self-Regulatory Processes among Novice, Non-Expert, and Expert Volleyball Players: A Microanalytic Study," *Journal of Applied Sports Psychology* 14 (2010): 91–105.

61. R. Rosenthal and L. Jacobson, "Pygmalion in the Classroom," *Urban Review* 3 (1968): 16–20.

62. Unpublished interview.

63. Ibid.

64. Kiewra et al., "Developing Young Chess Masters," 103.

65. Ibid., 103–104.

66. Witte et al., "Parenting Talent," 93.

67. Ibid.

68. Waitzkin, *The Art of Learning,* 17.

69. Witte et al., "Parenting Talent," 92.

70. K. A. Kiewra and A. Witte, "How to Parent Chess Talent: Classic and Modern Stories," in *The Nurturing of Talent, Skills and Abilities,* ed. M. Shaughnessy (Hauppauge, NY: NOVA Science Publishers, 2013), 155.

71. C. Davis, "Teen Tommy John Surgeries, Youth Sports Injuries Reach Epidemic Proportions," *Sun Sentinel,* June 28, 2018, http://www.sun-sentinel.com /sports/fl-sp-tommy-john-youth-injuries-20180618-story.html.

72. Ibid.

73. Jaimie Duffek, "Specialization or Multisport Participation? Here's What the Data Says," *USA Today,* February 8, 2018, https://usatodayhss.com/2018 /specialization-or-multisport-participation-heres-what-the-data-says.

74. Ibid.

75. Kiewra et al., "Developing Young Chess Masters," 104.

76. Ibid., 105.

77. Henry Emerson Fosdick quotation, PassItOn, https://www.passiton.com /inspirational-quotes/5383-no-steam-or-gas-drives-anything-until-it-is.

78. Les Brown quotation, Quotefancy, https://quotefancy.com/quote/853069 /Les-Brown-When-you-are-not-pursuing-your-goal-you-are-literally-committing -spiritual.

79. Woodrow Wilson quotation, AZ Quotes, http://www.azquotes.com /quote/1138033.

80. Killigrew, "Player of the Month," 340–342.

Chapter 8

1. Information in this section comes from an interview with Joyce Svitak, mother of Adora. Some quotations appear in part in A. Witte, K. A. Kiewra, S. C. Kasson, and K. Perry, "Parenting Talent: A Qualitative Investigation of the Roles Parents Play in Talent Development," *Roeper Review* 37 (2015): 84–96.

2. K. A. Kiewra and A. Witte, "Prodigies of the Prairie: The Talent Development Stories of Four Elite Nebraska Youth Performers," *Roeper Review* 40(3) (2018): 185. Information in this section comes from interviews with McKenzie Steiner and her parents, softball coach, and bandmate; some quotations appear in part in Kiewra and Witte, "Prodigies of the Prairie."

3. Ibid., 185.

4. Ibid.

5. Ibid.

6. Ibid., 186.

7. Unpublished interview.

8. Ibid.

9. Ibid.

10. Witte et al., "Parenting Talent," 90, 93.

11. Unpublished interview.

12. G. Robson, *Chess Child: The Story of Ray Robson, America's Youngest Grandmaster* (Seminole, FL: Nipa Hut, 2010), 125.

13. Unpublished interview.

14. Unpublished interview.

15. K. A. Kiewra and A. Witte, "How to Parent Chess Talent: Classic and Modern Stories," in *The Nurturing of Talent, Skills and Abilities,* ed. M. Shaughnessy (Hauppauge, NY: NOVA Science Publishers, 2013), 120; Unpublished interview.

16. K. A. Kiewra, T. O'Connor, M. McCrudden, and X. Liu, "Developing Young Chess Masters: A Collective Case Study," in *Chess in Education: Selected Essays from the Koltanowski Conference,* ed. T. Redman (Richardson: Chess Program at the University of Texas at Dallas, 2006), 103.

17. Unpublished interview.

18. Ibid.

19. Ibid.

20. Ibid.

21. Ibid.

22. K. A. Kiewra and A. Witte, "How to Parent Baton Twirling Talent," *Talent Development and Excellence* 7 (2015), 25.

23. Unpublished interview.

24. Kiewra and Witte, "How to Parent Baton Twirling Talent," 20.

25. Kiewra and Witte, "How to Parent Chess Talent," 151.

26. Robson, *Chess Child,* 41.

27. Unpublished interview.

28. Ibid.

29. Ibid.

30. Ibid.

31. Unpublished interview.

32. Ibid.

Chapter 9

1. T. Daher and K. A. Kiewra, "An Investigation of SOAR Study Strategies for Learning from Multiple Online Resources," *Contemporary Educational Psychology* 46 (2016): 10–21; D. Jairam, K. A. Kiewra, S. Rogers-Kasson, M. Patterson-Hazley, and K. Marxhausen, "SOAR versus SQ3R: A Test of Two Study Systems," *Instructional Science* 41 (2013): 409–420; D. Jairam and K. A. Kiewra, "Helping Students Soar to Success on Computers: An Investigation of the SOAR Study Method," *Journal of Educational Psychology* 102 (2010): 601–614; D. Jairam and K. A. Kiewra, "An Investigation of the SOAR Study Method," *Journal of Advanced Academics* 20 (2009): 602–609.

2. K. A. Kiewra, *Learn How to Study and SOAR to Success* (Upper Saddle River, NJ: Pearson Prentice Hall, 2005); K. A. Kiewra, *Teaching How to Learn: The Teacher's Guide to Student Success* (Thousand Oaks, CA: Corwin, 2009).

3. Symbiosis material adapted from Kiewra, *Teaching How to Learn,* 40.

4. K. A. Kiewra, "A Review of Note Taking: The Encoding-Storage Paradigm and Beyond," *Educational Psychology Review* 1 (1989): 147–172.

5. Planet material adapted from Kiewra, *Teaching How to Learn,* 6–7.

6. Medical marijuana information and image retrieved from James, "King MAP: Medical Marijuana Laws State by State," Brookings, April 11, 2016, https://www.brookings.edu/blog/brookings-now/2016/04/11/map-medical-marijuana-laws-state-by-state/.

7. Musical instruments example adapted from Kiewra, *Teaching How to Learn,* 45.

8. Experimental procedure material adapted from Kiewra, *Learn How to Study and SOAR to Success,* 56.

9. Dollar bill and telephone material from Kiewra, *Teaching How to Learn,* 68.

10. Daher and Kiewra, "An Investigation of SOAR Study Strategies for Learning from Multiple Online Resources"; Jairam, Kiewra, Rogers-Kasson, Patterson-Hazley, and Marxhausen, "SOAR versus SQ3R"; Jairam and Kiewra, "Helping Students Soar to Success on Computers"; Jairam and Kiewra, "An Investigation of the SOAR Study Method."

11. K. A. Kiewra and P. S. Gubbels, "Are Educational Psychology Courses Educationally and Psychologically Sound? What Textbooks and Teachers Say," *Educational Psychology Review* 9 (1997): 121–149.

12. The nervous and endocrine systems example were adapted from Kiewra, *Teaching How to Learn,* 73–74.

Chapter 10

1. J. B. Watson, *Behaviorism* (New York: People's Institute Publishing, 1924), 104.

2. B. Bloom, *Developing Talent in Young People* (New York: Ballantine Books, 1985), 4.

3. K. A. Kiewra and A. Witte, "How to Parent Baton Twirling Talent: Four Success Stories," *Talent Development and Excellence* 7 (2015): 17.

4. H. Gardner, *Creativity & Leadership: In Depth* (n.p.: Into the Classroom Media, 1998).

5. The Les Brown quotation is from Quote Fancy, https://quotefancy.com /quote/853069/Les-Brown-When-you-are-not-pursuing-your-goal-you-are-liter ally-committing-spiritual.

6. K. A. Kiewra, T. O'Connor, M. McCrudden, and X. Liu, "Developing Young Chess Masters: A Collective Case Study," in *Chess in Education: Selected Essays from the Koltanowski Conference,* ed. T. Redman (Richardson: Chess Program at the University of Texas at Dallas, 2006), 103.

7. K. A. Kiewra and J. W. Creswell, "Conversations with Three Highly Productive Educational Psychologists: Richard Anderson, Richard Mayer, and Michael Pressley," *Educational Psychology Review* 12 (2000): 135–161.

8. Ibid., 154.

9. Bloom, *Developing Talent in Young People.*

10. Unpublished interview.

11. Kiewra et al., "Developing Young Chess Masters," 103.

12. A. Witte, K. A. Kiewra, S. C. Kasson, and K. Perry, "Parenting Talent: A Qualitative Investigation of the Roles Parents Play in Talent Development," *Roeper Review* 37 (2015), 91.

13. G. Robson, *Chess Child: The Story of Ray Robson, America's Youngest Grandmaster* (Seminole, FL: Nipa Hut, 2010), 249.

14. "Stephen King on Writing for the Money," Kaye Dacus Humor, Hope, and Happily Ever Afters, May 20, 2014, https://kayedacus.com/2014/05/20/stephen -king-on-writing-for-the-money/.

15. Z. Ziglar, *Biscuits, Fleas, and Pump Handles* (Dallas, TX: Crescendo Publications, 1974), 171.

16. Unpublished interview.

17. Kiewra et al., "Developing Young Chess Masters," 102.

18. Witte et al., "Parenting Talent," 93.

19. R. Powell, "Empty Nest: Reckeweys Leave Home for Tennis," *Lincoln Journal Star,* June 28, 1998, 3C.

20. Kiewra et al., "Developing Young Chess Masters," 104.

21. R. Garlinghouse, "The Best Gifts I Can Give My Children to Ensure Their Success," Huffington Post, December 6, 2017, https://www.huffingtonpost.com /rachel-garlinghouse/the-best-gifts-i-can-give-my-children-to-ensure-their -success_b_7186792.html.

22. R. Louv, *Last Child in the Woods* (Chapel Hill, NC: Algonquin Books, 2008).

23. Reprinted in K. A. Kiewra, *Learn How to Study and SOAR to Success* (Upper Saddle River, NJ: Pearson Prentice Hall, 2005), 155.

24. Bloom, *Developing Talent in Young People.*

25. R. W. Emerson, *Letters and Social Aims* (Boston: Houghton Mifflin, 1904).

26. Sharyn Alfonsi, "Chess Instills New Dreams in Kids from Rural Mississippi County: Grade-School Chess Teams from Franklin County, Mississippi, Blow Past Stereotypes about Who Can Play Chess and Win National Recognition," CBS News, June 18, 2017, https://www.cbsnews.com/news/chess -instills-new-dreams-in-kids-from-rural-mississippi-county/.

27. Ibid.

28. Ibid.

29. Ibid.

30. Ibid.

31. Ibid.

32. Ibid.

33. Ibid.

34. Ibid.

35. K. Robinson, "Do Schools Kill Creativity," YouTube, January 6, 2007, https://www.youtube.com/watch?v=iG9CE55wbtY.

Index

About the Author

Kenneth A. Kiewra is a professor of educational psychology at the University of Nebraska–Lincoln. He earned his PhD in educational psychology from Florida State University and was also on the faculty at Kansas State University and Utah State University. His research pertains to the SOAR teaching and study method he developed and to talent development, particularly the roles that parents play. Kiewra has published more than 100 articles, authored 3 other books (*Learning to Learn: Making the Transition from Student to Life-Long Learner; Learn How to Study and SOAR to Success;* and *Teaching How to Learn*), and has made presentations to over 500 educational or corporate groups. Dr. Kiewra is also the former director of the University of Nebraska's Academic Success Center and the former editor of *Educational Psychology Review*. He can be contacted via his website, https://cehs.unl.edu /kiewra/, which showcases other talent-related projects.

DEVOTIONS EMPOWERED BY
BIBLICAL STATEMENTS OF FAITH

GOD
IS

KEN HEMPHILL

PUBLISHING GROUP

NASHVILLE, TENNESSEE

KINGDOM PROMISES: GOD IS

B&H Publishing Group
Nashville, Tennessee
www.BHPublishingGroup.com

Dewey Decimal Classification: 242.5
God—Attributes /
Devotional Literature / God—Name

Printed in the United States
1 2 3 4 5 12 11 10 09 08

I dedicate this book to my wife Paula's
sister and her husband:

{ Jimmy and Gretchen Epting }

Jimmy and Gretchen's love for
students has been evident in the growth
of North Greenville University,
where Christ makes the difference!
The rebirth of that school
demonstrates "God Is"
all we need.

PREFACE

Studying God's Word always brings its own rewards. I have been deeply moved by the study of these simple statements that are scattered throughout the Word of God. It is my prayer that they will minister in your life as they have mine. I thank you for your willingness to buy this book and allow me to be your guide as the Holy Spirit informs your mind and transforms your heart.

As always, I am indebted to my wife, who is my partner in ministry and my encourager in this ministry of writing. She brings the order and solitude to our home that makes it possible for me to reflect and write. She is often the source of ideas that soon appear in my books. Our devotional times together frequently become theological discussions which enrich my understanding.

My children are a constant joy to me, and our growing family provides a rich context for writing. Tina and Brett have been blessed with a daughter, Lois, who is as active as her "papa." Rachael and Trey have a daughter, Emerson, and a new son, Ward, whose smiles light up a room. Katie and Daniel and their daughter Aubrey are even further blessings from the Lord. My family is the context for my entire ministry.

I want to thank Morris Chapman, the visionary, former leader of the Southern Baptist Convention, for calling our denomination to focus on God's kingdom. He gave me freedom to write the things God laid on my heart. All of my colleagues at the Executive Committee of the Southern Baptist Convention have encouraged me in this phase of ministry.

As usual, the good folks at Broadman and Holman have been my partners in this ministry. I am challenged by the trust they place in me and inspired by their integrity. I can't begin to express my gratitude to Lawrence Kimbrough, my partner in this writing adventure. Lawrence is far more than an editor. He is a friend, colleague, and artist. What he does with a rough draft is a thing of beauty.

This book is somewhat of a new genre. It looks like a daily devotional in its format, but it is written to be "bite-sized" theology.

I have attempted to explain each of these great Kingdom Promises in its original context and then to apply it to life. Thus, I highly recommend that you read this book with your Bible open, because the focal passages will have the greatest impact on you as you see them in context. You might also want to consider using these verses as a Scripture memory project while you're reading.

I pray God will use his Word to bring encouragement to your heart. And if this book of Kingdom Promises speaks life to you and ministers to your needs, I hope you'll pass it along to someone else.

Ken Hemphill
Travelers Rest, South Carolina
Spring 2008

GOD IS
THE ALPHA

{ **Revelation 1:8** I am the Alpha and the Omega . . . the One who is, who was, and who is coming, the Almighty. }

He is the beginning and the end—and the Lord of everything in between! What an incredible statement! But that is precisely what this verse indicates.

When we speak of Jesus being the Alpha or the "first," we are speaking of his pre-existence—the fact that he has always been. *Alpha* is the first letter of the Greek alphabet. *Omega* is the last. By this affirmation, then, John was pointing to Christ's preeminence both in terms of authority and eternity.

Writing also in his Gospel (chapter 8), John recorded an interesting conversation between Jesus and the Jewish leaders. Jesus referred to the fact that their father Abraham had been overjoyed to know that he would witness Jesus' appearance. They responded that Jesus was not even fifty years old. How could he claim to have seen Abraham? Jesus responded, "I assure you:

'Before Abraham was, I am'" (John 5:58).

His listeners, shocked at what they were hearing, picked up rocks to stone him for such brazen blasphemy. They knew that Jesus' declaration of his preexistence, as well as his use of the name "I am" in reference to himself, was an affirmation that he was (and is) God, both pre-existent and self-existent, needing nothing else to create him.

Paul wrote about Jesus as the Alpha in Colossians 1:17–18. "He is before all things . . . the beginning, the firstborn from the dead, so that He might come to have first place in everything."

Jesus is timeless. The fullness of God indwells him. Therefore he is the only means of redemption and reconciliation between God and man. Everything rides on this singular affirmation. If Christ is not eternal, he is a created being, and therefore he lacks the quality of God.

But I have good news: he is the Alpha. No matter your present circumstances, he is sovereign God and he will bring his kingdom to victory. Now one question: Is Jesus the Alpha (the first) in your life?

GOD IS
OUR ADVOCATE

> **1 John 2:1** If anyone does sin, we have an advocate with the Father—Jesus Christ the righteous One.

We have witnessed several trials in the last several years involving well-known people. As we follow these cases in the newspaper or on television, we are given a great deal of information about the famous lawyers who have been hired to defend the people convicted of the crime. I know if I were accused of a crime, I would want the best person available to be my advocate.

John declared that we have one. Jesus is our Advocate.

Having a top-rate advocate, of course, might cause a client to become cavalier about sin, to think he could get away with anything. John addressed this without delay. He indicated that his purpose in writing his letter was "so that you may not sin" (verse 1). By indicating that we have an advocate, therefore, John was not suggesting that sin should be seen as a light matter. Still, we need to know that sin is not impossible to remedy. When Christians sin, we have an advocate with the Father.

The word translated "advocate" is used by John in his Gospel to refer to the Holy Spirit, who is our "Helper" or "Counselor" (John 14:16, 26). In 1 John, however, he used it to refer to Jesus, who pleads our case with the Father, who comes alongside us in our time of need as our spokesman.

Yes, our advocate is none other than Jesus Christ, the righteous one. It is the glorified and perfected Christ who pleads our case. He alone is qualified to represent those less righteous than himself before holy God. The entire picture points us to the high priestly role of Jesus, who became our holy and blameless sacrifice and who lives forever to be our advocate before the throne of God, ensuring that our sins do not hinder our constant fellowship with the Father.

This beautiful reality should relieve us of any anxiety about our salvation. But further, it should keep us from any desire to sin. If he died for us and continues to advocate our case for us, our greatest desire should be to live in holiness.

GOD IS
THE ALMIGHTY

> **Revelation 15:3** Great and
> awe-inspiring are Your works,
> Lord God, the Almighty.

We marvel at mighty people —
powerful politicians, bigger-than-life
athletes, wealthy individuals who could
buy and sell most of us many times over.
We have a fascination with strength and
might, whether it be megawatts, money, or
horsepower. But all the mighty persons in
our pantheon of heroes have weaknesses.
Only Christ is the Almighty.

In this chapter from Revelation, John
spoke of the seven last plagues as being
poured out on the earth — God's wrath
against sin. The sea of glass is mixed with
fire, symbolizing God's judgment. The
martyrs are standing by (or "on") the sea.
They are singing the song of Moses and the
Lamb — a song of deliverance. They know
that nothing evil can triumph over God's
people, for he is the Almighty.

The word translated "Almighty" is a
composite of two Greek words translated

"all" and "ruler." The Almighty is one without possibility of equal. When those who have "won the victory from the beast" hail Jesus as "Lord God, the Almighty," (verse 2), they are declaring that his power is unlimited. The power of the beast and the false wonders he has worked on the earth cannot compare with the "great and awe-inspiring" works of God.

Notice further in this verse that the thought moves from awe-inspiring power to righteousness and truth. Furthermore, he is "King of the Nations." This not only speaks to his universal sovereignty but of his heartbeat for the peoples of the world, a consistent theme of the entire Bible — particularly of the book of Revelation. The final victory for the nations has been won by the power of the cross of Christ and heralded by the testimony of his followers.

In the darkest hour of human history, when it seems the god of this age has won, the conquerors will sing a song of praise to the Almighty. Have you been singing the song of the Lamb today? Sing it whatever your circumstances, because the final victory has been won. He is the Almighty!

GOD IS
THE AMEN

> **Revelation 3:14** To the angel
> of the church in Laodicea
> write: "The Amen, the faithful
> and true Witness."

Anyone who has attended a church
service has heard someone utter the word
"amen." Perhaps it was spoken reverently
at the end of a heartfelt prayer. In some
contexts, it may have been shouted boister-
ously by someone who agreed with a major
point of the message. What, then, does it
mean to call Jesus the "Amen"?

The verse above is in a section of
Revelation where the seven churches are
being addressed, and the church of the
moment is the church in Laodicea. It was
located at the junction of the Lycus and
Maeander valleys at the convergence of
three important roads. It was one of the
richest commercial centers in the world,
noted for its banking and manufacture of
clothing from local black wool.

The church in Laodicea was established by the preaching of Epaphras (Col.
1:7 and 4:12–13). But its spiritual condition

had deteriorated to such an extent that it received the severest condemnation of the seven mentioned in Revelation. They are indicted for being "lukewarm" (verse 16), a spiritual condition which had resulted from their great material wealth.

In contrast to the unfaithful people of Laodicea, Jesus is said to be "the Amen, the faithful and true witness." *Amen* is a Hebrew word whose root meaning contains the idea of strength, firmness, and integrity. The idea is that God is faithful, reliable, and trustworthy. He can be trusted to keep his covenant.

Isaiah 65:16 speaks of God in the same manner: "Whoever is blessed in the land will be blessed by the God of truth." The word "Amen" as applied to Christ guarantees the truthfulness of his words, which is further defined by his title as the "faithful and true Witness."

The word "amen" reminds us that Jesus is God's "yes" to all of his promises. How would it change your attitude today knowing that Christ, through his life and character, is your assurance that all of God's promises are true?

GOD IS
THE AUTHOR & FINISHER

> **Hebrews 12:1–2** (NASB) Let us run with endurance the race set before us . . . fixing our eyes on Jesus, the author and perfecter of our faith.

Little things have a way of burning themselves into your memory bank. For example, I loved to go down to our garden with my dad. He was a little old-fashioned, and thus he liked to plow with a mule rather than a tractor. I enjoyed watching the battle of wills as my dad worked with an old mule that was nearly as stubborn as he was.

Once in a while, he would let me put my hands on the plow handles and guide the process. After finishing a row, I would look back with frustration to see that my row wandered across the hillside while Dad's seemed perfectly straight. He told me the secret was to focus on a tree or stump on the other side of the field and go straight for it.

In our present context, the author of Hebrews described life as a race to be run, an enduring struggle. And he told us if we want to run successfully, we need more than just the encouragement of a large crowd of witnesses surrounding us. We must keep our eyes on the goal.

Our focal point for the race is not a mere marker in the distance but a person — Jesus. As the "author," he is the source, guide, or pioneer of the successful race. He has already been down this path. Of course, his was not an easy race. He "endured a cross and despised the shame." But as the "finisher," he is the lone example of one who completed the race successfully, the one who has now become our guide and example for life, start to finish. He is now exalted at the right hand of the Father.

What motivated him to run the race with such focus and victory? He did so for the joy that lay before him, the joy of eternal sonship.

When you find yourself struggling in the journey, when you look back and see that you've plowed a crooked row, focus on Jesus and rejoice in his promises. When you consider eternity, you often find your present challenges becoming relatively insignificant.

GOD IS
THE BELOVED SON

> **Matthew 3:17** There came a
> voice from heaven: "This is
> My beloved Son. I take delight
> in Him!"

I am blessed to be the father of three
wonderful girls. They are now married
adults, two with children of their own.
But even though they are grown, I love
to affirm my girls, and they love to hear it.
It doesn't surprise me, then, that on three
separate occasions, God spoke from heaven
affirming his Son, twice with the simple
affirmation—"This is My beloved Son."

I think it is important that the first time
this occurred, it happened before Jesus
had begun any of his earthly ministry. The
Father's words must have steeled the Son
in his resolve to obey and glorify him.

This statement is drawn from Psalm
2:7—"You are My Son; today I have
become Your Father," as well as Isaiah
42:1—"This is My Chosen One; I delight
in Him." It was not as if Jesus in this
moment became something he wasn't.
He was eternally God's Son, the Davidic

Messiah, the Suffering Servant who would die for the sins of his people.

In Matthew 17, we are privileged to listen in once again, hearing the Father declare that he delights in his beloved Son. This time, the Father gave a command— "Listen to Him!" The command is a present imperative in the Greek, indicating that the disciples should *always* listen to him. He speaks with the authority of God, for the beloved Son is the Word of God.

The final word of affirmation from the Father takes a little different form, but it makes essentially the same point. Jesus had just predicted his own crucifixion. The Son then cried out to the Father, requesting only that the Father glorify his own name. The word from the Father was succinct but clear—"I have glorified it, and I will glorify it again!" (John 12:28). The beloved Son had lived in such a way that people had seen him and recognized his Father. Now he would die in such a manner that he would glorify the Father.

How wonderful to hear the Father declare, "Well done, good and faithful servant."

GOD IS
THE BREAD OF LIFE

> **John 6:35** "I am the bread
> of life," Jesus told them.
> "No one who comes to Me
> will ever be hungry."

One of my favorite Bible stories as a
child was the feeding of the five thousand.
I don't know if it was the sheer magnitude
of the miracle or the fact that a young lad
was given the opportunity to participate in
it, but I loved to read that story.

This story actually provides the setting for the first of seven emphatic "I am"
statements of Jesus—"I am the bread of
life." After feeding the five thousand, he
had withdrawn to join his disciples the
next day in Capernaum. When the crowd
discovered that he had departed, they got
into their boats and headed to Capernaum
looking for him.

There he confronted them with this
truth: they were seeking him only because
he had provided a free meal. They tried to
avoid his accusation by asking him what
kind of sign he would give them to encourage their belief, like when Moses provided

their forefathers manna in the wilderness. Wouldn't that make them more likely to believe in him?

Jesus quickly corrected their misunderstanding. The manna had not been provided by Moses. It had come from God the Father; therefore, it was life-giving and abundant. "For the bread of God is the One who comes down from heaven and gives life to the world" (verse 33). There is no room for misunderstanding—Jesus himself is the "bread of life."

This great "I am" statement has clear overtones of divinity and links our life in the closest fashion with Christ. He is the bread who gives and sustains spiritual life. When we feast on him, we are assured of being constantly satisfied. Our only hunger will be for more of him.

My mom had a simple formula for determining whether I was sick or not: my appetite. In much the same way, spiritual hunger is a pretty good sign of one's spiritual well-being. Do you hunger for the Bread of Life? Are you feasting on his Word? Are you seeking his presence in prayer? Then expect to be filled.

GOD IS
THE BRIGHT MORNING STAR

> **Revelation 22:16** I am the Root
> and the Offspring of David, the
> Bright Morning Star.

The darkness of night can be terrifying.
The smallest sound is magnified. The least
movement takes on frightening proportions. But the morning star that proclaims
the advent of dawn changes everything. I
can still hear my dad's words, "Son, everything will look different in the morning."

John's readers were living in dark
days filled with intense persecution. They
needed reassurance that a new day was
dawning. And they found it in Jesus. He
was not only the man who lived and died in
Palestine; He is the Messiah—"the Root
and the Offspring of David."

We could actually isolate "Root and
Offspring of David" as a separate title,
but when linked with Bright Morning Star,
it carries an even greater impact. The
first-century readers would have remem-
bered the promise of Isaiah 11:1—"A shoot
will grow from the stump of Jesse, and a

branch from his roots will bear fruit." But note the subtle yet significant alteration. Jesus declared that he is actually the root from which David grew. He is the very source of the Davidic line! Only one who is eternal can be both root and offspring.

So the Bright Morning Star heralds the dawning of a new day. This reference recalls the prophecy of Balaam. In Numbers 22–24, we find the intriguing story of Balaam, a prophet hired to curse Israel. In his final oracle, he declared, "I see him, but not now; I perceive him, but not near. A star will come from Jacob" (Num. 24:17). The Jewish people had long understood this as messianic prophecy.

In our sky, the "morning star" is the planet Venus. In ancient times Venus was seen as a symbol of victory and sovereignty over the nations. Roman generals sought the morning star as a good omen. But where Christ is present, the night is truly passing and a new day is dawning. The Lord of history is the crucified and risen Christ in whom a new day has been heralded and will soon be seen in its full glory.

GOD IS
CAPTAIN OF OUR SALVATION

> **Hebrews 2:10 (NKJV)** It was
> fitting for Him . . . to make the
> captain of their salvation perfect
> through sufferings.

I had the privilege of being pastor in
Norfolk, Virginia, to a large number of our
military, and I gained a great appreciation
for those whose rank made them leaders.
They not only gave orders; they led by
pace and example. They blazed the way
and represented well those who served
under them.

In the book of Hebrews, Jesus is
described as the "captain" of our salvation.
The word translated "captain" is variously
translated as "founder, author, or source."
These all point to the same truth: Jesus is
the means through which God has made
possible our redemption.

Man was created by God for his
glory, and yet we have been prevented
from attaining that glory by sin. It was
therefore "fitting" or "appropriate" for God
to provide a way to bring many sons to
glory. It was consistent with the character

of our loving and merciful God to provide a means of redemption.

We cannot overlook the fact that this required the suffering of his Son. It is in the self-giving of the Son that we see God's heart laid bare. It is "in Christ" that God was at work "reconciling the world to Himself" (2 Cor. 5:19). "He made the One who did not know sin to be sin for us, so that we might become the righteousness of God in Him" (2 Cor. 5:21). How can mortal man ever understand the depth of God's love that led him to give his own Son to atone for our sins?

Yet here it is in its stark reality. The captain of our salvation was made "perfect through sufferings." This does not suggest that Jesus was morally imperfect prior to his death. (This is explicitly denied in Hebrews 4:15, where he is shown to be "tested in every way as we are, yet without sin.") Rather, his death is described as perfectly completing his life and purpose, enabling him to purchase salvation for us, thus becoming our captain, our pathfinder.

Do you know the captain of salvation, and are you following his commands?

GOD IS
THE CHIEF SHEPHERD

> **1 Peter 5:4** When the chief Shepherd appears, you will receive the unfading crown of glory.

There are perhaps few images of Jesus that evoke more emotion than that of the shepherd. When I was a child attending Sunday school, we received colored cards with pictures of biblical scenes and Scripture verses. I particularly loved the picture of Jesus with a small sheep over his shoulders.

And to prove we don't change much as we grow up—at a shop I've visited in the Holy Land that sells olive wood carvings, the two items most in demand are the nativity set and the Good Shepherd.

In the verse above, Peter was exhorting his fellow church leaders to shepherd those under their leadership freely and joyously. Like a shepherd, they were to lead as examples and not to lord their authority over the sheep. In response, the "chief Shepherd" would give them an "unfading crown" upon his return. The adjective translated "unfading" referred to an amaranth, a flower which doesn't wither and revives when moistened with water.

Earlier in this same letter, Peter first introduced the shepherd idea: "For you were like sheep going astray, but you have now returned to the shepherd and guardian of your souls" (1 Pet. 2:25). The writer of Hebrews likewise referred to Jesus as the great "Shepherd of the sheep" (Heb. 13:20).

One wonders whether the New Testament writers chose this analogy because of the beautiful image of the shepherd in Psalm 23. Yet they likely had something else in mind, for Jesus stood out in contrast to perhaps the greatest threat of all to the early church—false shepherds. "I am the good shepherd," Jesus said by comparison. "The good shepherd lays down his life for the sheep" (John 10:11). "I know My own sheep, and they know Me" (John 10:14).

Therefore, he is the model for all other shepherds—not just church leaders but also parents who desire to guide their own children. Look to the chief Shepherd.

GOD IS
THE CORNERSTONE

> **Ephesians 2:20** [You are] built
> on the foundation of the apostles
> and prophets, with Christ Jesus
> Himself as the cornerstone.

In this section of Ephesians, Paul was celebrating the fact that Jew and Gentile alike have access through one Spirit to the Father. Thus, he declared that they are no longer "foreigners and strangers, but fellow citizens with the saints, and members of God's household, built on the foundation of the apostles and prophets" (v. 19).

Perhaps that last phrase sounds inaccurate to you. You may be thinking of 1 Corinthians 3:11, where Paul stated that Christ *alone* was the foundation. You are correct. Yet there is no contradiction here, just a difference in emphasis. The church stands on a totally unique event—of which Christ is the center—but the apostles and prophets fulfilled a foundational role, bearing witness to Christ and ministering through his church (see Eph. 3:5 and 4:11).

Yet our focus should always be on the cornerstone—the central foundational stone which binds the whole structure together and serves as the stone of testing. It shows whether the building carries out the master architect's specifications. The use of "cornerstone" in reference to Christ not only denotes his position of honor. It also implies that each successive stone must be fitted into him if it is to discover its place and usefulness in the building.

This imagery of "cornerstone" has great Old Testament lineage. The psalmist declared, "The stone that the builders rejected has become the cornerstone" (Ps. 118:22). The prophet Isaiah wrote: "Look, I have laid a stone in Zion, a tested stone, a precious cornerstone, a sure foundation; the one who believes will be unshakable" (Isa. 28:16). The apostle Peter used this imagery to speak of the crucified and resurrected Lord when called before the rulers of the Jews (Acts 4:11). Is it any wonder that he would use the cornerstone imagery on three occasions in his letter?

When you believe in Christ, you can "never be put to shame" (1 Pet. 2:6). When everything around you seems to be unstable, you can build upon the Cornerstone.

GOD IS
OUR COUNSELOR

> **Isaiah 9:6** He will be named
> Wonderful Counselor, Mighty
> God, Eternal Father, Prince
> of Peace.

We seem to have plenty of counselors today. We have both the secular and the Christian varieties, the paid and the unpaid, the good and the bad, the invited and the uninvited. It seems like everyone has a solution to our problems . . . even if they can't solve their own! A good counselor will listen, empathize, and point the way to healing, perfectly balancing grace and truth.

And during the dark days in which Isaiah wrote, the people were in great need of one. So he swept back the dark clouds, promising that the gloom of the distressed land would one day be lifted, and those "walking in darkness" would admit to seeing "a great light."

The cause of this celebration would be the birth of a child. But not just any child! The breadth of what is said of him so far exceeds human boundaries, even the most profound skeptic would have trouble arguing that the prophet had an earthly prince in mind. He must have been looking forward to the day of the Messiah, the Anointed One, the rightful King.

Isaiah saw the child with the royal symbol of government flowing from his shoulders, yet the child was so glorious that one name proved insufficient to describe him. Therefore we find five descriptive titles, including this one: Counselor.

In chapter 11, the prophet identified him as a shoot growing from the stump of Jesse. "The Spirit of the Lord will rest on Him—a Spirit of wisdom and understanding, a Spirit of counsel and strength, a Spirit of knowledge and of the fear of the Lord" (verse 2). This coming one was to be the counselor of his people.

Look at Jesus later as he counseled the woman taken in adultery. He offered her grace but confronted her with the truth. Yes, we have a perfect Counselor in Jesus. But to benefit from his counseling, we must be willing to listen to him, meditating on his Word, and taking his prescription for our healing: our total obedience.

GOD IS
OUR CREATOR

> **Colossians 1:16** By Him everything was created . . . all things have been created through Him and for Him.

The Bible begins with the incredible affirmation that the entire creation—all of nature and the whole of mankind—are the love gift of God. They all function for him. Nothing exists apart from him, and everything exists for him.

But nowhere do we find a more eloquent statement of this truth than in Paul's great hymn in praise of the cosmic Christ. In verse 15, Paul declared him to be the "firstborn over all creation." As the context makes clear, this in no way suggests that Christ is *part* of creation. On the contrary, he stands above and beyond creation. "Firstborn" denotes both priority in time and supremacy in rank.

Paul made it crystal clear that Christ is the firstborn precisely because he made all things, and therefore everything owes its very existence to him. Everything came into being *by* him, *through* him and *for* him.

It came into being *by* (or *in*) him because it occurred in the sphere of his person and power; *through* him, because he was the mediating agent through which it came to be; and *for* him, in the sense that he is the end purpose for which all things exist. The created purpose of everything on earth is to bear witness to him and thus to contribute to his glory.

Also, don't miss the emphasis on the totality of Christ's creative activity — "everything" and "all things." Paul further clarified this by listing Christ's creation of things "in heaven and on earth, the visible and the invisible, whether thrones or dominions or rulers or authorities." It is possible that this list includes a supposed hierarchy of spiritual beings that the false teachers of Paul's day found fascinating. But whatever spiritual beings exist, Christ is both before them and over them.

There are people still today, of course, who are fascinated by spiritual powers and beings, who chase after the new age rage. But why would anyone find such inferior spiritual beings intriguing when they can know and worship the Creator of all?

GOD IS
OUR DELIVERER

> **Romans 11:26 (NASB)**
> The Deliverer will come
> from Zion, He will remove
> ungodliness from Jacob.

In my many preaching engagements, I have the privilege of worshiping in a variety of churches with different worship traditions. I have learned to experience God's presence in these various musical contexts. Yet while I enjoy the freedom of much of the contemporary praise songs, I sometimes miss the depth of teaching in many of the great hymns of the faith.

An eighteenth century hymn, "Guide Me, O Thou Great Jehovah" by William Williams, speaks with great passion about the Lord as our deliverer: "Open now the crystal fountain, / Whence the healing stream doth flow, / Let the fire and cloudy pillar / Lead me all my journey through; / Strong Deliverer, be Thou still my strength and shield."

Paul, speaking about the unfolding of God's plan of salvation in history, looked to the day when all Israel would be saved.

The phrase "all Israel" does not mean every Jew without exception. Rather, it refers to Israel as a whole. In this context, Paul was concerned about the restoration of Israel to gospel favor and blessing as they turned from unbelief to repentance and faith in Christ.

The imagery behind the word "Deliverer" or "Liberator" is a powerful one. The picture that first comes to mind is that of a commanding officer who has just liberated a people held captive. We have all seen such images on television at the end of a long and costly battle.

Our Deliverer set us free from godlessness by taking away our sin. The Bible is clear about man's condition—he is enslaved to sin and thus held captive to death. But Christ is our Deliverer, ready to free us from the restraints of sin, to provide liberty and release from the power of sin and the penalty of death.

Have you met the Deliverer? He stands ready to take away your sins. If you already have a personal knowledge of him, does your life and demeanor give testimony that you have been delivered from sin?

GOD IS
THE DOOR

> **John 10:9** I am the door. If anyone enters by Me, he will be saved and will come in and go out and find pasture.

When I was a child, there was a popular game show that hid prizes behind three doors. The participants had to choose one of the three to unveil their prize. There was always a bit of mystery and anxiety as the prize behind the door was revealed. Sometimes the participant selected the door with the booby prize. But when Jesus declared that he is "the door," he made it clear what we would find.

If you read this passage in its entire context (verses 7–18), you see that Jesus repeated the declaration that he is "the door" in verses 7 and 9. In the first one, he pointed to himself as the singular, authentic point of entry, that all who came before him were thieves and robbers. This is a clear reference to false teachers whose only desire was the destruction of the sheep.

In contrast, Jesus promised that those who enter through him will be saved. He alone is the agent of wholeness and eternal life. His very purpose in coming to earth was that those who enter through him might "have life and have it in abundance" (verse 10).

It is possible that the image of the door is also tied to the reference of him as one who "lays down his life for his sheep" (verse 11). The ancient shepherd would gather his sheep into the fold and lay his own body over the entrance, preventing any of the sheep from leaving and also keeping any wild animals out. Jesus is the door of entrance at the cost of his life.

Yet the door has at least two other functions. First, it emphasizes security and safe haven for those within the sheepfold. And secondly, the reference to the sheep who "come in and go out and find pasture" indicates that Jesus provides for all the needs of the sheep. They have free, secure movement and rich pasture as they go in and out through him.

I'm glad that when I entered in through "the door," I wasn't holding my breath to see what was behind it. I found eternal life in him.

GOD IS
THE EVERLASTING FATHER

> **Isaiah 9:6** For a child will be born for us, a son will be given to us. . . . He will be named . . . Eternal Father.

The term "Father" has great meaning to me. My father was my pastor, my friend, my confidant, my counselor. Yes, I was a "preacher's kid," but I never had even the slightest desire to live in rebellion from the principles my dad taught me. In truth, I wanted to embody his godly teaching because I saw the integrity of his life and I knew of his passionate love for me.

The early disciples must have been shell-shocked when Jesus taught them to address the sovereign God of the universe with the intimate term "Father," translated from the Aramaic *abba*. This word was certainly one of endearment and intimacy that transcended their expectations. Paul wrote in Romans 8:15, "For you did not receive a spirit of slavery to fall back into fear, but you received the Spirit of adoption, by whom we cry out, 'Abba, Father!'" Through Christ, he had become a son —

a spiritual reality that seemed to never stop astonishing Paul all the days of his life.

We have already looked at Isaiah 9:6 in our consideration of Christ as our Counselor. We will have occasion to look at it on three other occasions later in this book, but here our focus is on Jesus as the "Eternal" or "Everlasting Father"—the Father of all eternity.

This mention of "eternity" indicates a timeless quality. It means his kingdom has no end. Only one who possesses eternity in his own being can give everlasting life, and this is the nature of the God we serve. Yet it not only speaks of eternity; it speaks of intimacy. This great King of ours cares for his children like a loving father. As the eternal or everlasting Father, he is always present and ever caring.

In Matthew 7:11, Jesus spoke to this intimate care. If an earthly Father knows how to give good gifts to his children, how much more does God desire to give good things to his? I confess that I miss my earthly dad, but I rejoice that in Christ I have an everlasting Father who always cares for me.

GOD IS
THE FAITHFUL WITNESS

{ **Revelation 1:4–5** Grace and
peace to you . . . from Jesus
Christ, the faithful witness, the
firstborn from the dead. }

We have all seen enough courtroom
dramas to know that an entire case can
turn on the integrity and reliability of a
witness. If one of the lawyers can catch a
witness in an untruth or a half-truth, the
entire case can fall like a house of cards.

John began the book of Revelation
by calling Jesus as a "faithful witness."
Christ's purpose, in fact, had always been
to obey his Father and make his name
known. Think for a moment about the
great prayer that stands at the end of his
earthly ministry: "I have glorified You on
the earth by completing the work You gave
Me to do" (John 17:4). He further indicated, "I have revealed Your name to the
men You gave Me from the world" (17:6).
In his life and through his death, Jesus was
indeed a "faithful witness."

In addition — by virtue of his resurrection — he became the "firstborn of the

dead." We will return to this great title of Jesus in the next reading, but his resurrection also proved him to be a faithful witness to the Father, "established as the powerful Son of God by the resurrection from the dead" (Rom. 1:4).

His coming, too, while revealing him as the ruler over all earthly kings when he establishes his own people "as a kingdom, priests to His God and Father" (Rev. 1:6), will also show him to be a faithful witness of God's eternal reality. John must have had in mind the promise recorded in Psalm 89:27 — "I will also make him My firstborn, greatest of the kings of the earth."

This must have seemed an incredible statement to John's first readers. By all appearances Rome ruled without rival. But the "faithful witness" assured them that beyond the chaos of what appeared, the Son was seated at the right hand of the Father, ruling over all rulers, now and forevermore. Though they were facing the supreme trial of their faith, they could be assured that they had a "faithful witness" — one who was unerring, unimpeachable, and unchanging. So can we.

GOD IS
THE FIRST AND THE LAST

> **Revelation 1:17–18** I am the
> First and the Last, and the Living
> One. I was dead, but look — I am
> alive forever and ever.

Our mind cannot comprehend something being both first and last. But such is the character of our wonderful Savior. He is "the First and the Last."

This phrase, combined with the phrase "the Living One," is an exposition of the truth contained in our earlier discussion of Christ as "the Alpha and the Omega" (Rev. 1:8). This affirmation majestically declares that Christ stands above all limitations of time. He is eternally "the Living One."

John's use of this title links the affirmation of Isaiah 44:6 with the covenant name Yahweh—meaning "I Am"—that was given at the burning bush. Listen with awe to Isaiah 44:6—"This is what the Lord, the King of Israel and its Redeemer, the Lord of Hosts, says: 'I am the first and I am the last. There is no God but Me.'" God is one, and he is God alone. Yet Jesus, too, is fully God.

While the mention of "first" reminds us of his creative activity, the focus on "last" pictures him as the finisher. The eternal "Living One" accomplished the incomprehensible: he died, yet he was not simply raised from the dead—he is alive forever and ever! By virtue of his resurrection, "the keys of death and Hades" were given to him (Rev. 1:19). The "keys" signify his authority over man's ultimate enemy. If you know Christ as Savior, you need not fear death. Death is his defeated foe.

"The First and the Last" is repeated in the final chapter of Revelation: "Look! I am coming quickly, and My reward is with Me to repay each person according to what he has done. I am the Alpha and the Omega, the First and the Last, the Beginning and the End" (22:12–13). Here the emphasis is on Jesus' return and judgment. He says: "Blessed are those who wash their robes, so that they may have the right to the tree of life and may enter the city by the gates" (22:14).

The single issue of life and death is this: how have you responded to the one who is both first and last?

GOD IS
THE FIRST BEGOTTEN

> **Colossians 1:18** He is the beginning, the firstborn from the dead, so that He might come to have first place in everything.

We are regularly learning more about the impact of birth order. I am the youngest of three. My other two siblings will argue (perhaps correctly) that our parents spoiled me. My sister was the firstborn; thus, she was accorded both privilege and responsibility. But I am sure she would argue that responsibility outweighed privilege in her case. My brother would likely argue, furthermore, that as the middle child he was often overlooked.

Whatever the modern day situation, we do know that in the Jewish home the firstborn had unique responsibility that would not be fully shared by the other children.

The term "firstborn" is rendered in other translations as "first begotten." This unique phrase is used in two different but complementary ways, one referring to Christ's entry into the world through human flesh, the other referring to his resurrection. In the case of the first use, I prefer the translation "first begotten" because it avoids the possible suggestion that Jesus was included among the created world.

In Colossians 1:15, we read that Jesus was the "first begotten over all creation," begotten of the Father before any created thing. The writer to the Hebrews used the word in a similar way, declaring that all the angels should worship him as the "firstborn into the world" (Heb. 1:6). Isn't it tragic that some today revere angels and nature when they should be worshiping the first begotten?

The second usage of firstborn, however, relates to Jesus' resurrection. In this case, being the "firstborn" obviously points to the fact that Jesus was the first to rise from the dead; therefore, he is the "firstfruits" of the resurrection" (1 Cor. 15:20).

And as the firstborn from the dead, Christ will lead all God's people to resurrection. Here again we see the majesty of the Christ—raised from the dead, taking us to glory to be with him forever.

GOD IS
THE GOOD SHEPHERD

> **John 10:11** I am the good
> shepherd. The good shepherd
> lays down his life for the sheep.

My wife and I lived in England for
three years. Because Paula has a love for
sheep, we enjoyed driving through the
English countryside looking for them.
Occasionally we were privileged to see a
shepherd and his dog bringing the sheep
in from pasture. Therefore, this theme of
Jesus as the Good Shepherd is endearing
to most of us, even if we are an urbanite
who has only seen sheep at the petting zoo
and has never seen a real shepherd.

The word "good" can certainly not be
overlooked as a key part of this title. It not
only refers to Jesus as *morally* good but
may include the ideas of "beautiful" and
"authentic." While the Pharisees claimed to
be morally upright, their legalism was
repulsive and deadly. Jesus' goodness,
however, was attractive and appealing.

Also, when we refer to Jesus as good,
it is the same as declaring he is God. A man

once called Jesus by the name "Good Teacher," to which Jesus responded; "Why do you call Me good? No one is good but One—God" (Mark 10:18). Jesus is indeed the "*good* shepherd."

It must have been rare for a Palestinian shepherd to actually risk his life for his sheep. When he did, it was most likely by accident. In other words, he would have attempted to save the sheep without losing his own life. Not so with our Shepherd. He chose to lay down his life for the sheep, not as a martyr but as a substitute.

The title Good Shepherd also draws attention to another aspect of the ministry of Jesus: "I know My own sheep, and they know Me" (verse 14). This does not speak of a superficial knowledge but an intimate relationship. Jesus compared his knowing of his sheep with the knowing that exists between him and his Father.

The Good Shepherd then made a profound statement about his sheep: "My sheep hear My voice, I know them, and they follow Me" (John 10:27). Do you know his voice and follow him? Then you have eternal life and absolute security.

GOD IS
THE GREAT HIGH PRIEST

> **Hebrews 4:14** We have a
> great high priest who has
> passed through the heavens —
> Jesus the Son of God.

Would it help you to know that you
have a high priest who can sympathize
with your weakness and who desires to
plead your case before the Father? Such a
truth should give you boldness to approach
the throne of grace right now.

The writer to the Hebrews had already
referred to Jesus as a "merciful and faithful
high priest" in Hebrews 2:17. In Hebrews
4:14, however, the use of the word "great"
in relation to Jesus' high priesthood
characterizes his supreme dignity. He is
seen as being different from and greater
than any Levitical high priest.

An earthly priest was allowed to pass
through the veil of the temple, but Jesus
has passed through the heavens, receiving
access to the very throne of God. "The One
who descended is the same as the One who
ascended far above all the heavens that He
might fill all things" (Eph. 4:10).

The linking of Jesus with the phrase "Son of God" may be intended to suggest the two natures of our high priest. Because he is fully human, we can be assured that he can understand and relate to what we're going through. "For we do not have a high priest who is unable to sympathize with our weaknesses, but One who has been tested in every way as we are, yet without sin" (verse 15). Yes, he can sympathize with us in our testing, but he can also give us real help because he is God, because he is genuinely without sin.

Once we understand the greatness of our High Priest, it gives us strength to hold fast to our confession. Do you sometimes feel like you can't hold on in your own strength? That is precisely why we must go to the throne of grace. "Let us approach the throne of grace with boldness, so that we may receive mercy and find grace to help us at the proper time" (verse 16).

Right now is the proper time! You can approach the throne of God with assurance through prayer, knowing that you will be greeted by him with his tender mercy and sufficient grace.

GOD IS
HEAD OF THE CHURCH

> **Colossians 1:18** He is also the head of the body, the church.

I was once preaching at a rural meeting in North Carolina, where a number of people from various local churches had come together. After the meeting was over, an elderly man approached to tell me that he had known my father when he was alive. He then remarked that I had both my dad's voice and his passion for the local church. I don't know about the voice, but I do have a love for the church. And why not? It is the body of Christ!

Colossians 1:15–20 is one of the most magnificent passages ever penned about the centrality and supremacy of Christ. Paul spoke of Christ as the "image of the invisible God" and the "firstborn over all creation." But while creation declares the glory of God, there is nothing on earth that reveals Christ like his church. It stands as the zenith of God's creative and revelatory activity.

In Matthew 16, we are told that Jesus established the church, declaring it to be the primary means by which God advances his kingdom on planet earth. He told us that the church is triumphant, that not even the gates of death can stand against it. He died to redeem it, was raised from the dead to empower it, sent his Spirit to infill it, and will present it to himself as his bride. Christ purifies, preserves, and empowers his church. He is supreme over it.

In Ephesians, the companion letter to Colossians, Paul looked at the resurrection and exaltation of Christ in terms of the church. "He put everything under His feet and appointed Him as head over everything for the church, which is His body, the fullness of the One who fills all things in every way" (Eph. 1:22–23). Now that Christ is at the right hand of the Father, the church is empowered to express God's fullness in the world today as Christ did during his incarnation.

Anyone who loves Christ will love his church. The kingdom person will of necessity be intimately involved in the life of a local church.

GOD IS
THE HOLY CHILD

> **Acts 4:27** Herod and Pontius Pilate . . . assembled together against Your holy Servant Jesus, whom You anointed.

The dean of the school of music at Southwestern Seminary, Benjamin Harlan, looked for every possible opportunity to sing "Holy, Holy, Holy." I can't blame him. If you review the words of that great hymn, you will grasp the significance of calling Jesus the "holy child" or "holy servant."

Luke, the author of Acts, said even the demons recognized the holiness of God's Son. He reported how a man with a demonic spirit once cried out to Jesus in a loud voice: "I know who You are—the Holy One of God!" (Luke 4:34). Isaiah the prophet repeated the phrase "Holy One of Israel" twenty-five times in his book. It was the prophet's favorite designation of God in his covenant relationship with Israel.

This reference to Jesus as the "holy child" clearly has messianic overtones. The phrase "whom You anointed" refers to God's setting apart Jesus as Messiah, a likely reference to Jesus' baptism, when the Father declared, "You are My beloved Son. I take delight in You" (Luke 3:22).

The context is most significant. Peter and John had just been released by the Sanhedrin, the Jewish high court, and had rejoined their friends. This caused the disciples to break forth in praise, quoting from Psalm 2 about the raging of the Gentiles, the people who imagine vain things, the rulers who set themselves against the Lord and his Anointed.

They understood that the words of this Psalm had been fulfilled. The "Gentiles" were the Romans who sentenced Jesus to death. The "peoples" were his Jewish enemies. "Kings" were represented by Herod Antipas, who attempted to kill Jesus at birth. "Rulers" were represented by Pontius Pilate, who surrendered Christ to a mob.

The disciples saw that all these forces could not thwart God's eternal plan for his "holy child." Psalm 2 was being fulfilled before their eyes. The long view of history gave them boldness. Doesn't it give you confidence to know that God is in control?

GOD IS
THE I AM

> **John 8:58** Jesus said to them, "I assure you: Before Abraham was, I am."

In elementary English, we were taught that proper names are always nouns. But on this occasion, we have to throw out that lesson. The name translated "I am" is an emphatic form of the verb "to be." One of Jesus' names is "I am."

When Jesus said of himself, "I am the light of the world" (John 8:12), this prompted an argument. How could this man give testimony like this about himself? Much of the discussion centered on Jesus' statements about doing his Father's will, causing the Jews to affirm the greatness of their forefather Abraham. But when Jesus said that their father Abraham had rejoiced when he saw Jesus' day, they were totally confused. "You aren't 50 years old yet, and You've seen Abraham?" (verse 57).

Then the bombshell: "Before Abraham was, I am" (verse 58). Jesus was aware of the gravity of this statement. This is why he prepared them for it with a twofold "amen," rendered by the words "I assure you" in our translation. They had encountered "I am" in combinations such as "I am the light of the world." But here the full impact was felt.

This statement identified Jesus with the covenant God of Israel. When God appeared to Moses in a burning bush, Moses demanded to know his name. God declared: "I Am Who I Am. . . . This is My name forever" (Exod. 3:14–15). Isaiah, in contrasting God with the many gods of the nations, noted, "Who has performed and done this, calling the generations from the beginning? I, the Lord, am the first, and with the last—I am He" (Isa. 41:4).

Do you understand now why the Jews picked up stones to kill him? They were left with only two options: he was either the greatest fraud and blasphemer of all time, or he was and is the incarnate God. Therefore, when we read "I am," we know Jesus was declaring himself to be the promised Messiah, God in flesh. This is Jesus' boldest declaration about himself. Where Jesus is, God is!

GOD IS

IMMANUEL

> **Isaiah 7:14** The Lord Himself
> will give you a sign: The virgin
> will conceive, have a son, and
> name him Immanuel.

We have all experienced the power of
"presence" when we were afraid. We have
caressed the brow of our fevered child and
watched as our presence brought a sense
of peace. We have been in the hospital
waiting room when no one knew exactly
what to say, but the physical presence of
family and friends was all that was required to bring comfort.

The name "Immanuel" assures us that
God is always "with us."

During the time of King Ahaz, the
house of David was beset with enemies,
and the king was weak in faith. In contrast
to the worldly power on which Ahaz had
put his hope, the prophet Isaiah spoke
about the wondrous birth of a child whose
very name signified a redemption only God
could bring. The ultimate fulfillment of this
promise would not occur for generations,
but the promise was one that brought hope.

A few scholars have argued against the translation "virgin" for the Hebrew word *alma*, which means "young woman." But contrary to what some have argued, the use of the words "young woman" (rather than "wife") suggests a birth outside the normal pattern of childbirth. What we sometimes forget is that a young unmarried woman in Isaiah's day would have been expected to be a virgin. Together with other passages from Isaiah that use the term Immanuel and speak of a coming birth, it is clear that the promise of Isaiah 7:14 is preparing the way for a developing messianic theme.

A few years ago when I embarked on a study of several of the Old Testament names of God, I was intrigued to discover that the last of the names, occurring in Ezekiel 48:35, was Jehovah Shammah, which means "The Lord is there." Ezekiel was speaking of the rebuilding of the temple—the earthly reminder of God's presence. The promise of God's presence was not to be accomplished by an earthly temple, however, but by the birth of Jesus. Only our Savior, Jesus, allows us to experience "God with us."

GOD IS
JESUS

> **Matthew 1:21** She will give birth to a son, and you are to name Him Jesus, because He will save His people from their sins.

"Jesus, Jesus, Jesus, there's just something about that name," the familiar Bill Gaither tune goes. While all the names or titles we have discussed have significant meaning, none have the emotional impact as the simple declaration "Jesus." We shout it in praise and we whisper it in prayer. We weep his name over our loved one's sick bed, and we breathe it when the storm clouds are gathering. It is a name that brings comfort, strength, and joy.

In the verse above, we have been ushered into the prayer closet of Joseph, who has just discovered that Mary, his fiancée, is pregnant. And to avoid public disgrace, he has decided to divorce her secretly. Yet the messenger of the Lord tells him not to fear, for the child whom Mary is bearing has been conceived by the Holy Spirit. Joseph is to take Mary as his wife and name the child Jesus.

Names, especially divinely given names, are full of meaning. "Jesus" is actually the Greek word for the common Hebrew name Joshua. Isn't it interesting that God gave his own son a name that would have been as common in his day as John is in ours?

But the significance of his name is anything but common. The name means "Yahweh is salvation." *Yahweh* is the great memorial name of God, and *salvation* is a prominent element of Old Testament hope. This pronouncement set the tone for Jesus' ministry. He was surely not going to fit the popular mold of messianic expectation as a national liberator, but he would deal with a much more universal problem—the sin that enslaves man and keeps him from fellowship with holy God.

The name Jesus has become precious because those of us who have come to know him as our personal Savior comprehend the cost of our forgiveness. "What can wash away my sin? Nothing but the blood of Jesus!"

I sincerely hope and pray that you can say the same.

GOD IS
THE JUST ONE

> Acts 3:14 (NKJV) But you
> denied the Holy One and the
> Just, and asked for a murderer
> to be granted to you.

The healing of a lame man created
quite a stir in the temple complex, and his
victory dance gathered quite a crowd. With
the man still clutching Peter's robe, the
great apostle seized the moment.

Peter's message was short and to the
point. This feat had not been accomplished
by either his or John's own power or
godliness. Kingdom people recognize their
dependence on God, wanting him alone to
receive glory. Furthermore, the Jews had
handed Jesus over to Roman authorities
for a death sentence, but God's purpose
was to glorify him. The full impact of their
guilt is felt in our focal verse—"You denied
the Holy One!"

You may have noticed that there is
actually a twofold title given to Jesus in
this verse, and both terms have their roots
in the Old Testament. "The Holy One" was
actually uttered first by a man with an

unclean spirit—"I know who You are—The Holy One of God!" (Mark 1:24). The demons inhabiting the man knew the truth God's own people refused to accept.

The "Just" or "Righteous One" clearly alludes to Jesus as the Suffering Servant of Isaiah's prophecy. This term is used two more times in the book of Acts—at the stoning of Stephen (Acts 7:52) and at Paul's defense before the Jerusalem mob (Acts 22:14).

The writer of Hebrews also made it clear why seeing Jesus as the "Righteous One" is so important: "For this is the kind of high priest we need: holy, innocent, undefiled, separated from sinners, and exalted above the heavens" (Heb. 7:26). The Holy One was without sin; thus, he alone can forgive sin.

When we understand the impact of this great affirmation, we understand why Peter saw their denial of the Holy One as so incongruous. They had killed their "source of life" (Acts 3:15). But before we point our finger at the first century Jews, we must be bold enough to ask, "What have I done with the Just One?"

GOD IS
THE LAMB OF GOD

> **John 1:29** Here is the Lamb of
> God, who takes away the sin of
> the world!

John the Baptist accumulated quite a
following with his fiery preaching and his
message of repentance. Nonetheless, he
continually deflected every attempt by the
crowd to exalt him. He was only the voice
in the wilderness. There was one who was
coming, however, whose stature was such
that John would be unworthy to untie his
sandal strap.

When John saw Jesus approaching,
he announced, "Here is the Lamb of
God"—a title found only in John's Gospel
(verses 29, 36). The same Greek term is
used in Acts 8:32, when Philip helped
the Ethiopian official understand that the
Suffering Servant of Isaiah 53 had come in
the person of Christ. The term appears
again in 1 Peter 1:19, when he declared
that people are not saved by perishable
things but through the precious blood of
Christ, "a lamb without defect or blemish."

It is likely that the Gospel writer John picked up on this phrase to present Jesus as more than the Passover lamb. The motif of the Passover runs throughout the Gospel of John, binding his message together. In the Old Testament, the blood of the Passover lamb was placed on the doorpost, covering over the sin of the people. Jesus, however, did not merely cover over; he took away. No longer is man's sin covered in a sacrifice which must be continually repeated, but it has been washed away by the death of the Lamb.

The genitive in the phrase "Lamb of God" can either mean "Lamb *belonging* to God" or "Lamb *provided* by God." Both are true. The sacrifice provided by God belongs to God, in that he sent his own Son as our sin offering. The wages of sin bring death; therefore, all of mankind deserved to die. The only alternative was for one who was without sin to die in our place. Jesus—the Lamb provided by God—has made redemption for the "sin of the world."

There was nothing limited in his atonement. His sacrifice is sufficient for anyone who will turn to him in faith.

GOD IS
THE LIFE

> **John 14:6** I am the way,
> the truth, and the life. No one
> comes to the Father except
> through Me.

One of the most endearing discourses
of John's Gospel is interrupted by a rather
abrupt question — "'Lord,' Thomas said,
'we don't know where You're going. How
can we know the way?'" (verse 5).

Jesus was celebrating a final Passover
with his disciples. And wanting to reassure
them in light of his impending death, he
told them about a place where he was
going, a place where he would prepare a
lasting home for them in his Father's house,
a place he promised to return from to take
them back with him.

It was at this point that Thomas
interjected his honest yet somewhat negative appraisal of the situation. He voiced
his deep despair and confusion about the
riddles of life. You may recall that Thomas
had expressed his willingness to die with
Jesus when he agreed to accompany him
on his journey to Bethany (John 11:16).

He knew this was a real possibility if his Master continued on his chosen path.

But why must Jesus leave? Where was he going? And how could they follow him when they didn't know the way?

Do you wish you had the courage to be as brutally honest as Thomas? Do you desire to know the answers to life's greatest questions? Then don't miss the radical nature of this claim. Jesus is not a mere philosopher or religious leader who suggests that we follow a certain way, some principle that has given meaning to his own life. No, he *is* life! Jesus doesn't simply hazard an answer to life's great questions; he provides life in himself. His solution is neither a recipe nor a religion; it is a relationship with him.

The Jews had denied the one whom God had glorified, and in so doing they had "killed the source of life, whom God raised from the dead" (Acts 3:15). Truly, Jesus alone can give life, because he alone is the resurrected one. "I am the resurrection and the life. The one who believes in Me, even if he dies, will live" (John 11:25).

Do you have life?

GOD IS
THE LIGHT OF THE WORLD

> **John 8:12** I am the light of the world. Anyone who follows Me will never walk in the darkness.

When I was a child, my bedroom was on the back of the house. And just outside my window, a weeping willow tree stood backlit by a streetlight. On windy nights, my room would fill with what appeared to be demons and dragons as the shadows of willow tree limbs played across the walls. When I could take it no longer, I would cry out to my father, who with one flip of a switch would bathe my room in light. The shadows of childhood fear would vanish.

Jesus' declaration that "I am the light of the world" would have instantly and dramatically caught everyone's attention. The setting was the Feast of Tabernacles. A part of that celebration was the much anticipated lighting of the festive golden lamps. These lamps reminded the worshipers of the pillar of fire which God had used to lead Israel during those long-ago years of wilderness wandering.

Perhaps you have already noticed that Jesus never said he would provide enlightenment, as other religious leaders claimed. He declared instead that he was the source of all light. It was Yahweh (Jehovah) who spoke light into being, and the connection of the word "light" with the declaration "I am" made this declaration even more stunning. Jesus was the very glory of God. He was and is that pillar of light which gives life.

But this light does not belong to mankind in general. Only those who follow him are delivered from darkness. The word "follows" in verse 12 carries the idea of *continuously* following. We experience the light of his presence only as we are wholeheartedly following him. We don't have to walk in darkness.

One final note: you may recall that Jesus also said that his kingdom followers would be the "light of the world" (Matt. 5:14). Our light is not of the same essence as his, but it is the clear reflection of it. Like the moon reflects the light of the sun, so we are intended to reflect the light of God's Son.

GOD IS
THE LION OF JUDAH

{ **Revelation 5:5** The Lion from the tribe of Judah, the Root of David, has been victorious. }

The lion has long been a symbol of strength and victory. From antiquity we find it emblazoned on armor and standards carried into battle. We refer to the lion as the king of the jungle. If you are a C. S. Lewis fan, you fell in love with Aslan the lion that was slain.

In the last book of the Bible, John gives us a glimpse into the heavenlies. He was grieved that "no one in heaven or on the earth or under the earth" was able to break the seven seals and open the scroll (Rev. 5:3). But his wailing was stopped by one of the elders, who comforted him with the news that the Lion of Judah had won the victory and thus was qualified to open the scroll.

The expression "Lion of Judah" occurs only here in the Bible, alluding to the first messianic prophecy in Genesis 49:9–10. Judah is pictured in that passage as a young lion that has returned from victory, about whom it is said, "The scepter will not depart from Judah, or the staff from between his feet, until He whose right it is comes and the obedience of the peoples belongs to Him," until all nations of the earth come under the reign of their rightful King.

Notice, too, that John identified the Lion of Judah with the "Root of David." This is likely an allusion to the prophecy in Isaiah 11:1 — "A shoot will grow from the stump of Jesse, and a branch from His roots will bear fruit." The royal family of David was pictured as a tree that had fallen, but out of it had sprung the one who would restore the kingly rule.

When John looked for the Lion, he saw instead "one like a slaughtered lamb" (verse 6). The final victory of Christ is possible only because he willingly suffered as the Lamb of sacrifice.

All these images point to an incredible truth: the Messiah "has been victorious." By his incarnation, death, and resurrection, Christ has triumphed over all the powers of Satan. Are you experiencing his victory?

GOD IS
THE LORD OF ALL

{ **Acts 10:36** He sent the message . . . proclaiming the good news of peace through Jesus Christ—He is Lord of all. }

There are certain events in life that help us to see a fundamental truth in bold relief. Once seen, it becomes forever etched on our hearts and it impacts all we do. Such an event for Peter and for the early church was the conversion of Cornelius.

Cornelius was a centurion of the Italian Regiment. He was a Gentile who feared God, prayed always to him, and did good deeds for the Jewish people. God honored the desire of this devout man who was earnestly seeking him, and instructed him to send for Peter.

As Peter was praying on the housetop, the Lord spoke to him in a vision. He saw a sheet being lowered to the earth filled with animals considered unclean by the Jews. He was instructed to eat but he refused. Yet the voice continued to repeat the same instruction three times, saying, "What God has made clean, you must not call common" (verse 15). While Peter was pondering this vision, the men from Cornelius came for him.

After arriving at the house of Cornelius, Peter began his speech to them with a confession: "In truth, I understand that God doesn't show favoritism" (verse 34). What an insight! This had been a truth the Old Testament Jews had failed to comprehend—that God had chosen them to join him in reaching the nations. Even the early Jews who accepted Jesus as their Messiah had the same parochial view of God.

Thus, Peter admitted that his mind was just now taking hold of a truth which should have been clear to him at Pentecost, when the message was declared in every man's tongue. He now understood that the person who fears God in every nation is "acceptable" to him (verse 35). Relationship with God was never intended to be exclusive to the Jews, because he is "Lord of all."

Do you believe that Jesus is Lord of all? Does your giving and your going reflect the desire of the Lord that all may come to know him?

GOD IS
THE LORD OF GLORY

> **1 Corinthians 2:8** If they had known it, they would not have crucified the Lord of glory.

The Corinthian letter has always been one of my favorites. The church family in Corinth was diverse, to say the least. And sometimes this diversity led to a factious spirit.

There were some in Corinth who were impressed by flowery speech and the rhetoric of wisdom. Thus, Paul had determined to focus on preaching Jesus simply, for he knew that those who were "mature" would recognize the wisdom of Christ without all the lofty language (2:6).

The wisdom that Paul preached was "hidden in a mystery" (verse 7), unable to be discerned by human wisdom. It is a wisdom that must be revealed by the Spirit of God, who searches "the deep things of God" (verse 10). And the sure evidence that none of the rulers of this age understood God's wisdom was their role in the crucifixion of the "Lord of glory."

What divine irony! The very men who attempted to do away with Jesus unwittingly participated in carrying out God's divine purpose determined before the ages. They thought they were killing a messianic pretender, a blasphemer. But if they had understood the enormity of rejecting him, they would not have done so.

The title "Lord of glory" is seen by many to be the most magnificent title given to Christ. James referred to Jesus as our "glorious Lord" (James 2:1). A similar idea surfaces in John's Gospel: "We observed His glory, the glory as the One and Only Son from the Father, full of grace and truth" (John 1:14). In the Old Testament, God's glory was manifest on a smoke-shrouded mountain, the pillar of fire, and the cloud filling the temple. But once Jesus came, God's glory was manifest in *him*.

The Lord of all ages is thus the Lord of final glory, for himself and for all his people. Paul concluded that if the rulers of this age had understood this, they never would have rejected him. But *we* understand! May we never be guilty of rejecting him through our apathy or unbelief.

GOD IS
THE MAN OF SORROWS

> **Isaiah 53:3 (NASB)** He was despised and forsaken of men, a man of sorrows and acquainted with grief.

"Man of sorrows" has a rather somber feel, doesn't it? Yet I think you may discover that this name will become one of the titles of Jesus that will grow to be the most precious to you.

When Isaiah first began to describe him, he saw him as a "young plant," like a shoot that is often cut off before maturity, like a "root out of dry ground" (verse 2). No one expects much from a plant like that. Jesus' background was such that few could suspect that he was born with royal blood, that he was in the lineage of Jesse and David.

We have so romanticized the story of Jesus' beginnings, we forget that his conception through a virgin left many scandalized. For some, he would always be an illegitimate child. Remember the accusation of the Jews: "We weren't born of sexual immorality" (John 8:41). For others, he was nothing more than a carpenter's son, a handyman (Matt. 13:55).

Thus Isaiah prophesied, "He was despised and rejected by men." John stated this same truth in blunt form: "He came to His own, and His own people did not receive Him" (John 1:11). But the deep sorrow of Jesus came when he took upon himself the sin of the world and received the chastisement that belonged to us.

I can still vividly remember watching *The Passion of the Christ* by Mel Gibson. During the brutal beatings, most viewers had to look away. We could not bear to look upon him. But as we watched the drama unfold, tears of joy welled up in our eyes as we comprehended the truth of his suffering. "He Himself bore our sicknesses, and He carried our pains . . . pierced because of our transgressions, crushed because of our iniquities. . . . The Lord has punished Him for the iniquity of us all" (verses 4–6).

The Man of Sorrows took our place. He "who did not know sin" bore our sins, "so that we might become the righteousness of God in Him" (2 Cor. 5:21).

GOD IS
OUR MASTER

> **Luke 5:5** "Master," Simon replied, "we've worked hard all night long and caught nothing! But at Your word, I'll let down the nets."

Can you sense Peter's frustration? He may not have been an expert at many things, but he knew fishing. This was his turf, and now a novice fisherman was telling him what to do.

You are probably familiar with the story. Jesus was teaching by the side of Lake Gennesaret when the crowd literally pressed him to the water's edge. Seeing two fishing boats nearby, he commandeered one for his floating platform and continued his message. When the sermon was complete, he instructed Simon, "Put out into deep water and let down your nets for a catch" (Luke 5:4).

Do you identify with the conflict raging in Peter's mind? He and his partners had fished all night with nothing to show for it. They were exhausted and frustrated because there would be no paycheck today. He must have thought,

"This guy may be a great teacher, but I'm the expert here." Yet to Peter's credit, he obeyed the one he called "Master."

The term "master" only occurs on six occasions in the Bible, and all are found in Luke's Gospel. It means "one who is set over," such as a military officer or the commander of a ship.

In fact, these same fishermen later uttered this word again in a slightly different setting. In Luke 8:24, while out on a boat in the middle of a stormy night, they cried out; "Master, Master, we're going to die." They had used all of their considerable knowledge and skill to save themselves. But in a final act of desperation, they woke Jesus, who calmed the storm and rebuked his disciples for their unbelief. "Who can this be?" they asked themselves. "He commands even the winds and the waves, and they obey Him!" (Luke 8:25).

All of these stories have a common theme: Jesus has absolute authority over our lives. Thus, like the fishermen, we must obey when all the circumstances of life and reason dictate against it. There is no realm where he is not qualified as Master.

GOD IS
OUR MEDIATOR

> **1 Timothy 2:5** For there is one God and one mediator between God and man, a man, Christ Jesus.

One of the intriguing personalities of the Old Testament is Job. You may recall that he underwent severe testing and yet remained faithful to the Lord. But he pled for someone who would mediate between himself and God. After all, the Lord was not a man Job could just sit and talk to. "There is no one to judge between us, to lay his hand on both of us" (Job 9:33).

Job's plea has now been answered in Christ Jesus, who is the one mediator between God and man.

Notice that this great "God Is" statement is found in a section where Paul was encouraging believers to pray for all men. Have you ever paused to think that the foundation of all prayer is the mediatory role of Christ? He is our mediator both in terms of redemption and intercession.

The essence of kingdom-focused praying is found in verses 3–4: "It pleases

God our Savior, who wants everyone to be saved and to come to the knowledge of the truth." We are required to pray for all persons because there is only one God, who created all peoples and thus desires them to be saved.

Since there is only one God, there can likewise only be one mediator. And only Christ is qualified, because he is fully God and fully man. Through his perfect life and substitutionary death, he met the demands of God's law and gave himself as a "ransom for all" (v. 6), as the price required to free us from slavery. Don't forget that sin enslaves us all. Therefore, all of us require a mediator who can free us from slavery and rightly relate us to a holy God.

Jesus Christ died for all the people of the earth, and his desire is that all be saved. But how will this good news get to those at the ends of the earth?

Prayer is the foundation for kingdom advance. We must follow Paul's direction that "petitions, prayers, intercessions, and thanksgivings be made for everyone" (verse 1). Our prayers open the doors for those who herald the gospel.

GOD IS
THE MESSIAH

{ **Luke 2:11** Today a Savior, who is Messiah the Lord, was born for you in the city of David. }

Have you ever heard a story so many times that it begins to lose its impact? As my dad aged, he would often repeat a story about his childhood that I had heard on numerous occasions. Because of my great love for my dad, however, I would listen with rapt attention as if I were hearing the story for the first time.

Now that my dad is gone, I am glad that he repeated those great stories—just as today we are looking at a verse that should grow more precious to us every time we hear it.

The story of Jesus' birth was heralded by an angel of the Lord to lowly shepherds. Isn't it interesting that a history-altering event like this would be declared to ordinary men busy at a rather mundane task? At the heart of the story is the incredible good news that the long awaited Messiah had been born.

The Greek *christos* translates the Hebrew *messiah*, which means "anointed one." *Anointing* in the Old Testament was reserved for special servants like the priest or king. Yet the Jews looked for a day when God would send a unique Messiah to be the deliverer of his people.

Thus, we are told that the Messiah is also Savior, a title used only here in the synoptic gospels. Our Messiah is the one who saves us from sin and alienation, from all dangers . . . ultimately from death.

So hear this story again for the first time. Our Savior is the one anointed by God as prophet, priest, and king. As such, he is Lord—a word often used in the Old Testament to translate the great covenant name Yahweh. Our Messiah is God in the flesh.

As you hear this familiar story, I challenge you to think seriously about a couple of questions. Is the Messiah your personal Savior? Have you turned from your self-rule and asked him to be your Savior and Lord? If not, why not do so right now? If so, do you trust him to provide for your every need?

GOD IS
THE MIGHTY GOD

> **Isaiah 9:6** He will be named
> Wonderful Counselor, Mighty
> God, Eternal Father, Prince
> of Peace.

"What a mighty God we serve! /
Angels bow before him / Heaven and earth
adore him." So goes a portion of the lyrics
from a song that has had a long run of
popularity. Perhaps its hand-clapping
rhythm is what has made it popular, but
the truth of its words is what is most
important.

We have already looked at two titles
that come from this text—Counselor and
Everlasting Father. We will look at two
others before this book is ended—Prince
of Peace and Wonderful. For now, we
focus on him as Mighty God.

Isaiah wrote to a suffering people
whose life had been one of gloom and
despair. They needed a word of hope.
Yet Isaiah promised that hope was on the
way. He saw the dawn of a new light for
the people walking in darkness, those who
had dwelt in the shadow of death (verse 2).

Hope would come through the birth of a child, whose greatness is such that one name will not suffice.

The title "Mighty God" speaks of his sovereign might and heroic nature. Like the Israelites of old, we should take comfort in knowing that we serve a God whose power is unlimited. There is nothing you will face today that moves beyond the power of Mighty God.

Do you remember the song of praise that Mary sang to God when she visited Elizabeth after learning of the babe in her womb? "Surely, from now on all generations will call me blessed, because the Mighty One has done great things for me" (Luke 1:48–49). She recognized that the miracle in her womb was only possible through the action of sovereign, almighty God.

What do you need to surrender to Mighty God? What keeps you from doing so? Is it your lack of conviction that God has all might? Remember Daniel's conclusion: "The people who know their God will be strong and take action" (Daniel 11:32). Those of us who know him by faith can trust in his power and victory.

GOD IS
THE ONLY BEGOTTEN SON

> **John 3:18 (NASB)** He has not believed in the name of the only begotten Son of God.

Nicodemus was a good, religious man. One might even call him a seeker. He came to Jesus with a level of belief. But based on Jesus' response to him, he must have been troubled by a single issue: How can any person enter the kingdom of God?

It is in this context that we find the favorite verse of many — John 3:16. It contains such profound truths, we stand before it speechless. It speaks of God's infinite and profound love, his universal love, his sacrificial, initiating love. The immensity of the gift is staggering — his one and only Son.

Why was God moved to provide such a unique and priceless gift? Because everything was at stake! God's heartbeat, echoed throughout Scripture, is that all the peoples of the earth would escape judgment and enjoy salvation — "that the world might be saved through Him" (v. 17).

Verse 18, then, puts everything in perspective. The Scripture is clear that God's intention is for all humanity to be saved (Acts 17:30–31 and 1 Tim. 2:4). Yet man, created in God's image, has been given free will which requires a personal response.

John actually repeated some form of the word "believe" three times in verse 18, underlining the enormity of refusing to accept God's Son. The place where we will spend eternity is not based on some uncaring force or irresistible fate. It is based on our response to God's "only begotten Son."

We encountered this phrase for the first time in John 1 — "The Word became flesh and took up residence among us. We observed His glory, the glory as the One and Only Son from the Father, full of grace and truth" (John 1:14). The title "only begotten" assures us that Jesus eternally has the same nature as the Father. Furthermore, it declares his absolute uniqueness in providing the way to the Father. Since Jesus is the "one and only Son," to reject him brings condemnation. God's desire is that all men receive him.

GOD IS
THE PRINCE OF PEACE

{ **Isaiah 9:6** He will be named
Wonderful Counselor, Mighty
God, Eternal Father, Prince
of Peace. }

I grew up in an era marked by the
peace symbol, a time when the Vietnam
War polarized the nation. I was in college
when the draft was enacted, and I still
remember the day when I was told that
one of my college friends was killed in
that conflict.

Peace seems even more elusive today
than it was when I graduated from college.
War came to our shores on September 11,
2001, and our new enemy—the terrorists—
are elusive and more difficult to defeat.
Will our children and our children's
children ever know peace?

We return once again to the promise
of Isaiah 9:6. All the names mentioned in
this verse find their climax in this great
affirmation—"Prince of Peace." Again,
these words were written to a people living
in deep despair and darkness. Yet one was
prohesied who would shatter the burden-

some yoke of their oppressors. No promise of peace could be more vivid than verse 5: "For the trampling boot of battle and the bloodied garments of war will be burned as fuel for the fire."

But his peace is not simply a cessation of strife. It is much more! It is a life of personal well-being and hope—of salvation, blessing, happiness, and fullness. Just listen to the implications as spelled out in verse 7: "The dominion will be vast, and its prosperity will never end. He will reign on the throne of David and over his kingdom to establish and sustain it with justice and righteousness from now on and forever. The zeal of the Lord of Hosts will accomplish this."

Ultimately, his peace will envelop all the earth and its peoples. "I will cut off the chariot from Ephraim and the horse from Jerusalem. The bow of war will be removed, and He will proclaim peace to the nations" (Zech. 9:10). Those who know the Prince of Peace will one day join him in extending his reign to the nations. We know the message that will bring peace, and we must declare it to the nations.

GOD IS
OUR REDEEMER

> **Job 19:25** But I know my living Redeemer, and He will stand on the dust at last.

Job was placed under severe testing when the circumstances of his life were radically changed for the worse. Perhaps the most difficult element of it was the accusation of his friends, who were quick to give their diagnosis of the situation.

In his response to one of them, Job made a great declaration—"I know my living Redeemer"—echoing his conviction that one day he would see God. This one who was his redeemer would also become his vindicator.

The idea of a "redeemer" is a concept which the Jew would clearly understand. Leviticus 25 taught that the land belonged to the Lord and was given in stewardship to man. For this reason, it could not be permanently sold (verse 23). If a man became destitute and had to sell his land, his nearest relative could come and redeem what his brother had sold (verse 25).

Later, the psalmist wrote: "May the words of my mouth and the meditation of my heart be acceptable to You, Lord, my rock and my Redeemer" (Ps. 19:14). The image of the rock indicates refuge, and the word "Redeemer" indicates that God was his champion.

The most moving picture of a redeemer in the Old Testament, however, is the story of Hosea and Gomer. Hosea was a prophet who was married to a harlot. One day, Hosea saw Gomer being sold on the slave market. But with unprecedented love and grace, he bought his wife's freedom. He became her redeemer.

The story doesn't stop here, though. All the images of a redeemer point to Christ, who "has redeemed us from the curse of the law by becoming a curse for us" (Gal. 3:13). "God sent His Son . . . to redeem those under the law" (Gal. 4:4–5). "He gave Himself for us to redeem us from all lawlessness and to cleanse for Himself a special people, eager to do good works" (Titus 2:14).

Do you know your Redeemer? And are you eager to please him?

GOD IS
RESURRECTION & LIFE

{
John 11:25 I am the
resurrection and the life.
The one who believes in Me,
even if he dies, will live.
}

As a pastor, I accompanied many
families on that difficult trip to the grave-
yard as they buried a family member or
loved one. In recent years, I have had to
make that same trip myself—first with my
dad, then my mom.

But I cannot imagine how intense the
pain must be for the individual who has no
hope or assurance of ever seeing their dear
one again. While my grief was profound, it
was tempered by the firm assurance that
Jesus is "the resurrection and the life."

The two sisters of Lazarus struggled
with the death of their brother. Typical
of grief, Martha was looking for someone
to blame, and Jesus was the most likely
candidate. She asserted that if he had been
present, Lazarus would not have died.
And though she properly understood and
believed he would be resurrected at the last
day, Jesus' reply to her was startling: "I am

the resurrection"—not just in the future but in the present tense.

Martha spoke of resurrection as if it were only a future gift of God to be dispensed by Christ at the end of time. But Christ's assertion required that she focus not on resurrection but on him. He is not the *dispenser* of resurrection; he *is* resurrection!

Notice that "resurrection" is the first word Jesus mentioned. But it is taken up into the larger concept of "life," which is already ours today in Christ.

We are reminded of Paul's shout of triumph: "Death has been swallowed up in victory" (1 Cor. 15:54). This victory is a present tense reality for those who are in Christ. It is why Jesus could promise, "Everyone who lives and believes in Me will never die—ever" (John 11:26). When we are hidden in Christ, death has no authority over us. When we lay down this earthly body, our life in Christ will become resurrection life!

There is only one permanent cure for the fear of death—life! Eternal life! And this life is only found in our Lord and Savior, Jesus Christ.

GOD IS
OUR ROCK

> **1 Corinthians 10:4** They
> drank from a spiritual rock
> that followed them, and that
> rock was Christ.

The Corinthian church was anything
but boring. There were believers who saw
themselves as spiritually exalted, which left
others feeling spiritually inferior. This led
to divisions in the church and distorted
understandings of biblical truths.

Some Corinthians, for example, had
developed a view of the Lord's Supper
which bordered on the magical. If they
took the elements on a regular basis, they
thought they could live as they pleased. We
see a similar disconnect today when people
wear a cross as a good luck charm or treat
church membership as little more than a
fire insurance policy.

Paul warned the Corinthians about
such spiritual arrogance by reminding
them of the judgment that came upon the
Israelites, who had likewise enjoyed God's
rich supply of spiritual blessings as they
traveled in the wilderness. The linking of

"rock" and "spiritual drink" would have brought to mind the stories of the striking of the rock from which water miraculously flowed (Exod. 17 and Num. 20).

Yet Paul quickly focused this analogy on Christ, identifying him with the "rock" image of the Old Testament, thus identifying him as Jehovah.

In the Song of Moses, recorded in Deuteronomy 32, the image of Yahweh as the "Rock" occurs frequently (verses 4, 15, 18, 30, 31). Listen to verse 4: "The Rock — His work is perfect; all His ways are entirely just." He warned them about scorning or ignoring the Rock. In speaking of other nations, Moses declared: "But their 'rock' is not like our Rock" (verse 31). The psalmist also picked up on this imagery, declaring, "The Lord is my rock, my fortress, and my deliverer" (Ps. 18:2).

There are certainly implications here of the pre-existent Christ and the oneness of God, the source of all the blessings Israel received as they traveled. But the overwhelming truth is that he is our Rock today — our provider, the source of all good things, our rock of refuge, our strength.

GOD IS
THE ROSE OF SHARON

> **Song of Songs 2:1** I am a rose
> of Sharon, a lily of the valleys.

My dad loved roses. I remember the
excitement that any gardening catalog
produced within him upon its arrival. Dad
would quickly flip to the section containing
roses to see if a new variety was being
offered. The new rose was quickly ordered
and planted, and the entire family waited
with rapt eagerness to see it in bloom.

This title "Rose of Sharon" has likewise
become precious to many believers, yet it
occurs only once in the Bible. The Song of
Songs tells of the great love between
Solomon and his bride, Shulamith. In the
first chapter, the couple exchanges expressions of desire, encouragement, and endearment as they ponder their great love
for one another. Some of the images seem
a bit quaint to us since they come from a
rural setting long ago. Nonetheless, it is
clear that Solomon greatly admires her
stunning beauty.

Shulamith's response to Solomon, which contains the description "rose of Sharon" and "lily of the valleys," may seem boastful, but the very opposite is true. The beloved modestly and humbly compares herself to the common wildflowers of the valley of Sharon.

The word translated "rose" is derived from a Hebrew word meaning "to form bulbs," and thus may be more akin to a crocus, narcissus, or daffodil. The reference to the lily may be used of any one of a number of flowers, ranging from the lotus of the Nile to the wildflowers of Palestine. Thus, the bride humbly compares herself to a common wildflower that bursts into bloom in the midst of the everyday brambles of life. She is not locked up in some private garden but is available to all.

Isaiah described the coming Messiah as one who had "no form of splendor that we should look at Him, no appearance that we should desire Him" (Isa. 53:2). Yet like Solomon, when you have fallen in love with Christ, he is like a rose among thorns. Daily he bursts into glorious bloom in the midst of the brambles of your life.

GOD IS
OUR SAVIOR

{ **2 Timothy 1:10** This has
now been made evident
through the appearing of our
Savior Christ Jesus. }

The announcement that opens the
pages of the New Testament brings this
hope: "She will give birth to a son, and you
are to name Him Jesus, because He will
save His people from their sins" (Matt.
1:21). This declaration is made all the more
precious because it addresses our greatest
need. Our sin has alienated us from a holy
God who created us to live in a permanent
relationship with him. Thus, our greatest
need is for a Savior who can deliver us
from our sin.

In the above text from 2 Timothy,
Paul was encouraging his readers from
prison. He spoke of their salvation and
calling, purposed by God in Christ Jesus
before time began. The idea of God's
eternal purpose from eternity past may be
beyond our comprehension, but it has now
been made evident by the birth of "our
Savior Christ Jesus."

To begin with, he has "abolished death" (verse 10). "Abolished" is a favorite term of the apostle Paul. In 1 Corinthians, he spoke of death as the last of man's enemies to be abolished (15:56). But our Savior is not just a destroyer; he is also an illuminator who "has brought life and immortality to light" (2 Tim. 1:10). Life and immortality had been obscured until the coming of the Savior, but they have now been flooded with light, revealing the "mystery" of God's love for all in Christ (Eph. 3:9).

The abundant life we receive in Christ is immortal. Although we still face physical death, it no longer holds us in its dread. As Paul declared in 1 Corinthians 15, the sting of death has been removed. The word "gospel" speaks of the entire revelation of God in Christ—his life, teaching, death, and resurrection.

Can you call him Savior? Have you stepped into the light of Christ and appropriated his everlasting life? Then notice how immediately Paul spoke of his desire to declare this good news (verse 11). How long has it been since you told anyone about your Savior?

GOD IS
THE SON OF GOD

> **Matthew 16:16** Simon Peter
> answered, "You are the
> Messiah, the Son of the
> living God!"

Speculation had been growing as to the true identity of Jesus. The suggestions ran from John the Baptist to Elijah to Jeremiah. Yes, people were confident that Jesus was unlike any teacher they had ever heard, causing them to think of him as a prophet. But all their estimations fell short. He was not a spokesman from God; he was God speaking in the flesh.

In response to Jesus' query about this to his disciples, Peter spoke for the Twelve, declaring him to be "the Messiah, the Son of the living God." The title "Son of God" had likely come into use as a messianic title in pre-Christian Judaism, indicative of God's vice-regent in his kingdom. In later Christian thought, it was applied to Jesus to affirm both his divine origin and nature.

Another text that clarifies the work of the Son of God is 1 John 3:8 — "The one who commits sin is of the Devil, for the

Devil has sinned from the beginning. The Son of God was revealed for this purpose: to destroy the Devil's works."

Interesting, isn't it, that the Bible declares the devil has been sinning from the beginning of time. This reference to "beginning" probably refers to the time when Satan first sinned against God. To suggest that sin existed *before* Satan's rebellion would clearly stand against the teaching of Scripture. But prior to the creation of man, the devil was already sinning. And ever since the creation of man, he has been attempting to make sin a ceaseless way of life for his followers.

Yet as John declared, "The Son of God was revealed for this purpose: to destroy the Devil's works." So when we recall that Jesus is the Son of God, we need to let this also assure us that Satan is a defeated foe. Jesus has the power to undo the penalty and power of sin in your life and to loose you from its power. When you find yourself tempted to sin and you think you are too weak to resist, call upon the one who has already won the victory — Jesus Christ, the Son of God.

GOD IS
THE SON OF MAN

{ **Matthew 9:6** The Son of Man has authority on earth to forgive sins. }

What do we need most? While some might sing, "Love, sweet love," the truth is, we need forgiveness. All of mankind shares the same dilemma. We are sinners by nature and we have sinned in practice. Religion is man's attempt to discover the answer to this sin problem. But the thing religion cannot provide, the Son of Man has authority to give—forgiveness.

The title "Son of Man" occurs around eighty-four times in the Gospels, and all but one comes from the lips of Jesus. The largest number of these sayings relate to the end of time, when Jesus will descend to the earth to gather the elect and judge the nations. One example is found in Matthew 25:31—"When the Son of Man comes in His glory, and all the angels with Him, then He will sit on the throne of His glory."

The second largest group is connected with his suffering, death, resurrection, and return. On three occasions, he predicted that the Son of Man would be rejected by men, resulting in his death and resurrection (Mark 8:31; 9:31; 10:33–34). The linking of the Son of Man as both Messianic Judge and Suffering Servant is unique to the teaching of Jesus. "Then the sign of the Son of Man will appear in the sky, and then all the peoples of the earth will mourn; and they will see the Son of Man coming on the clouds of heaven with power and great glory" (Matt. 24:30).

The final group of Son of Man sayings relate to Jesus' earthly ministry. As we have seen in the Matthew 9:6 passage, he has the authority as the Son of Man to forgive sins. In his preaching, he sowed the seed of God's kingdom (Matt. 13:37), reinterpreted the Sabbath and the law (Matt. 12:8), and brought salvation to the lost (Luke 19:10).

Aren't you glad that the Son of Man has forgiven your sin and promised you life with him forever? He will one day gather his forgiven elect "from the four winds" (Matt. 24:31) so that we mere men might live forever with him, the Son of Man.

GOD IS
THE TRUE LIGHT

{ **John 1:9** The true light, who
gives light to everyone, was
coming into the world. }

Reflected or partial light can play
tricks on the eyes, but "true light" makes
everything clear. Even familiar objects that
wouldn't warrant a second glance in broad
daylight can be made to look frightening or
suspicious in the dark of night or in the
half-lit shadows before sunrise.

Our title for this reading occurs in
the wonderful prologue to John's Gospel.
John had already referred to Jesus as the
pre-existent *logos* or Word of God. He then
declared: "Life was in Him, and that life
was the light of men" (verse 4). This light
penetrated the darkness and was so intense
that the darkness could not overcome it.
He then spoke of John the Baptist, the
witness who testified about the light. John,
however, was not the source of light; he
could only point people to the "true light."

The word "true" captures the ideas of
completeness, authenticity, dependability,

and steadfastness. While some other lights may have had elements of the truth or, like John, had testified to the truth, only Jesus was the full embodiment of the truth. He did not simply bear witness to the truth; he was truth in flesh. There was and is nothing shadowy or unseen in the light Christ brings.

His light is available to all men. God has revealed something of himself to all mankind (Rom. 1:20), sufficient enough to allow them to choose the light. Yet this does not suggest that everyone will come to the light. The tragedy is found in John 1:10–11. The world he created "did not recognize Him" and "His own people did not receive Him." John repeated this tragic situation in 3:19: "This, then, is the judgment: the light has come into the world, and people loved darkness rather than the light because their deeds were evil."

Once we have "seen the light" by seeing Christ, we must bear witness to him, so that all may see him and know him. Kingdom-focused people are concerned that all the nations have equal opportunity to see the "true light."

GOD IS
THE TRUE VINE

{ **John 15:1** I am the true
vine, and My Father is the
vineyard keeper. }

I inherited a great deal from my dad,
but a green thumb was not one of them.
My dad seemed to have a way with plants.
He loved roses and cultivated a love for
them in my life, although I admit I find it
easier to enjoy them than to grow them.

When I planted my first roses, Dad
taught me to watch for "sucker growth,"
where the wild vine would re-emerge and
take valuable energy from the plant. He
taught me that pruning was essential if the
rose bush was ever to provide abundant
blossoms.

Jesus referred to himself as the "true
vine." In the Old Testament, the "vine" is
frequently used as a symbol for Israel.
Tragically, however, Israel is often pictured
as a faithless and fruitless vine, which
through disobedience had become a wild
vine (Jer. 2:21). In contrast to fruitless
Israel, however, Jesus is the "true vine,"

accomplishing perfectly that which God purposed for him.

We might expect Jesus to say that the *church* is the vine, drawing a parallelism with the wild vine of Israel. But, no, Jesus is the vine. He stands as a sort of bridge or source of life between the vineyard keeper (the Father) and the branches (his church). Because he gives life to the branches, the fruit they bear is the natural consequence of abiding in him. Just as a branch is not a self-sufficient entity, neither is the believer.

The role of the Father is also decisive in this process. He watches over the vine to ensure fruitfulness. Left to itself, the vine will produce unproductive growth; therefore, pruning is essential. This does not suggest that a genuine believer can be cut from the vine, but it does mean that fruitfulness is the test of belonging to the "true vine." And we can trust the vinedresser to know the difference, removing unproductive branches and cleansing productive ones so that they will be even more fruitful.

And because you are his, you will most definitely bear fruit for him, for his power flows to you from the Vine—the *True* Vine.

GOD IS
THE TRUTH

> **John 14:6** I am the way,
> the truth, and the life. No one
> comes to the Father except
> through Me.

I recall standing on the bridge of a
destroyer headed from Norfolk to York-
town, Virginia, on a short cruise. My
friend, the captain of the ship, was all
smiles until the ship was underway. Then
I watched in fascination as he constantly
monitored the ship's course.

I knew he had taken this ship out of
port hundreds of times. But when I ques-
tioned him about why he was so diligent to
track the course of the ship, he told me that
the turbulence of the water, as well as the
small opening that was provided over the
bay bridge tunnel, left him no room for
deviation. Truth was definitely not relative
in his case.

Neither is it relative when it determines
where we will spend eternity. Jesus had
just told his disciples that he was returning
to his Father. Thomas, perplexed by this
announcement, asked the question every-

one else must have been thinking—"We don't know where You're going. How can we know the way?" (verse 5). In response, Jesus declared that he is the way, the truth, and the life. This trilogy fits naturally with each other, knitting together several themes of John's Gospel. It serves as a summation of Jesus' mission to the world.

The question of "the way" obviously raises the question of truth. If various individuals or religious groups espouse a "way" of life, how are we to know the truth of the various claims? Everyone suggests they are telling you the truth. The radical difference, though, is that Jesus does not merely *declare* the truth; he *is* the truth! Truth reminds us of the complete integrity and reliability of all that Jesus does and is.

Thus, the declaration that Jesus is "the truth" does not simply speak of illumination but of revelation. Jesus is God's final word to man. God added the exclamation mark to Jesus' affirmation that he is "the truth" by establishing him "as the powerful Son of God by the resurrection from the dead according to the Spirit of holiness" (Rom. 1:4). Any questions?

GOD IS
WONDERFUL

> **Isaiah 9:6** He will be named
> Wonderful Counselor, Mighty
> God, Eternal Father, Prince
> of Peace.

This is our fourth and final visit to Isaiah 9:6. As we read the titles applied to the child born for us, it becomes apparent they could not refer to King Ahaz's baby or any subsequent earthly child. This prophecy would not be fulfilled, in fact, for over 700 years, when a messenger of the Lord would appear to ordinary shepherds with a startling word: "Don't be afraid, for look, I proclaim to you good news of great joy that will be for all the people: today a Savior, who is Messiah the Lord, was born for you in the city of David" (Luke 2:10–11).

The context in Isaiah 9 declared that those in darkness would see a "great light" (verse 2), that their burdensome yoke would be shattered and their joy restored. When Jesus began his ministry in Capernaum, Matthew reiterated this hope. The idea of "great light" flooding the land was a favorite symbol of deliverance and of its accompanying joy and happiness. Jesus is indeed the one to bring about this "wonderful" event!

"Wonderful" indicates that Jesus exceeds the limits of human understanding and transcends the boundaries of human existence and power. When God sent an angelic messenger to Manoah to tell him of the impending birth of his son Samson, Manoah wanted to know this angelic one's name so he could honor him. The messenger responded, "Why do you ask My name . . . since it is wonderful" (Judg. 13:18).

If the name of a *messenger* is wonderful, how much more the name of the Son?

Jesus once told his listeners a parable about an owner of a vineyard whose tenants killed both his messengers and his son. He then concluded the story with a quotation from Psalm 118—"The stone that the builders rejected has become the cornerstone. This came from the Lord and is wonderful in our eyes" (Matt. 21:42).

When we come to know him as Savior, this experience will fill every fiber of our being and every event of our daily existence with wonder—for he is Wonderful.

GOD IS
THE WORD OF GOD

{ **Revelation 19:13** He wore
a robe stained with blood,
and His name is called
the Word of God. }

It would be insufficient to discuss the
name "Word of God" without full attention
to the imagery of our Savior's dress. What
is the meaning of the robe stained with
blood?

Various interpreters have suggested
that the blood is (a) that of the martyrs,
(b) the blood of the cross, or (c) the blood
of the enemy. The latter two are the most
likely. Those who suggest it's the blood of
the defeated enemy take their cue from the
victorious conqueror pictured in Isaiah
63:1 — "Who is this coming from Edom in
crimson-stained garments from Bozrah —
this One who is splendid in His apparel,
rising up proudly in His great might?"

Nevertheless, it is difficult not to think
of the blood on his robe as the blood of
Calvary. The concept of the Lamb that was
slain is so integral to the book of Revelation, it is hard to dismiss it from this

context. It is not impossible to think, in fact, that both ideas are present at the same time in this powerful symbol.

Christ has set us free by his blood. It is through his death that ultimate victory has been won, and thus the Lamb seen in Revelation receives glory and honor and praise. The Redeemer as well as the Judge of all the earth are one and the same—the Word of God.

This reference to "the Word" also reminds us of John's earlier writings: "In the beginning was the Word, and the Word was with God, and the Word was God" (John 1:1; see also 1 John 1:1). Jesus was no mere prophet speaking on behalf of God. He was God in flesh, embodying the word in his life of redemption and his judgment at the end of time. Jesus as the "Word of God" is God's final and complete word to man.

The writer of Hebrews put it this way: "Long ago God spoke to the fathers by the prophets at different times and in different ways. In these last days, He has spoken to us by His Son" (Heb. 1:1–2). He is the Word—the Word of God.

GOD IS
THE WAY

{
John 14:6 I am the way,
the truth, and the life. No one
comes to the Father except
through Me.
}

Have you ever been lost? I mean
sufficiently lost that you swallowed your
pride and actually asked for directions?
Before the advent of GPS guidance systems, this was an all too common experience for me. I am directionally challenged.
When I am in a strange place and ask
directions, I don't want several suggestions
about optional routes. All this does is add
to my present confusion.

But confusion about earthly directions
is merely an issue of inconvenience. Confusion about *heavenly* directions has eternal
consequences.

In response to Thomas' impassioned
cry that the disciples could never join
Jesus when he returned to the Father,
Jesus declared that he is "the way." If you
read this entire section, you will notice that
the word "way" is repeated in verses 4, 5,
and 6. Jesus is not simply offering to guide

men to God by *revealing* the way; he is offering to bring them to God by redeeming them. Fallen man doesn't simply need a guide to show him the way to the Father. He needs a Redeemer who can make it possible for him to enter the presence of holy God. We don't need illumination or direction; we need redemption.

That's because the way to the Father has been blocked by our sin. For us to live in the presence of holy God, we must have the way prepared by the forgiveness of our sins. And only Christ is the Way, because he alone is both God and man. "Now everything is from God, who reconciled us to Himself through Christ" (2 Cor. 5:18).

Make special note, though, that Jesus is not merely *a* way but *the* way. There is no possibility of confusion because there are not any alternative means of approaching the Father. Only the Son of God is qualified to be "the way." So to declare that Christ is the Way is not simply praying for direction. It is the sinner's cry for provision. Have you discovered Christ as the way to the Father? If not, why not ask him to provide access to the Father for you?

GOD IS
THE OMEGA

{
Revelation 21:6 It is done!
I am the Alpha and the Omega,
the Beginning and the End.
}

We have a saying that someone "saves the best for last." We seem to use this most often in relation to food—in particular, dessert. We want to savor that last morsel since it is the final flavor on our tongues.

All of the great "God Is" promises are so flavorful, it would be challenging to suggest that any one of them is best. But the affirmation that he is "Omega" is last, not only in terms of this book but because *omega* is the last letter in the Greek alphabet.

The affirmation "first and last" occurs on four occasions in the book of Revelation. At first, the reference is to God, who is declared to be the beginning and end of all things—the sovereign, eternal, transcendent one who is in control of history. What a word of encouragement this must have been to those first-century Christians who were facing persecution and death.

And even today, in spite of the chaotic appearance of the world, the promises of God can be spoken of as if they are already accomplished, because God's purposes in redemption are that certain. The one who created everything will oversee the new creation in the eternal order.

In chapters 21 and 22, the identical expression is applied to Christ himself, setting him apart from all created things. His authority rests in a singular fact: he shares the eternal nature of God. Thus, he is the beginning and end of all history and the Lord of all that comes between.

The translation of the phrase "It is done" is actually plural, so it can be rightly translated "*They* are done." And when all the world events that must take place have been completed, the triune God will clearly be seen as the one in command. In the end, God works all things according to his perfect, sovereign will.

He is the end of suffering, pain, and darkness—of death and of the curse! When Christ is the beginning of life for you—your Alpha—he is the culmination of all you have desired—your Omega!

APPENDIX

The promises of this book are based on one's relationship to Christ. If you have not yet entered a personal relationship with Jesus Christ, I encourage you to make this wonderful discovery today. I like to use the very simple acrostic—LIFE—to explain this, knowing that God wants you not only to inherit *eternal* life but also to experience *earthly* life to its fullest.

L = LOVE
It all begins with God's love. God created you in his image. This means you were created to live in relationship with him. *"For God loved the world in this way: He gave His One and Only Son, so that everyone who believes in Him will not perish but have eternal life"* (John 3:16).

But if God loves you and desires a relationship with you, why do you feel so isolated from him?

I = ISOLATION
This isolation is created by our sin—our rebellion against God—which separates us from him and from others. *"For all have sinned and fall short of the glory of God"* (Rom. 3:23). *"For the wages of sin is death, but the gift of God is eternal life in Christ Jesus our Lord"* (Rom. 6:23).

You might wonder how you can overcome this isolation and have an intimate relationship with God.

F = FORGIVENESS

The only solution to man's isolation and separation from a holy God is forgiveness. *"For Christ also suffered for sins once for all, the righteous for the unrighteous, that He might bring you to God, after being put to death in the fleshly realm but made alive in the spiritual realm"* (1 Pet. 3:18).

The only way our relationship can be restored with God is through the forgiveness of our sins. Jesus Christ died on the cross for this very purpose.

E = ETERNAL LIFE

You can have full and abundant life in this present life . . . and eternal life when you die. *"But to all who did receive Him, He gave them the right to be children of God, to those who believe in His name"* (John 1:12). *"A thief comes only to steal and to kill and to destroy. I have come that they may have life and have it in abundance"* (John 10:10).

Is there any reason you wouldn't like to have a personal relationship with God?

THE PLAN OF SALVATION

It's as simple as ABC. All you have to do is:

A = Admit you are a sinner. Turn from your sin and turn to God. *"Repent and turn back, that your sins may be wiped out so that seasons of refreshing may come from the presence of the Lord"* (Acts 3:19).

B = Believe that Jesus died for your sins and rose from the dead enabling you to have life. *"I have written these things to you who believe in the name of the Son of God, so that you may know that you have eternal life"* (1 John 5:13).

C = Confess verbally and publicly your belief in Jesus Christ. *"If you confess with your mouth, 'Jesus is Lord,' and believe in your heart that God raised Him from the dead, you will be saved. With the heart one believes, resulting in righteousness, and with the mouth one confesses, resulting in salvation"* (Rom. 10:9–10).

You can invite Jesus Christ to come into your life right now. Pray something like this:

"God, I admit that I am a sinner. I believe that you sent Jesus, who died on the cross and rose from the dead, paying the penalty for my sins. I am asking that you forgive me of my sin, and I receive your gift of eternal life. It is in Jesus' name that I ask for this gift. Amen."

Signed _____

Date _____

If you have a friend or family member who is a Christian, tell them about your decision. Then find a church that teaches the Bible, and let them help you go deeper with Christ.

KINGDOM PROMISES

If you've enjoyed this book of Kingdom Promises, you may want to consider reading one of the others in the series:

God Will
978-0-8054-4768-2

We Are
978-0-8054-2783-7

We Can
978-0-8054-2780-6

But God
978-0-8054-2782-0

Available in stores nationwide and through major online retailers. For a complete look at Ken Hemphill titles, make sure to visit www.bhpublishinggroup.com/hemphill.